"Driscoll and Breshears have teamed up to provide a new generation of pastors and Christian leaders with a biblically sound, tartly relevant, and crisply practical guide to understanding the church. This book lives up to its subtitle, *Timeless Truths and Timely Methods*. The authors' wit, grit, and gravitas combine to make it an enjoyable and thought provoking must-read for twenty-first-century spiritual leadership."
  —Rick Booye, Senior Pastor, Trail Christian Fellowship, Eagle Point,
    Oregon; President, Pacific Bible College

"Having treated us to *Vintage Jesus* and *Death by Love,* Mark Driscoll and Gerry Breshears team up again to provide a third installment that addresses the nature, life, and missional character of the church of Jesus Christ. Pastors, church members, and those who are just wondering about Jesus and his church will find this book to be very helpful. The expected topics—church leadership, preaching, baptism, the Lord's Supper—are covered clearly and practically. What I especially appreciate is the discussion of often overlooked topics such as church unity, discipline, and love, and the attention given to new topics such as multi-site campuses and the use of technology. 'Timeless' and 'timely' are apt descriptions of this book on the church that is must reading!"
  —Gregg R. Allison, Associate Professor of Christian Theology,
    Southern Baptist Theological Seminary

"Vintage Church is a remarkable book. Mark and Gerry seek to be rigorously biblical and theologically faithful as they address the doctrine of the church. However, the real uniqueness to this book is its personal and practical insights. Remaining faithful to the gospel of Jesus, the authors help us think and see how to do church in a twenty-first-century context that presents both challenges and opportunities to the body of Christ. Timeless truths and timely methods indeed are woven together in a beautiful tapestry. This is a valuable work."
  —Daniel L. Akin, President, Southeastern Baptist Theological Seminary

"Gerry Breshears and Mark Driscoll combine the thinking of a theologian with the experience of an innovative church leader to bring us fresh approaches to ministry that are more relevant without being less biblical. This book is an inspiring application of what it means for the body of Christ to be 'in the world but not of it.'"
  —Dan Jarrell, Teaching Pastor, ChangePoint Church, Anchorage, Alaska

"Clarity and biblical fidelity on what church is in relation to culture is harder and harder to find in our consumer-dominated culture. *Vintage Church* stands out as a book willing to tackle the difficult issues and willing to keep flexible within the constraints of culture—both without losing a fervent commitment to the Scriptures as our unshakable foundation. May God give all of us the grace to live out what Driscoll and Breshears exemplify."

—Scott Moreau, Professor of Intercultural Studies, Wheaton College; editor, *Evangelical Missions Quarterly*

"*Vintage Church* is full of ideas on how to do church. But it really is a story of a pastor who struggles to live what he preaches in the crucible that is spiritual leadership. What a glorious day it is when we understand that our character is our influence. Mark Driscoll not only owns his influence in a 'gutsy' way, but in humility he also offers his church the very best he has—his example. It is easy to follow a man who follows Christ in humility, submission, obedience, and sacrifice."

—Bill Hull, author, *Jesus Christ Disciple Maker; The Disciple Making Pastor;* and *The Disciple Making Church*

"Carefully reasoned, clearly-written volumes on the nature of the church are indeed rare. Here, the overall impression is that of decades of research being condensed into a highly readable form. Treading through so many difficult and delicate waters is seldom done so succinctly, with key issues being discussed concisely, buttressed by multiple explanations. This is an exceptional text that should be digested by anyone who cares about this subject. Once again, Crossway has added to their fine collection of solid books."

—Gary R. Habermas, Distinguished Research Professor, Liberty University

"Of all the established entities and organizations on earth, none has enjoyed as much glory, faced as much scrutiny, or endured as much persecution as the church. Even today, questions and doubts abound when it comes to explaining the only thing Jesus himself instituted. But here Mark Driscoll and Gerry Breshears continue the tradition they began in *Vintage Jesus* of providing clarity and direction to something many people approach with caution and confusion. And as they point us to answers about the church, such as its role, purpose, and potential, they help us all realize the true essence of the church today and the eternal influence it can have in our lives."

—Ed Young, Senior Pastor, Fellowship Church; author, *The Creative Leader*

VINTAGE CHURCH

Re:Lit Books

Vintage Jesus, Mark Driscoll and Gerry Breshears
On Church Leadership, Mark Driscoll
On the New Testament, Mark Driscoll
On the Old Testament, Mark Driscoll
On Who Is God? Mark Driscoll
Practical Theology for Women, Wendy Alsup
Death by Love, Mark Driscoll and Gerry Breshears
Total Church, Tim Chester and Steve Timmis

TIMELESS TRUTHS *and* TIMELY METHODS

MARK DRISCOLL
& GERRY BRESHEARS

CROSSWAY BOOKS
WHEATON, ILLINOIS

Cover design: Patrick Mahoney

Cover photo: Jerad Knudson

First printing 2008

Printed in the United States of America

PDF ISBN: 978-1-4335-0569-0

Mobipocket ISBN: 978-1-4335-0570-6

Library of Congress Cataloging-in-Publication Data
Driscoll, Mark, 1970–
    Vintage church : timeless truths and timely methods / Mark
Driscoll and Gerry Breshears.
        p. cm. (Re:Lit theology series)
    Includes bibliographical references and index.
    ISBN 978-1-4335-0130-2 (hc)
    1. Church. I. Breshears, Gerry, 1947–   . II. Title. III. Series.
BV600.3.D74   2009
262—dc22   2008028615

LB		18	17	16	15	14	13	12	11	10	09	08
15	14	13	12	11	10	9	8	7	6	5	4	3	2	1

contents

PREFACE

✝

This book is about the church of Jesus Christ. Thus, before examining his church we must exalt him by explaining his relationship to the church.

Jesus died and rose to reconcile sinners to God as Christians and to one another as the church.[1] Jesus is the head or preeminent authority over the church.[2] Jesus is the apostle who plants a church.[3] Jesus is the leader who builds the church.[4] Jesus is the senior pastor and Chief Shepherd who rules the church.[5] It is ultimately Jesus who closes churches down when they have become faithless or fruitless.[6]

During his earthly ministry, Jesus ministered as prophet, priest, and king. Following his ascension back into heaven after his death and resurrection, Jesus sent the Holy Spirit to enable and empower Christians to continue his ministry on the earth, which is an overriding theme of this entire book. To be absolutely clear, the people who make up the church must have a living connection to the true Jesus rather than to one of the many popular idols that litter our cultural landscape under the name "God" or even "Jesus." The real Jesus of Scripture is the virgin-born incarnation of the second person of the Trinity, the Word come in the flesh and the gift given to the church.

Within the Protestant theological tradition of which we are a part,

---

[1]Eph. 5:25–27. For further study on Jesus see Mark Driscoll and Gerry Breshears, *Vintage Jesus: Timeless Answers to Timely Questions* (Wheaton, IL: Crossway Books, 2008); and for further study on the cross see Mark Driscoll and Gerry Breshears, *Death by Love: Letters from the Cross* (Wheaton, IL: Crossway Books, 2008).
[2]Eph. 1:9, 19–23; 4:15–16; 5:23.
[3]Heb. 3:1.
[4]Matt. 16:18.
[5]1 Pet. 5:4.
[6]Rev. 2:5.

there is a long history of seeing Jesus in his three offices of prophet, priest, and king. These are megathemes of Scripture connected to Jesus from Genesis to Revelation. As prophet, Jesus preached and taught Scripture with authority and has now commissioned preachers filled with his Spirit to proclaim his Word. As priest, Jesus cares for people and deals with their sin compassionately and calls his people to join him in these ministries of mercy. As king, Jesus demonstrated his rule over creation through miracles while on the earth and today leads his people, the spiritual "body of Christ," into all nations and cultures through church leaders, principles, and systems by the Holy Spirit and according to his Word.

Subsequently, throughout this book there are some sections that are more prophetic and others that are more priestly or kingly. Where we explore the prophetic functions of the church, the importance of confessing the truth of Scripture and contending for it against false teaching will be stressed. The confessional nature of the church requires that the essential truths of biblical Christian faith be declared, defined, and defended. These chapters will resonate with those Christians who are deeply committed to such things as doctrinal and apologetical precision within the church.

In the more priestly sections of the book we will examine the experiential nature of the church, by which Christians covenant to live for Jesus as Jesus' people gathered, scattered, and led. We will stress that the church is a community of the Spirit made up of sinners who have new hearts, are indwelt and unified by the Spirit, and have Jesus' life in them as the source of new life. The priestly, experiential nature of the church requires that the new life that Jesus gives to his people be visible when the church both gathers and scatters with Jesus. These chapters will resonate with those Christians who are deeply committed to such things as loving community, living worship, and practical ministry for the well-being of the church.

In the more kingly sections of the book we will examine the function of the church to bring the gospel of Jesus Christ into all the world, over which Jesus is the anointed king.[7] In this way, the body of Christ continues the mission of Jesus as an outpost of Christ's coming kingdom. This missional nature of the church requires that the truth and

---

[7] Acts 3:19–21; 4:26–27.

love of Jesus be extended to the cultures and subcultures of the earth. These chapters will resonate with those Christians who are deeply committed to such things as gospel contextualization, evangelism, church planting, and overseas missions.

Sadly, great imbalance and unhealthiness occurs when any one of these aspects of the church is either neglected or overly emphasized at the expense of the others. When the prophetic, confessional nature of the church is inordinately emphasized, the result is cruel fundamentalism. When the priestly, experiential nature of the church is inordinately emphasized, the result is compromised liberalism. When the kingly, missional nature of the church is inordinately emphasized, the result is cowardly evangelicalism, which either capitulates to modernity in a seeker fashion or to postmodernity in an emergent fashion.

This book is admittedly one of tension. We seek to take what is best from various prophetic, priestly, and kingly Christian traditions and tribes in order to be faithful to all of Scripture without neglecting any part of Scripture. In so doing, we anticipate finding ourselves in the middle of a shootout of sorts between various teams. Some will appreciate the prophetic/confessional aspects, others will prefer the priestly/experiential ones, and still others will value the kingly/missional portions—each seeing the others as good for no more than target practice in Jesus' name.

Underlying this book is the belief that the church and its leaders and people need both humility and discernment. If we are humble, we can learn from those with whom we disagree. If we are discerning, we will not agree with everything or everyone but rather ultimately submit everything to Scripture and "test everything; hold fast [to] what is good."[8] The result will be a church that is biblically rooted (prophetic/confessional), grace centered (priestly/experiential), and culturally connected (kingly/missional).

Before moving on with the rest of the book, we want to thank you for giving us some of your time to read our work. It is my (Mark's) voice you will find on the pages ahead, but many of the concepts were shaped by Gerry. He lent his editing skills to much of the material, and he also wrote most of the "Answers to Common Questions" found at the end of each chapter.

---

[8]1 Thess. 5:21.

We deeply love the church and have both given our lives to serving as pastors in a local church. Gerry is an unpaid pastor-elder on the preaching team at Grace Community Church in Gresham, Oregon, where he has served since 1996. He has also given his life to training pastors as professor of theology at Western Seminary in Portland, as well as teaching at seminaries around the world. I have pastored Mars Hill Church since founding it in 1996 and have seen it grow from the size of a Mormon family to multiple campuses supporting multiple church plants. Gerry and I have given our lives in a very real sense to serving the church of Jesus Christ both locally and globally. We spend considerable amounts of our energy serving fellow pastors as best we are able. Therefore, this book is very close to our hearts because the church is what Jesus gave his life for and what we have given our lives to. Our prayer is that this book would in some humble way, by God's grace, help the church be faithful to Jesus and fruitful in culture.

Mark Driscoll

CHAPTER ONE

WHAT IS THE CHRISTIAN LIFE?

**Therefore, as you received Christ Jesus the Lord,
so walk in him.**

COLOSSIANS 2:6

✝

Jesus. If one word were to be chosen as the most important word in the history of the world, it would be the name Jesus.

God preached the first gospel to our parents, Adam and Eve, shortly following their sin in Genesis 3; he promised that Jesus would come. From that day onward, God inspired his prophets to reveal in great detail the events surrounding the coming of Jesus.[1] Consequently, for roughly a few thousand years God's people longed for Jesus' arrival.

Jesus came into history in the most humble manner. He was born roughly two thousand years ago in a barn to a poor, young virgin woman named Mary. Although he was God, Jesus' first earthly throne was the feeding trough of an animal, which was used for his crib.

Jesus' unparalleled humility is one of his most shocking attributes.[2] Our culture believes that pride is our greatest friend although it is the reason why Satan himself was kicked out of heaven. Pride covets the success of others and is about self—*my* glory, *my* arrogance, and *my* independence. Our culture, tragically, considers pride a virtue rather

---

[1] For further study on this see chap. 3 of Mark Driscoll and Gerry Breshears, *Vintage Jesus: Timeless Answers to Timely Questions* (Wheaton, IL: Crossway Books, 2008).
[2] For further study on humility see C. J. Mahaney, *Humility: True Greatness* (Sisters, OR: Multnomah, 2005).

than a vice. Conversely, Jesus came in great humility and lived his life in great humility. Before repeatedly and emphatically declaring himself to be God,[3] Jesus spent the first roughly thirty years of his life in relative obscurity in a humble town with humble parents working a humble job as a carpenter.

Theologians use the word *incarnation* as shorthand to explain the coming of the second member of the Trinity into human history as the man Jesus Christ. *Incarnation* is taken from the Latin translation of John 1:14 and literally means "becoming flesh." The word speaks of Jesus' humility in temporarily forgoing being worshiped by angels as God in glory to come instead on a mission to glorify God in heaven and save sinners on the earth.[4]

In 451 the Christian Council of Chalcedon confirmed the biblical position regarding the divinity and humanity of Jesus that remains the accepted doctrine of Protestant, Catholic, and Orthodox Christians alike, despite their other differences. Using the phrase "hypostatic union," they rightly declared that Jesus was one person with two natures, human and divine. Jesus is both fully God and fully man, or as the Bible says, "Immanuel," which means God with us.

As God who became a man, Jesus came to fully identify with our humanity and serve as the mediator between us and God to deal with our sin problem and reconcile us back to God.[5]

Significantly, Jesus lived his sinless life on the earth in large part by the power of the Holy Spirit. This does not mean that Jesus in any way ceased to be fully God while on the earth, but rather that he humbly chose to limit the continual use of his divine attributes. Thus, he lived as we must live—by the enabling power of God the Holy Spirit. We want to be clear: Jesus remained fully man and fully God during his incarnation, and he maintained all of his divine attributes and did avail himself of them upon occasion, such as to forgive human sin, which God alone can do.[6] Nonetheless, Jesus' life was lived as fully human in that he lived it by the power of the Holy Spirit.[7]

---

[3]Matt. 26:63–65; Mark 14:61–64; John 8:58–59; 10:30–33.
[4]John 1:14; Phil. 2:5–6; Col. 2:9; 1 John 4:2.
[5]1 Tim. 2:5.
[6]Mark 2:1–7.
[7]For a more thorough study of this and other issues regarding the Holy Spirit, a helpful resource is Graham A. Cole, *He Who Gives Life: The Doctrine of the Holy Spirit* (Wheaton, IL: Crossway Books, 2007).

As the church father Augustine rightly said, by becoming a man Jesus did not lose anything; rather, he added humanity to his divinity. Echoing this point, Bruce Milne writes, "The biblical equation is . . . incarnation = God plus. In becoming incarnate the divine Word did not relinquish his deity; he added to it, if one may so speak, by taking a full human nature into hypostatic union with the Word."[8]

The most thorough section of Scripture regarding the incarnation is Philippians 2:5–11:

> Have this mind among yourselves, which is yours in Christ Jesus, who, though he was in the form of God, did not count equality with God a thing to be grasped, but made himself nothing, taking the form of a servant, being born in the likeness of men. And being found in human form, he humbled himself by becoming obedient to the point of death, even death on a cross. Therefore God has highly exalted him and bestowed on him the name that is above every name, so that at the name of Jesus every knee should bow, in heaven and on earth and under the earth, and every tongue confess that Jesus Christ is Lord, to the glory of God the Father.

Jesus had the divine life and full equality with God in every way, yet he emptied himself of that divine way of living. He who created and rules the universe became a servant. He took on flesh with the same image and likeness of God that Adam had, while keeping his identity as the second person of the Trinity. In that humble state, he obeyed God the Father in every way. He lowered himself even further to the point of shameful death on the cross. So, God exalted him as Messiah and bestowed on him "the Name," that is, "Yahweh," the personal name of God that he always had as second person of the Trinity but now has as the God-man, Messiah Jesus.

The confession of Jesus as God come in the flesh is a biblical test of orthodoxy. Any person or group who compromises this ceases to be part of the church and is a false prophet, serving the devil rather than Jesus.[9] It is of greatest concern that many professed Christians never confess this truth plainly. They use the name "Jesus" but never clearly declare him to be God in the flesh. On the other hand, some have effectively

---

[8]Bruce Milne, *Know the Truth: A Handbook of Christian Belief* (Downers Grove, IL: InterVarsity, 1998), 185.
[9]Matt. 24:4–5; Rom. 16:17–19; Gal. 1:7–9; 1 John 4:1–4.

denied his true humanity in their zeal to protect his divinity. They miss the power of the Holy Spirit in Jesus. To understand how Jesus' life of sinless humility was empowered, we will now investigate his relationship to God the Holy Spirit while he was on the earth.

SPIRIT-FILLED JESUS

Jesus grew from infancy to adulthood, lived among a family, worked a job, ate meals, increased his knowledge through learning, told jokes, attended funerals, had male and female friends, celebrated holidays, went to parties, loved his mom, felt the pain of betrayal and lies told about him, and experienced the full range of human emotions from stress to astonishment, joy, compassion, and sorrow. Furthermore, Jesus experienced the same sorts of trials and temptations that we do,[10] with the exception that he never did sin.[11] Subsequently, Jesus lived the sinless life that we were supposed to live but have not, both in our place and as our example.

Sadly, all of the major creeds compiled during the early church ignore the missional life of Jesus between his birth and death. The Apostles' Creed, Nicene Creed, and Athanasian Creed all declare that Jesus was born to the Virgin Mary and then skip forward to his suffering under the rule of Pilate without speaking a word about the years in between. What is lost is the example of Jesus' life, in general, and his exemplary relationship with God the Holy Spirit, in particular.

Regarding the relationship between Jesus and the Holy Spirit, Abraham Kuyper wrote:

> This ought to be carefully noticed, especially since the Church has never sufficiently confessed the influence of the Holy Spirit exerted upon the work of Christ. The general impression is that the work of the Holy Spirit begins when the work of the Mediator on earth is finished, as tho [sic] until that time the Holy Spirit celebrated His divine day of rest. Yet the Scripture teaches us again and again that Christ performed His mediatorial work controlled and impelled by the Holy Spirit.[12]

---

[10]For example, Matt. 4:1–10 and Heb. 4:14–16.
[11]John 8:46; 2 Cor. 5:21; Heb. 4:14–16; 1 Pet. 1:19.
[12]Abraham Kuyper, *The Work of the Holy Spirit*, trans. Henri de Vries (Grand Rapids, MI: Eerdmans, 1975), 97.

The empowerment of Jesus through God the Holy Spirit is repeatedly stressed in the Gospel of Luke. There we find that Jesus was conceived by the Holy Spirit and given the title "Christ," which means anointed by the Holy Spirit.[13] Jesus' aunt Elizabeth was "filled with the Holy Spirit" when greeting Jesus' pregnant mother, Mary, and his uncle Zechariah went on to prophesy that their son John was appointed by God to prepare the way for Jesus.[14] An angel had revealed to Mary that she would give birth to Jesus; when Mary asked how that was possible since she was a virgin, the angel said, "The Holy Spirit will come upon you."[15]

Once born, Jesus was dedicated to the Lord in the temple according to the demands of the law by Simeon; "the Holy Spirit was upon [Simeon]" and the Holy Spirit had revealed to him that he would not die until seeing Jesus Christ.[16] Simeon was "in the Spirit" when he prophesied about Jesus' ministry to Jews and Gentiles to the glory of God.[17] John later prophesied that one day Jesus would baptize people with the Holy Spirit.[18] The Holy Spirit descended upon Jesus at his own baptism.[19] It is curious that while the Gospels give scant information about Jesus' childhood, all four include the account of Jesus' baptism. Matthew adds the interesting statement that the Spirit rested on Jesus, as if to suggest that the remainder of his life and ministry on the earth would be done under the anointing and power of the Holy Spirit.[20]

Regarding Jesus' baptism, Graham Cole writes, "The symbol of the dove and Jesus' emerging from the waters, soon to reenter the land, possibly conjure up the old stories of Noah's flood and Israel's exodus from Egypt and its eventual crossing over the Jordan into the Promised Land. God is about to do something of extraordinary significance in salvation-history."[21]

In the remainder of Luke's Gospel we discover that Jesus was "full of the Holy Spirit," "led by the Spirit,"[22] and came "in the power of the

---

[13]Luke 1–2.
[14]Luke 1:41–43, 67, 76.
[15]Luke 1:35–37.
[16]Luke 2:25–27.
[17]Luke 2:27–34.
[18]John 1:14; Phil. 2:5–6; Col. 2:9; 1 John 4:2.
[19]For example, Matt. 4:1–10 and Heb. 4:14–16.
[20]Matt. 3:16.
[21]Cole, *He Who Gives Life*, 158.
[22]Luke 4:1–2.

Spirit."[23] After reading Isaiah 61:1–2, which says, "The Spirit of the Lord is upon me, because he has anointed me to proclaim good news to the poor. He has sent me to proclaim liberty to the captives and recovering of sight to the blind, to set at liberty those who are oppressed, to proclaim the year of the Lord's favor," Jesus declared, "Today this Scripture has been fulfilled in your hearing."[24] Luke continues by revealing that Jesus also "rejoiced in the Holy Spirit."[25] Regarding the Holy Spirit's ministry to and through Christians, Jesus promised that God the Father would "give the Holy Spirit to those who ask him"[26] and that the Holy Spirit would teach us once he was sent.[27]

In the charismatic and Pentecostal traditions of the church there has been a great devotion to the person and work of God the Holy Spirit. However, sometimes the emphasis on the Holy Spirit comes at the expense of a full appreciation of the person and work of Jesus and/or a subtle impression that somehow Jesus and the Holy Spirit are competing for glory. This is Holy Spirit-olatry.

In some Reformed and dispensational traditions there is a devotion to Jesus that results in a practical denial of the work of the Holy Spirit in Jesus and in the church today. This is Jesus-olatry. They affirm the reality of the Spirit, but in their zeal to glorify only Jesus and to protect the uniqueness of the Bible, or in their fear of falling into emotionalism, they stress the cessation of the work of the Spirit. They limit the work of the Spirit in pointing to Jesus instead of empowering the church to continue the mission of Jesus.

Gerald Hawthorne, who has written one of the most compelling books on the subject of Jesus' relationship with the Holy Spirit, says, "Not only is Jesus their Savior because of who he was and because of his own complete obedience to the Father's will (cf. Heb. 10:5-7), but he is the supreme example for them of what is possible in a human life because of his total dependence upon the Spirit of God."[28] By closely examining the relationship between Jesus and God the Holy Spirit during Jesus' earthly life, we see that they work in cooperation, not in

[23]Luke 4:14.
[24]Luke 4:14–21.
[25]Luke 10:21.
[26]Luke 11:13.
[27]Luke 12:12.
[28]Gerald F. Hawthorne, *The Presence and the Power: The Significance of the Spirit in the Life and Ministry of Jesus* (Dallas, TX: Word, 1991), 234.

competition. Furthermore, we see that Jesus and not some goofy guru is the quintessential example of what it means to live a Spirit-filled life. Important also is the fact that Jesus' life was lived by the power of the Spirit as a missionary in culture.

SPIRIT-FILLED MISSIONARY JESUS

Jesus is the greatest missionary who has ever lived or will ever live. In fact, Jesus' incarnation was in many ways a mission trip led and empowered by God the Holy Spirit.

First, Jesus came into a sinful culture. As a missionary, Jesus left the culture of heaven to come into a sinful culture on the earth. This cross-cultural transition was starker than any missionary has ever experienced. Jesus came from the culture of heaven, where there is no temptation, sin, sinners, or death. In entering into culture on earth, Jesus was tempted by Satan to sin, surrounded by sinners, and both witnessed and experienced death as the penalty for sin.

Second, Jesus learned firsthand about a sinful culture. As the perfect missionary, Jesus did not learn about the sinful culture from a careful and safe distance. No, Jesus built friendships with sinners, Jesus learned the language of sinners, Jesus ate food with sinners, Jesus drank wine with sinners, and Jesus participated in the parties and holidays of sinners. The religious types in Jesus' day were incensed by his participation in sinful culture with sinners, and Jesus himself reports that when they saw him they would rebuke and mock him, saying, "Look at him! A glutton and a drunkard, a friend of tax collectors and sinners!"[29]

Third, Jesus did not condone sin, nor did he sin, himself. Jesus said that he never sinned.[30] Furthermore, the Bible elsewhere emphatically declares that Jesus is the only person who has never sinned.[31] While Jesus never broke any of God's laws as revealed in Scripture, he did not hold certain social and religious customs (those that do not find their authority in Scripture) in high regard. Subsequently, Jesus frequently broke various social and religious customs when he felt it was necessary to further the work of God. Examples include healing on the Sabbath,[32]

---

[29]Luke 7:34.
[30]John 8:46.
[31]Matt. 27:3–4; Luke 23:22, 41, 47; Acts 3:14; 2 Cor. 5:21; James 5:6; 1 Pet. 1:19; 2:22; 3:18; 1 John 3:5.
[32]Mark 1:21–27.

throwing over tables in the temple,[33] eating with godless sinners,[34] and not washing his hands before eating.[35]

Some people who were committed to defending their social and religious traditions, despite the lack of biblical support, were offended by Jesus' unwillingness to submit to their rules in addition to God's. Their tribe continues to this day among those who are prone to place the authority of cultural trends and religious traditions above Scripture. You can hear them saying, for example, that we who preach in jeans without tucking in our shirts dishonor God.

Furthermore, during his earthly missional ministry Jesus not only confessed that he was sent into culture as a missionary, but he also sent Christians on the exact same mission. For example, in John's Gospel alone, Jesus told us no less than thirty-nine times that he was a missionary from heaven who came to minister incarnationally in an earthly culture.[36] Jesus also commands us to be missionaries in culture as he was: "As you sent me into the world, so I have sent them into the world."[37] He also said, "As the Father has sent me, even so I am sending you."[38]

Before sending Christians on their mission, though, Jesus accomplished his mission by dying on the cross in our place for our sins. Theologically, we call this *penal substitutionary atonement*. In common vernacular, this means that our God became the man Jesus Christ who, though without sin, died on the cross in our place to pay the penalty of death for our sins. In the garden our first parents, Adam and Eve, substituted themselves for God, and since then we each have done the same by living as our own gods. Yet at the cross Jesus substituted himself for us to bring us back to the real God. The Bible uses the word *for* to explain that the historical fact of Jesus' death was for our sins:

- "But he was wounded *for* our transgressions; he was crushed *for* our iniquities; upon him was the chastisement that brought us peace, and with his stripes we are healed."[39]

- "[He] was delivered up *for* our trespasses."[40]

---

[33]John 2:14–17.
[34]Matt. 9:11.
[35]Mark 7:1–23.
[36]John 3:34; 4:34; 5:23, 24, 30, 36, 37, 38; 6:29, 38, 39, 44, 57; 7:16, 28, 29, 33; 8:16, 18, 26, 29, 42; 9:4; 10:36; 11:42; 12:44, 45, 49; 13:20; 14:24; 15:21; 16:5; 17:3, 8, 18, 21, 23, 25; 20:21.
[37]John 17:18.
[38]John 20:21.
[39]Isa. 53:5.
[40]Rom. 4:25.

- "But God shows his love for us in that while we were still sinners, Christ died *for* us."[41]
- "Christ died *for* our sins."[42]
- "For Christ also suffered once *for* sins, the righteous *for* the unrighteous, that he might bring us to God."[43]

The importance of the cross to the church is that apart from Jesus' death on it in our place for our sins, the church does not exist and has no good news to tell. Unless our sin is taken away, our new life as God's people cannot begin. It cannot be overemphasized that where the cross of Jesus is not exalted and proclaimed as the central act in all of history and in our own redemption, the church is not present. Spiritually speaking, the church is the community of people who gather around the cross of Jesus to humbly repent of sin, trust in him, sing his praises, and follow his example.

Furthermore, the church has as its answer to every important question the good news of the person and work of Jesus. His work includes the following ten things he accomplished for those who are saved by grace alone through faith alone in Jesus Christ alone without any false notion that they can in any way contribute to their salvation through human works such as morality, spirituality, or religious devotion.[44]

1) Jesus is our victor who conquered Satan and demons on the cross so that we could live a life free of slavery to sin, of vain regrets for past sin, of condemnation and torment.[45]

2) Jesus is our redeemer who freed us from slavery to sin and death, not unlike the Old Testament saints who were liberated from tyranny and oppression in Egypt to live new lives of worship, joy, and holy freedom.[46]

3) Jesus is our new-covenant sacrifice and our great high priest who offered his own body as a sacrifice in our place for our sins in fulfillment of the Old Testament sacrificial system.[47]

4) Jesus is our justification who takes away our sin and gives us his righteousness as a gift by exchanging places with us on the cross so that we can be justified in the sight of God.[48]

---

[41]Rom. 5:8.
[42]1 Cor. 15:3.
[43]1 Pet. 3:18.
[44]Isa. 64:6; Rom. 3–5; Gal. 2:16; Eph. 2:4–6; Phil. 3:8–9; Titus 3:7.
[45]Col. 2:13–15.
[46]Titus 2:13–14.
[47]1 Pet. 1:18–19.
[48]Gal. 2:16; 2 Cor. 5:21.

5) Jesus is our propitiation who stood in our place to divert the just wrath of God away from us by enduring it himself in love.[49]

6) Jesus is our expiation who cleanses us from the sins we have committed and the sins that have been committed against us, which commingle to make us dirty and defiled.[50]

7) Jesus is our ransom who has mediated between us and God and paid the price for our sins.[51]

8) Jesus is our example who has shown for us the perfect human life, which includes laying down our lives for brothers and sisters by the power of the Holy Spirit.[52]

9) Jesus is our reconciliation who has taken away our sin and reconciles us back into loving relationship with God and others.[53]

10) Jesus is our revelation, and on the cross we see God's wrath and love, justice and mercy, holiness and compassion revealed in perfection.[54]

In every way, the church is the people who have benefited from Jesus' work on the cross, live in light of it, and gladly proclaim it.

Following his death on the cross in our place for our sins, Jesus rose by the power of the Holy Spirit.[55] In the New Testament, the cross and the resurrection are treated as essentially one event because if Jesus had not risen to conquer Satan, sin, and death, all we would have is the death of a great man, not the remission of sin. Following his resurrection in victory over Satan, sin, and death, Jesus gave the Great Commission: "All authority in heaven and on earth has been given to me. Go therefore and make disciples of all nations, baptizing them in the name of the Father and of the Son and of the Holy Spirit, teaching them to observe all that I have commanded you. And behold, I am with you always, to the end of the age."[56] Indeed, the authority of our mission rests on nothing less than the authority delegated to us by the exalted Lord Jesus Christ who rules over all.

The sequel to Luke, the book of Acts, reveals how our mission is to occur. Whereas the Gospel of Luke focuses on the cultural life and missional ministry of Jesus in his physical body by the power of the Holy

[49] 1 John 4:10.
[50] 1 John 1:7.
[51] 1 Tim. 2:5–6.
[52] 1 John 3:16; 1 Pet. 2:21.
[53] Eph. 4:31–5:2.
[54] John 1:18; Col. 1:15.
[55] Rom. 1:4, 8:11; 1 Tim. 3:16; 1 Pet. 3:18.
[56] Matt. 28:18–20.

Spirit, the book of Acts reveals the continuing ministry of Jesus in his metaphorical body, the church, by the power of the same Holy Spirit.[57] With the ascension of Jesus, a great reversal of sorts occurred. While on the earth, Jesus bore the Spirit. Following his ascension and return to glory in heaven, however, Jesus bestowed the Spirit upon the church. This is precisely what we read of in Acts 2 where the Holy Spirit descends upon the church in much the same way that he did at the baptism of Jesus. We read in Acts 2:4 that "they were all filled with the Holy Spirit." After this birth of the church, many miraculous activites occurred. For example, Graham Cole says, "Just as there had been with the Messiah's birth an outburst of prophesying by various people filled with the Spirit (e.g., Luke 1:41, Elizabeth; v. 67, Zechariah) or having the Spirit upon them (e.g., Luke 2:25–26, Simeon), so too at the birth of the Messiah's eschatological community [the church] (Acts 2:17–18)."[58]

THE SPIRIT-EMPOWERED GOSPEL (ACTS 2)

Acts 2 is widely appreciated by Christians across varying denominational traditions and theological persuasions as the record of the dawning of the new covenant church. Jesus poured out his Spirit to begin and to commission the church—the community of Holy Spirit–regenerated and–empowered people who continue the ministry of Jesus.

Some people ask, "What is the gospel?" and then proceed with their own speculations, as if God never revealed it. A better answer is to read the Bible! There we find Peter's sermon in Acts 2, which summarizes the gospel, the power center of the mission of the church. The gospel pattern of Acts 2, as well as of other Scriptures, breaks down into three aspects: (1) *revelation*, or what God did; (2) *response*, or what we do; and (3) *results*, or what God gives.[59]

REVELATION: WHAT GOD DID

Peter begins by affirming that Jesus fulfills the promises of a divine Messiah, God come among us, as accredited him by miracles, signs, and wonders (v. 22). Next, Peter declares that Jesus died on the cross accord-

---

[57]Acts 1:1–9
[58]Cole, *He Who Gives Life*, 193.
[59]These three organizational points are adapted from Steve Walker, pastor of Redeemer's Fellowship, Roseburg, OR. The same basic outline can be seen in Luke 24:46–47; Acts 10:39–43; 13:26–39; Rom. 4:22–25; and 1 Cor. 15:1–8.

ing to God's prophetic purpose (v. 23). Peter proceeds to emphasize the reality that God raised Jesus from death in fulfillment of Old Testament prophecy (vv. 24–32). Peter concludes with the final acts of God exalting Jesus to the right hand of the Father and pouring out the Spirit in fulfillment of Old Testament prophecy (vv. 33–35).

response: what we do

The first thing we are to do in response to God's revelation is repent (vv. 36–37). Repentance is the Spirit-empowered acknowledgment of sin that results in a change of mind about who and what God is in my life, what is important, and what is good and bad. This is followed by a change of behavior flowing out of an internal change of values. The second response is to accept the revealed message about Jesus by Spirit-empowered faith (v. 41). Faith means taking God at his word and trusting my life and eternity to the truth of his revelation. All of this is seen in the act of baptism, which is the visible expression of our connection with the death and resurrection of Jesus through repentance and faith (vv. 38, 41).

results: what god gives

Peter immediately announces the gift of forgiveness of our sins, which is the result of the propitiatory death of Jesus (v. 38). This gift flows into justification, or the imputed righteousness of Jesus. Peter goes on to the second gift, the Holy Spirit and the new heart and new life of Christ (v. 38). This regeneration, or the imparted righteousness of Jesus, is for living a new life as a Christian with, like, for, to, and by the living Jesus. The third gift is membership in the body of Christ, the new community of the Spirit called the church. This community is a supernatural community where God's power is seen from miracles and supernatural signs to the sharing of possessions among the community members and giving to all in need (vv. 41–47).

This full and robust biblical understanding of the gospel is incredibly important. There are many truncations of the gospel in today's church. Some overemphasize the missional aspect of the church and in so doing abandon the theological truth that Jesus is God who came in the flesh to die and propitiate the just wrath of God toward sin. Others overemphasize the experiential aspect of the church and focus almost exclusively on renewal and worship while neglecting God's missional calling for the church to be incarnational like Jesus and actively involved in their community and its culture. Perhaps the most common overemphasis is the confessional reduction of the gospel to Jesus' death, forgiveness of sin, and imputed righteousness leading to eternal life in heaven. While this is true, it neglects Jesus' exemplary life, resurrection, imparted life of regeneration, and the rich life of the missional community of the church on the earth until we see him face-to-face.

Tragically, many Christians have lost the understanding of the new life of the Spirit. They do not preach or live the regeneration of believers. Rather than living out a joy-filled life flowing from their deepest desire to be like Jesus, they settle for being sinners saved by grace, obligated to do all they can to keep the law of God by duty rather than by delight. Subsequently, they have lost the double gift of imputed righteousness, which accompanies our justification, and the imparted righteousness of the indwelling Spirit, which accompanies our new heart and regeneration. On the cross God did a work for us by saving us through the death of Jesus in our place for our sins. At Pentecost we then see that God does a work in us through the Holy Spirit in our hearts for our regeneration. Together, both our eternity and every step along the way can be filled with hope, joy, purpose, and passion if we see the relationship between the cross and Pentecost.

God promised a new covenant when the Messiah came: "I will give you a new heart, and a new spirit I will put within you. And I will remove the heart of stone from your flesh and give you a heart of flesh. And I will put my Spirit within you, and cause you to walk in my statutes and be careful to obey my rules."[60] In the Bible, "heart" does not usually refer to the physical organ but rather the metaphorical center, seat, and sum of who we are. Proverbs 4:23 says, "Keep your heart with all vigilance, for from it flow the springs of life." Therefore, if our life is a river, it flows from the wellspring of our heart. The regenerating work of the Holy Spirit in the heart is the source of the Christian life and Christian church.

People who are regenerated are repeatedly spoken of throughout the New Testament as new people with a new identity, new mind, new desires, new emotions, new power, new hope, new joy, new love, new

---

[60]Ezek. 36:26–27.

passion, and new freedom to live a new life. Therefore, by the Spirit's power and our heart's desire, we live for, like, through, by, and with Jesus Christ for God's glory and our joy. We live as missionaries for Jesus in the world by loving our neighbors. We also gather together as the church to grow together in love for our spiritual brothers and sisters, all of which is done out of love for God because he has loved us so well.

One of the great debates among various denominations and theological traditions is how we can distinguish between Christians and non-Christians. Various answers such as being baptized, taking communion, asking Jesus into your heart, going to church, and living a good life are often given. The problem with each of these is that while true Christians do bear each of these marks, there are also non-Christians who do the acts without having regenerated hearts that belong to God. Such people are like the religious people God speaks of in Isaiah 29:13: "People draw near with their mouth and honor me with their lips, while their hearts are far from me, and their fear of me is a commandment taught by men." In the end, as 2 Timothy 2:19 says, "The Lord knows those who are his." This is because he alone knows our hearts and whether the Holy Spirit has regenerated them.

Regarding the regenerated heart, which is the mark of a true Christian, the theologian Millard J. Erickson has said,

> All of the people of God are marked with a special brand as it were. In the Old Testament, circumcision was the proof of divine ownership. It was required of all male children of the people of Israel, as well as of all male converts or proselytes. It was an external sign of the covenant which made them God's people. It was also a subjective sign of the covenant in that it was applied individually to each person, whereas the ark of the covenant served as an objective sign for the whole group.
>
> Instead of this external circumcision of the flesh, found in the administration of the old covenant, we find under the new covenant an inward circumcision of the heart. Paul wrote, "He is a Jew who is one inwardly, and real circumcision is a matter of the heart, spiritual and not literal" (Rom. 2:29; see also Phil. 3:3).[61]

The heart is both regenerated and empowered by God the Holy Spirit to live a life patterned after Jesus. In speaking of Jesus' earthly

---

[61]Millard J. Erickson, *Christian Theology* (Grand Rapids, MI: Baker, 1985), 1036.

ministry, Peter said, "God anointed Jesus of Nazareth with the Holy Spirit and with power. He went about doing good and healing all who were oppressed by the devil, for God was with him."[62] Likewise, prior to his death and resurrection, Jesus promised that those who believe in him would do greater works than he by the power of God the Holy Spirit who empowered his own life and ministry; we see this in the church spread across the earth to continue Jesus' ministry in a greater number of places than he could minister while limited by his human body.[63]

Before ascending into heaven, Jesus spoke of how the church was supposed to continue with Spirit-anointed ministry.[64] Just as Jesus promised, today Christians are sealed by the Holy Spirit at conversion and are able to be filled with the Holy Spirit like Jesus was.[65] This means that we can live like Jesus, doing what he did, with two exceptions. One, we must continually repent of personal sin, which is something the sinless Jesus never had to do. Two, we are not continually and perfectly able to live like Jesus because of our ongoing sinful desires.[66]

Subsequently, seeing Jesus as led and empowered by God the Holy Spirit eliminates any apparent conflict between the two for prominence. If Jesus was filled with the Holy Spirit, then Jesus and the Holy Spirit are obviously not in opposition but work together in perfect union. This allows us to love, worship, obey, and follow Jesus by the power of the Holy Spirit without any conflict in loyalty between Jesus and the Holy Spirit.

Additionally, seeing Jesus as Spirit-filled allows us to keep the cross at the center of our Bible and theological convictions rather than viewing the cross as the precursor to Pentecost, where the more important work of sending the Holy Spirit occurred. It allows us to see the crucifixion and resurrection of Jesus as the most important events in all of human history. It also allows us to see the outpouring of the Holy Spirit at Pentecost not as a distinct and greater work but as the application of the work of Jesus on the cross to sinners for their salvation, bringing the Holy Spirit to dwell in them and empower them to live the life of Jesus.

Practically, this also means that living the Spirit-filled life includes

---

[62]Acts 10:38.
[63]John 14:12–27.
[64]Acts 1:8.
[65]Eph. 1:13–14; 5:18.
[66]Gal. 5:16–18; Col. 3:5–8; James 4:1; 2 Pet. 2:4.

enduring hardship, pain, weakness, and loss as Jesus did. If we suffer while Spirit-filled, we will, like Jesus, grow in perfection through these hardships.[67] Therefore, we must embrace the truth that our joy lies through hardship, not in spite of hardship, if we remain led by the Spirit.[68] We must also accept that evil happens to even the most Spirit-filled people and is not an excuse for rebellious sin or a reason to believe that God is unjustly punishing us.[69] This Spirit-filled suffering is also required of whole churches, which suffer as the "body of Christ."[70] Therefore, being Spirit-filled like Jesus ultimately means denying ourselves, picking up our cross, and following him wherever the Spirit leads, which may include suffering and dying like Jesus.

This Spirit-filled perspective of Jesus' incarnation allows us to remain Jesus-centered in our thinking, Spirit-led in our practice, and humble in our hardships. This is made possible when we realize that because being Spirit-filled means being like Jesus, such things as poverty, sickness, and hardship are not incompatible with living a Spirit-filled life, as many false health-and-wealth teachers preach. Indeed, the only perfect Spirit-filled person who has ever lived, Jesus Christ, worked a simple job, lived a simple life, and died a painful death as a flat-broke homeless man by the power of the Holy Spirit as a missionary in a sinful culture.

Among many pastors today is a growing interest in the incarnation of Jesus Christ. Rightly understood, the incarnation of Jesus as a missionary in culture led and empowered by God the Holy Spirit serves as our pattern of life as Spirit-filled missionaries with regenerated hearts made possible by the cross. Wrongly understood, an overemphasis on the past humble incarnation of Jesus fails to see Jesus in his present glorious exaltation. If we were to see Jesus today we would not see him in his state of humble incarnation as a poor, homeless Galilean peasant. Rather, we would see Jesus as both Isaiah and John saw him[71]—enthroned in glory as King of kings and Lord of lords ruling over everyone and everything with "all authority in heaven and on earth," just as he said.[72]

[67] Heb. 5:8–9.
[68] Heb. 12:1–3.
[69] 1 Pet. 2:19–25.
[70] 1 Cor. 10:16; 12:13.
[71] Isa. 6:1–5 cf. John 12:41.
[72] Matt. 28:18.

Therefore, it is the supremacy of Jesus Christ as our sovereign and exalted God that is our authority for mission. There is not one inch of creation, one culture or subculture of people, one lifestyle or orientation, one religion or philosophical system, over which Jesus' throne does not rule. We derive our authority to preach the gospel to all peoples, times, and places from the glorious exaltation of our great God and savior, Jesus Christ. Jesus claimed all authority for himself and commanded us to go in his authority to preach the gospel truth: "that Christ died for our sins in accordance with the Scriptures, that he was buried, that he was raised on the third day in accordance with the Scriptures."[73] Jesus himself said, "All authority in heaven and on earth has been given to me. Go therefore and make disciples of all nations, baptizing them in the name of the Father and of the Son and of the Holy Spirit, teaching them to observe all that I have commanded you. And behold, I am with you always, to the end of the age."[74] Indeed, the authority of our mission rests on nothing less than the authority delegated to us by the exalted Lord Jesus Christ who rules over all. It is the one gospel of Jesus Christ that is needed by all tribes, races, nations, tongues, ethnicities, religions, and cultures.

Nevertheless, as we Christians enter into our local culture and its subcultures, we must also remember that it is Jesus who is sovereign, not us, and it is Jesus who rules over all, not the church. We are to come in the authority of the exalted Jesus, but we are also to come in the example of the humble incarnated Jesus. This means that we must come into culture like Jesus did—filled with the Holy Spirit, in constant prayer to the Father, saturated with the truth of Scripture, humble in our approach, loving in our truth, and serving in our deeds.

Jesus gave his life for the church and continually lives to care for his church. The connection between Jesus and the church is incredibly clear in Scripture. In Acts 6–8 we read of a zealous man named Saul who persecuted Christians and even oversaw the murder of a church deacon named Stephen. In Acts 9 the living Jesus actually got off his throne to come down and confront and convert Saul, saying, "Saul, Saul, why are you persecuting me?" Saul replied, "Who are you, Lord?" To which Jesus said, "I am Jesus, whom you are persecuting."[75] Thus, Jesus' own words

[73]1 Cor. 15:3–4.
[74]Matt. 28:18–20.
[75]Acts 9:4–5.

reveal that Jesus is so closely connected to the church that he too suffers when it is persecuted.

Perhaps the most vivid metaphor used in the New Testament for the church is Jesus' own words that he is the vine and we are the branches.[76] Therefore, both the life and unity of the church, despite all its diversity, is its connection to the living Jesus. One theologian has said:

> Unity, however, does not demand uniformity. Indeed, from the beginning the church has manifested itself in many local churches (in Jerusalem, Antioch, Corinth, Ephesus, etc.); and the one NT [*sic*] church had neither uniformity of worship nor structures, or even a uniform theology. . . . Unity is possible when we stop thinking of our church or denomination as the vine and all others as the branches. Rather, Jesus is the vine and all of us are branches.[77]

Because the church is so dear to Jesus, it is dear to Christians who love Jesus and are part of the church because of justification on the cross and regeneration in their hearts. This is why the church father Irenaeus rightly said, "Where the Church is, there is the Spirit of God; and where the Spirit of God is, there is the Church."[78]

---

[76]John 15:1–11.
[77]R. L. Omanson, "The Church," in *Evangelical Dictionary of Theology*, ed. Walter A. Elwell (Grand Rapids, MI: Baker, 1984), 232.
[78]Quoted in Douglas Wilson, *Mother Kirk: Essays and Forays in Practical Ecclesiology* (Moscow, ID: Canon Press, 2001), 34.

ANSWERS TO COMMON QUESTIONS ABOUT THE CHRISTIAN LIFE

HOW CAN SOMEONE KNOW THAT HE OR SHE IS A CHRISTIAN?

It is important to remember that the power of salvation is not in the strength of our faith but in the completeness of Jesus' saving work. Jesus said that even faith as small as a grain of mustard seed (Matt. 17:20) connects us to God's power, which raised Jesus from death, giving us new life and forgiveness of all sins (Col. 2:13). Through faith we can know the truth of what Paul said, "You were washed, you were sanctified, you were justified in the name of the Lord Jesus Christ and by the Spirit of our God" (1 Cor. 6:11).

The three dimensions of the Christian life are confession, experience, and mission. These dimensions are like the three legs of a stool on which you can sit solidly when you want to know that you are a Christian forgiven of sin, regenerated, and adopted as a child of the Most High God.

The first leg is confession. Being a Christian means that you "confess with your mouth, that Jesus is Lord and believe in your heart that God raised him from the dead" (Rom. 10:9). Ask yourself, "Am I trusting the truth of the gospel?" To help you answer this question, you may also want to reread chapter one and discuss it with a pastor or Christian friend.

Many people emphasize the moment when you prayed to accept Jesus. Some go so far as to declare that if you can't remember the moment you prayed, then you cannot even be a Christian. But if you look in the Bible, that kind of statement is never made. Conversely, 1 John 5:13 says, "I write these things to you who believe in the name of the Son of God that you may know that you have eternal life." It is real belief and not a magical prayer that saves a Christian. In fact, many who grew up in Christian homes never remember a time when they prayed a prayer or made a decision for Jesus, but they lovingly confess Jesus all the same.

The second leg is experience. A Christian experiences life change. Practically, this means that it is important for you to prayerfully examine yourself looking for evidences of God's Spirit-guided work in your life (John 14:26; 16:13; 1 Cor. 2:10). Do you see evidences of a new heart, a yearning to be like Jesus? Do you want to be with other believers in Jesus, as they "devote themselves to the apostles' teaching and the fellowship, to the breaking of bread and the prayers" (Acts 2:42)? Do you find that you wish you could stop doing sinful things? When you see these things, you are experiencing the fruit of "the washing of regeneration and renewal of the Holy Spirit, whom he poured out on us richly through Jesus Christ our Savior" (Titus 3:5–6).

The third leg is mission. Are you beginning to enjoy living a life in obedience to Jesus? Do you find that you want to join his rescue mission in the world? Do you want to help others to find forgiveness for their sins and healing for their brokenness? Do you want to help stop evil? Do you want to seek the welfare of the city in which you live? If so, then, as a Christian, you are becoming a missional follower of Jesus.

If you aren't quite sure whether you are a Christian, it will be helpful to find someone to speak with. Prayerfully seek out someone who lives for Jesus and has a knowledge of Scripture as well as compassion, kindness, humility, meekness, and patience (Col. 3:12) and talk to him or her about Jesus.

YOU DEFINED REGENERATION AS GOD GIVING US A NEW HEART BY THE POWER OF THE HOLY SPIRIT (P. 25). WHAT DOES IT MEAN TO LIVE A REGENERATED LIFE?

Living a regenerated life primarily means that our deepest desires are to live in loving obedience to Jesus out of our new heart by the power of the Holy Spirit. The opposite of this is either living in sin out of the deepest desires of an unregenerated heart or trying to live in compliance to a standard of righteousness without a new nature, when our deepest desires are for sin and not holiness. Like Jesus, regenerated living is serving not out of duty and fear of punishment but out of joy and delight (Heb. 12:2).

We want to please God, to be with him, to be like him. The longings of a regenerated heart are for his Word, for prayer, for worship, for fellowship with God and his people, for service, for holiness, for witness, and for being home with him in his eternal kingdom.

However, the conflict with sin continues because we still have sinful desires, what the Bible calls "flesh." The sinful desires are opposed to the desires of the new heart (Gal. 5:17). Romans 7:14–25 describes the conflict in the justified (Romans 4–5) and regenerated (Romans 6) believer. In regeneration, love for God and neighbor is written on our heart in the depth of our being. At this deep level, we can say, "I delight in the law of God, in my inner being" (Rom. 7:22). But Paul sees in himself "another law waging war against the law of my mind" (Rom. 7:23). This is the presence of sinful desires, and the conflict they cause makes us feel wretched. Paul's answer is not more law but instead more Spirit (Rom. 8:2–4).

This is also how Paul deals with the sins of the Corinthian believers who were involved in rampant sexual immorality, hostile factions, and even idolatry. Paul could have easily opened his Bible and thundered, "The Ten Commandments order us not to worship idols and to abstain from sexual immorality, so stop it!" But he didn't. Again and again he called them back to Jesus and their life with him. Don't go to prostitutes because you are united with Christ. Don't go to demon feasts, because that is not who you are in Jesus. It is the same principle in every case: Jesus, Spirit, life, heart—not law. Do right because of who you are in Christ and because he's in you. Everything is defined by our new identity and our new love.

If we take time to think and pray, consulting with other new covenant believers, and do what will give us the deepest joy, then we will almost always do the right thing. We serve God with delight rather than drudgery. Obedience, or keeping in step with the Spirit, means that we stop doing willful sins and do the things Christ asks us to do, because that will make us and Jesus happiest. We do this by the gracious direction and empowerment of the Spirit. Rather than focusing on mere morality, or conduct, we live transformation from the inside out. As we draw close to God and spend time in his presence, the Spirit progressively transforms our character into conformity with the character of Christ. As this happens, Jesus says, "You will find rest for your souls. For my yoke is easy, and my burden is light" (Matt. 11:29–30).

You can find more on this approach to the Christian life in books like Dallas Willard, *Renovation of the Heart*; John Piper, *Desiring God*; and Gary Thomas, *The Beautiful Fight*.

YOUR STATEMENT OF THE GOSPEL IS VERY DIFFERENT FROM WHAT I LEARNED IN CHURCH.

Sadly, you are not alone. Many Christians have learned only the forgiveness part of the gospel. These gospel presentations begin with our sinfulness, separation from God, and impending eternity in hell and go on to say that Jesus came to die to pay the penalty for our sin so that if we believe and receive him as Savior, we will have all our sins forgiven and spend eternity with him in heaven.

Everything in this outline is absolutely true. But it leaves out some vitally important aspects of the gospel as Peter preached it in Acts 2 (see page 23). For example, if we leave out regeneration, the Christian life is reduced to duty-based religion rather than the joyous spiritual life. Without membership in the community of the Spirit, people bring culturally conditioned values of radical individualism into their Christian experience. Subsequently, Christianity becomes only a matter of private devotion between me and God, something that's all about *me* and what *I* get from God instead of a participation in a community committed to fulfilling the mission of God. Without exaltation and the defeat of the powers of darkness, people are left thinking they are helpless in their subjugation to the pagan gods and evil spirits.

DIDN'T JESUS COME TO EARTH TO DIE FOR OUR SIN?

Absolutely! But that's not all he came for. In addition to coming to die for sin, Jesus came to redeem captives out of slavery into freedom (John 8:32–36), to destroy the authority of the powers of darkness (Eph. 1:20–23), to show us how to live (Phil. 2:1–5; 1 John 4:9–11), to reveal the Father to us (John 1:18; Rom. 5:8), and to bring us life. When Jesus speaks of this life, he exclaims, "I came that they may have life and have it abundantly" (John 10:10).

This life is not just being with Jesus in heaven after we die but having a Spirit-empowered relationship with Jesus in the present. John 17:21 says we actually share the life of the Trinity now. Jesus prays "that they may all be one, just as you, Father, are in me, and I in you, that they also may be in us, so that the world may believe that you have sent me." It is a serious mistake to affirm one facet of truth with the implication that it is the whole truth. Even if we do it with good intention, we still deny truth.

CHAPTER TWO

WHAT IS A CHRISTIAN CHURCH?

**And they devoted themselves to the apostles'
teaching and the fellowship, to the breaking of bread
and the prayers. And awe came upon every soul,
and many wonders and signs were being done.**

ACTS 2:42-43

✝

A few billion people worship Jesus Christ as God every week and do so in the church as the church. Yet, if you walk into various churches and ask the people who comprise that church what the word *church* means, the odds are that you will get either a blank stare or a series of conflicting definitions.

Sadly, this is even true from their pastors. In preparing for this book I asked various pastors of some of America's largest churches—godly men and dear friends—if they have a working definition of the church. And not one of them did; they confessed they were giving their lives to building something for which they did not even have a clear definition.

Their response was not surprising, because for much of the history of the church the definition of church has simply been assumed. For example, the Nicene Creed says, "We believe in one holy catholic and apostolic church." Yet, it does not define what is meant by "church" but rather assumes that we already know.

The assumption that Christians innately know what the church is has a long history. The early church debated many things, such as the Trinity and the relationship between the humanity and divinity of Jesus Christ. However, one issue it did not debate was what constitutes the church. After Cyprian, bishop of Carthage, wrote *The Unity of the Church* in AD 251 until Wycliffe wrote *The Church* in 1378, there was no significant monograph on the church.[1]

Everything changed in the sixteenth century when the Reformation forced Protestants and Roman Catholics alike to actually define church. This led to numerous definitions and debates, which continue to this day with no widespread agreement. For example, the *Evangelical Dictionary of Theology* says:

> The Arnoldists emphasized poverty and identification with the masses; the Waldenses stressed literal obedience to Jesus' teachings and emphasized evangelical preaching. Roman Catholics claimed that the only true church was that over which the pope was supreme as successor of the apostle Peter. The Reformers Martin Luther and John Calvin, following John Wycliffe, distinguished between the visible and invisible church, claiming that the invisible church consists of the elect only. Thus an individual, including the pope, might be a part of the visible church but not a part of the invisible and true church."[2]

Part of the confusion is that the Greek word *ekklēsia*, which is translated "church," has a wide range of meaning.[3] Originally, it sometimes designated any public assembly, including a full-blown riot.[4] In the Septuagint (the Greek translation of the Hebrew Old Testament), the word is translated *qāhāl*, which designates the assembly of God's people.[5] So in the New Testament *ekklēsia* may signify the assembly of the Israelites.[6] Most of the uses of the word *ekklēsia* in the New Testament designate the Christian church, both the local church[7] and the universal church.[8]

The English word *church* derives from the Greek word *kyriakon*,

---

[1]T. F. Torrance, *Theology in Reconstruction* (Grand Rapids, MI: Eerdmans, 1965), 266.
[2]R. L. Omanson, "The Church," in *Evangelical Dictionary of Theology*, ed. Walter A. Elwell (Grand Rapids, MI: Baker, 1984), 231.
[3]Ibid.
[4]Acts 19:32, 39, 41.
[5]Deut. 10:4; 23:2–3; 31:30; Ps. 22:23.
[6]Acts 7:38; Heb. 2:12.
[7]Matt. 18:17; Acts 15:41; Rom. 16:16; 1 Cor. 4:17; 7:17; 14:33; Col. 4:15.
[8]Matt. 16:18; Acts 20:28; 1 Cor. 12:28; 15:9; Eph. 1:22.

which means "the Lord's."[9] Later it came to mean the Lord's house, a church building. This increases the confusion because nowhere in the New Testament does *church* in any of its forms refer to a building. Wayne Grudem helpfully summarizes the uses of *church*:

> A "house church" is called a "church" in Romans 16:5 ("greet also *the church in their house*"), 1 Corinthians 16:19 ("Aquila and Prisca, together with *the church in their house*, send you hearty greetings in the Lord"). The church in an entire city is also called "a church" (1 Cor. 1:2; 2 Cor. 1:1; and 1 Thess. 1:1). The church in a region is referred to as a "church" in Acts 9:31: "So *the church throughout all Judea and Galilee and Samaria* had peace and was built up." Finally, the church throughout the entire world can be referred to as "the church." Paul says, "Christ loved *the church* and gave himself up for her" (Eph. 5:25) and says, "God has appointed *in the church* first apostles, second prophets, third teachers . . ." (1 Cor. 12:28). . . . We may conclude that the group of God's people considered at any level from local to universal may rightly be called "a church."[10]

Various Christian traditions are prone to define the church—or their church—in an unhealthy and reductionistic manner, focusing on one primary metaphor at the expense of the full breadth of New Testament teaching. As a result, they become imbalanced in some way and therefore unhealthy. For example, the corporate church is referred to as the bride of Christ. The result of overemphasizing this metaphor is the effeminate nature of much of evangelical preaching and singing.[11]

We must devote this chapter to defining the *being* of the church before we turn to the *well-being* of the church in the rest of the book. The definition of what constitutes a Christian church is vitally important, especially in our day when cultists and oddball, self-appointed spiritual gurus keep starting various kinds of pseudo-churches. The church is also a hot issue among younger pastors today. In previous generations, singles' ministry, student ministry, and parachurch ministry were the hot options for entrepreneurial young leaders. But today the hot ministry is church planting in every form. This includes churches within

---

[9]1 Cor. 11:20; Rev. 1:10.
[10]Wayne Grudem, *Systematic Theology: An Introduction to Biblical Doctrine* (Grand Rapids, MI: Zondervan, 1994), 857.
[11]This is what David Murrow speaks of in his book *Why Men Hate Going to Church* (Nashville: Thomas Nelson, 2004).

churches seeking to reach people outside the existing church, house churches, multi-campus churches, and traditional church planting. This phenomenon is spreading across all denominational and theological traditions, often with no clear understanding of exactly what a church is or does.

Furthermore, the effort to cultivate the most innovative and effective postmodern church has led to a market of books that nearly always start with some word followed by "church," such as *Liquid Church, Emerging Church, Organic Church, Missional Church, Multi-Site Church, Externally Focused Church, House Church, Future Church, Ancient-Future Church, Blogging Church,* and *Prevailing Church.* What is curious about most of the books on the church is that very rarely do any of them actually define what the church is, or even clarify what the church does. Instead, most of the books simply share best practices gleaned from "successful" churches. This is curious because without a definition of what a church is or does, I'm unsure how we can even deem one successful. Therefore, we will establish a definition of the local church:

> The local church is a community of regenerated believers who confess Jesus Christ as Lord. In obedience to Scripture they organize under qualified leadership, gather regularly for preaching and worship, observe the biblical sacraments of baptism and Communion, are unified by the Spirit, are disciplined for holiness, and scatter to fulfill the Great Commandment and the Great Commission as missionaries to the world for God's glory and their joy.

This definition is summarized from Acts 2. As we study through that text, we will see eight characteristics of the true local church, which is an incarnation of the universal church. I believe understanding these characteristics will be helpful to many churches and their leaders, thanks to Gerry's helpful insights gleaned over many decades of study on this issue. A true church is one characterized by:

1) Regenerated church membership
2) Qualified leadership
3) Preaching and worship
4) Rightly administered sacraments
5) Spirit unity
6) Holiness

7) The Great Commandment to love

8) The Great Commission to evangelize and make disciples.

1) The church is made up of regenerated believers in Jesus.[12] There are unbelievers and outsiders who join the meetings and have an important place in the extended community, as we see in passages such as 1 Corinthians 14:22–25. Likewise, children are welcomed into the church to be loved and served so that they will become Christians with saving faith and then church members. Therefore, the church is a community manifesting the supernatural life of the triune God.

2) The church is organized under qualified and competent leadership. For example, we see the leadership role of the apostles in Acts, including their unique role in teaching (2:42), their receiving of gifts (4:35–5:2), their leading the congregation in wise decision making about a potentially divisive problem (6:1–6), and their sending Peter and John to Samaria to confirm the authenticity of the evangelistic outbreak there (8:14). We also see the church appointment of elders in Acts 14:23. In Acts 15 they practice their leadership in a doctrinal dispute with the party of the Pharisees in Jerusalem. In Acts 6 is the beginning of what were likely deacons appointed to oversee service.

3) The church regularly gathers to hear God's Word rightly preached and to respond in worshipful ways. The church is under apostolic authority. As such, it is a learning and growing church. In the early church, people eagerly devoted themselves to the teaching of the apostles,[13] not because they had to but because their regenerated hearts wanted to. They had received the Spirit, seen remarkable miracles, and witnessed great conversion growth. But they also refused a simple experience-based Christianity.

As disciples, they knew they needed to learn, and so they studied not just for information but also for transformation in all of their life. Therefore, the church studies Scripture to show submission to the apostolic authority of the Word of God. We believe in the apostolic gift for church planting and movement leading, but we do not believe there are apostles in the same sense today, insofar as being able to write books of the Bible and such; rather, their teaching authority comes to us in Scripture. From the very beginning, the church recog-

---

[12] Acts 2:38–41.

[13] Acts 2:42.

nized the unique authority of the apostolic writings and immediately canonized them as divinely inspired, just like the Old Testament Scriptures.

The church was also a worshiping community where believers praised God and had favor with all people.[14] Worship is a response to the revelation of the Lord consisting of both adoration and proclamation of the greatness of God and his mighty works[15] and of serving him by living out his character in gracious service to others. It is both *proskuneo*, literally to fall down and kiss Jesus' feet in an expression of one's allegiance to and adoration for God,[16] and *latreia* or *leitourgeo*, which is ministering, or doing work and service in the world in the name of Jesus.[17]

4) The church is where the biblical sacraments of baptism and Communion are performed regularly.

5) The church is unified by God the Holy Spirit. In this way the unified life of the Trinity is manifested among God's people who live in loving unity together as the church.

6) The church is a holy people. When they sin, they repent of their sin. If someone should fail to repent, the church and its leaders lovingly enact biblical church discipline in hopes of bringing the sinner to repentance and to a reconciled relationship with God and his people.

7) The church is a loving community that devotes itself to fellowship, or *koinonia*. Fellowship includes God's people living together in intentional, relational community to seek the well-being of one another in every way, including physical, spiritual, material, and emotional. This most misunderstood word speaks of the church as having a close association involving mutual interests and sharing, characterized by an attitude of good will that manifests in generosity, altruism, and sharing one's possessions because of joint participation in the Spirit and mutual interest in Jesus.[18] For fellowship, the church gathers regularly[19] for such things as worship, learning, sacrament, and encouragement. But even when it is not gathered, it is still the church. There is a Spirit-bond of belonging and mission that unites the believers wherever they are,

[14]Act 2:47.
[15]Acts 2:11.
[16]Matt. 2:11; 4:9; 8:2; 28:9; Rev. 19:10.
[17]Rom. 1:9; 12:1; Rev. 7:15.
[18]"*Koinonia*," in *A Greek-English Lexicon of the New Testament and Other Early Christian Literature*, 3rd ed. (BDAG), ed. and rev. Frederick William Danker (Chicago: University of Chicago Press, 2000).
[19]Acts 20:7; 1 Cor. 5:4; 11:17–20; 14:23–26; Heb. 10:25.

in the same way that a family is still a family even when Dad is at work, Mom is at the store, and the kids are at school.

8) The church is an evangelistic community where the gospel of Jesus is constantly made visible by its preaching, its witness of the members, and its Spirit-empowered life of love. From the first day "the Lord added to their number day by day those who were being saved"[20] because they took Jesus' command seriously: "You will receive power when the Holy Spirit has come upon you, and you will be my witnesses in Jerusalem and in all Judea and Samaria, and to the end of the earth."[21]

As we now examine various ways that the church has been defined throughout history, our hope is to inform you of some of the important differences between definitions of what constitutes the true church and to help you be discerning in what church you would choose for fellowship. We will begin with the church in which I was baptized as an infant and raised, the Roman Catholic Church, before proceeding to other definitions held by Reformed Protestantism, which I have adhered to since Jesus saved me at the age of nineteen and which Gerry has been involved in since he was an infant.

CATHOLICS: ROMAN, EASTERN, AND ANGLICAN

Catholicism in its various forms stresses the historical and institutional nature of the church. We see this in the official definition of the Catholic Church as found in the documents of Vatican II in chapter 1 of "The Dogmatic Constitution on the Church": the church is defined as simultaneously "visible structure" and "the Mystical Body of Christ."[22] To further explain this, the document continues, "After his resurrection our Saviour handed her [the church] over to Peter to be shepherded (John 21:27), commissioning him and the other apostles to propagate and govern her.... This church, constituted and organized in the world as a society, subsists in the Catholic Church, which is governed by the successor of Peter and by the Bishops in communion with him."[23]

The document goes on to explain how the church is to be orga-

[20]Acts 2:47.
[21]Acts 1:8.
[22]W. Abbott and J. Gallagher, eds., "Lumen Gentium," 1, 8, in *The Documents of Vatican II* (USA: Geoffrey Chapman, 1966), 22. (Also available online here: http://www.vatican.va/archive/hist_ councils/ii_ vatican_council/documents/vat-ii_const_19641121_lumen-gentium_en.html).
[23]Ibid., 23.

nized. First, we are told that Jesus Christ appointed Peter to lead the apostles, granting to them special power and authority. Second, they then appointed bishops as their successors to continue this proverbial chain of command from one generation to the next, all the way to our present day. Third, the bishops appointed men as priests and deacons to assist them in ministry and "share the sacerdotal dignity" of the bishops and are granted special power, including the power to re-represent the sacrifice of Jesus Christ during the Mass.[24]

Summarily, the Catholic concept of the church as an institution inaugurated by God with a clear hierarchy that is to be maintained through successive generations "has been a standard feature of Roman Catholic ecclesiology from the late middle ages until the middle of the present century."[25]

Roman Catholic theologians see the church primarily as a worldwide clerical hierarchy under the bishops who are successors of the authority of the apostles, with the bishop of Rome being the successor of Peter. They support this from such passages as 2 Timothy 2:2, "What you have heard from me in the presence of many witnesses entrust to faithful men who will be able to teach others also." They also see the church as a eucharistic society, the organism through which God dispenses his grace through the sacraments. Subsequently, only in the Catholic Church can people receive the grace of God.

Anglican theologian Kevin Giles says, "Almost word for word, apart from the claim for the Papacy, Anglo Catholics [Anglicans] conceive of the church in exactly these terms. . . . For the Anglo Catholic, even more so than the Roman Catholic, the threefold form of the ministry (i.e., bishops, priests, and deacons) is constitutive of the being of the church."[26]

In response to the Protestant Reformation, the Roman Catholic Counter-Reformation emphasized the visible nature of the church as synonymous with the invisible nature of the church. Perhaps one of the clearest expressions of this error came from Robert Bellarmine (1542–1621) who said, "The church is a society as visible and as palpable as are the community of the people of Rome, or the kingdom of France, or the Republic of Venice."[27]

---

[24]Ibid., 53.
[25]Avery Dulles, *Models of the Church* (New York: Doubleday, 1991), 26.
[26]Kevin Giles, *What on Earth Is the Church? An Exploration in New Testament Theology* (Downers Grove, IL: InterVarsity, 1995), 9.
[27]Ibid., 192.

For me personally, this definition is very troubling. I was baptized and raised in the Catholic Church as a member of a practicing Catholic family. Furthermore, I spent a few years as an altar boy assisting the priest in Mass as a visible leader in the church. I too sadly believed that because I was a member of the church partaking in Communion, my eternal salvation was secure. I wrongly believed that the church was the mediator between me and God.

It was not until the age of nineteen, while reading Romans in my college dorm room, that God the Holy Spirit regenerated me, giving me faith to trust in Jesus alone for my salvation. This happened apart from any church. Both the teaching of Scripture and the work of the Holy Spirit to regenerate me through the power of the gospel made me a member of the invisible church despite the fact I had already lived my life as a member of the visible church. My point is that you can be baptized in the church, raised in the church, confirmed in the church, serve in the church, marry in the church, die in the church, and have your funeral in the church, and still wake up in hell if you are merely in the church and not in Christ.

This distinction was made most poignantly to me at the funeral of someone I knew very well. He had been baptized and confirmed in the Catholic Church but had not lived a life of repentance or love for Jesus at all. In fact, some of his coworkers showed up at his funeral to, in their own words, make sure he was dead because he had been so despicable. His funeral was held in a Catholic church and officiated by a priest who asked me to say a few words since I was a pastor. I will never forget, standing on the platform waiting to speak, when the priest walked in along with the processional and stood alongside me and declared to the almost entirely non-Christian gathering of friends and family, whom I knew were committing adultery and regularly abusing drugs and alcohol, that they could rest assured that their dead friend and relative was in heaven because he had been baptized as a member of the Catholic Church as a baby, and that if they too were Catholic, God was fine with them.

He then looked at me and said I was free to say a few words, which by God's grace alone did not include expletives. Instead, I briefly presented the gospel as the only assurance for eternal life. Simply, we reject the Catholic definition of the church as unbiblical, unfaithful, and unhelpful because it falls into the same trap as Judaism, believing that succession and not faith is the entry point into the community of God's people.

However, we do appreciate the Catholic Church's attempt to remain connected with and faithful to the apostles. We would argue, however, that it has wrongly defined how to be apostolically faithful. Paul's point in 2 Timothy isn't the establishment of a line of ordination, but that the men who are constituted leaders are faithful to the apostolic teaching, the faith once for all delivered to the saints.[28] Irenaeus, the second-century church father and grandson in the faith of John the apostle, expounds this point well:

> The Church having received this preaching and this faith, although scattered throughout the whole world, yet, as if occupying but one house, carefully preserves it. She also believed these points [of doctrine] just as if she had but one soul, and one and the same heart, and she proclaims them, and teaches them, and hands them down, with perfect harmony, as if she possessed one mouth.[29]

One theologian summarizes it well: "To claim that the church is apostolic is not to assert a direct line of succession through specific individuals. It is to recognize that the message and the mission of the apostles as mediated through Scripture must be that of the whole church."[30]

To be faithfully apostolic, a church must remain true to both the biblical message and mission of Jesus. For that and other reasons we are Protestants, which we will now examine.

PROTESTANT

The leaders of the Protestant Reformation rejected the Roman Catholic definition of the church on many grounds. (1) The church and its leaders and sacraments do not function between God and his people in a mediatorial manner, because in Scripture Jesus Christ alone is clearly said to be our only mediator and means of saving grace. First Timothy 2:5 says, "For there is one God, and there is *one mediator* between God and men, the man Christ Jesus." (2) There is no evidence anywhere in the New

---

[28]Jude 1:3.
[29]*Against Heresies*, I.10.2.
[30]R. L. Omanson, "The Church," 233.

Testament that Jesus Christ or his apostles called the church into being with such a rigidly structured institutional hierarchy as purported by Catholicism. (3) There is no evidence anywhere in the New Testament that the apostles appointed bishops. (4) Outside of Scripture the history of the early church flatly denies that it organized itself in the manner described by the Roman Catholic Church.[31] (5) The entire concept of the Roman Catholic priesthood contradicts the repeated New Testament teaching that in the new covenant there is not a special office of priest but rather a special priesthood.[32] As this priesthood, believers have direct access to God the Father through God the Son by God the Spirit,[33] live lives of worship as sacrifices to God,[34] hear the confessions of one another's sin,[35] and give spiritual guidance and counsel.[36] (6) The idea that the appointed leaders and members of the Roman Catholic Church were godly followers and obedient servants of Jesus Christ as the true church on earth simply contradicts even the Roman Catholic Church's historical record, as many leaders were godless men who served out of political and not spiritual motivation.

Augustine became the bishop of Hippo in AD 396 and saw the churches under his jurisdiction divided by heresy and many church members and leaders living unregenerate lives as "the covetous, the defrauders, the robbers, the usurers and the drunkards."[37] As a result, he developed a concept that distinguished between the visible and the invisible church, which later featured very prominently in the Protestant definition of the church during the Reformation.

This distinction is biblical and comes from Jesus Christ himself, who said that not everyone who is a member of the visible church on earth is truly a member of the invisible, historical church bound for heaven. Jesus distinguished between wheat and weeds, and wolves and sheep in the church.[38] Even Jesus himself had a non-Christian wolf among his little flock of twelve, Judas Iscariot.

---

[31]For example, see Edward Schillebeeckx, *Ministry: A Case for Change* (London: SCM, 1981) and *The Church With a Human Face* (London: SCM, 1985); Bernard Cooke, *Ministry to Word and Sacrament* (Philadelphia: Fortress, 1980); and Kenan Osborne, *Priesthood: A History of the Ordained Ministry in the Roman Catholic Church* (New York: Paulist, 1988).
[32]1 Pet. 2:5–9.
[33]Rom. 5:1–2; Eph. 2:18.
[34]Rom. 12:1.
[35]James 5:16.
[36]Col. 3:16.
[37]Kevin Giles, *What on Earth Is the Church?* 190.
[38]Matt. 7:15; 13:24–30.

The invisible church is the church as God perfectly sees it. The invisible church is the community of all Christians throughout history who have been or will be loved and saved by Jesus Christ,[39] including the believing people of the Old Testament.[40] While it is possible for us to know others who profess faith in Christ (e.g., the Bible often references people as Christian brothers and sisters), ultimately only the Lord knows exactly who is and is not a Christian.[41] In this sense, "invisible church" refers to every person of any age, race, and culture whose sins are forgiven through the death and resurrection of Jesus Christ.

On the topic of the invisible church, theologian Millard Erickson says, "In Ephesians, Paul gives particular emphasis to the universal nature of the church. . . . 'There is one body' (4:4). . . . Obviously, the church includes all persons anywhere in the world who are savingly related to Christ. It also includes all who have lived and been part of his body, and all who will live and be part of his body."[42] Likewise, Wayne Grudem says, "*The church is the community of all true believers for all time.* This definition understands the church to be made of all those who are truly saved. Paul says, 'Christ loved *the church* and gave himself up for her' (Eph. 5:25)."[43]

The visible church is the church as we imperfectly see it. The various congregations of the universal church that regularly meet together in a particular place at a set time for things such as teaching, fellowship, and worship are commonly called the "local church" or the "visible church."[44] Many of the letters in the New Testament were written to help inform and direct the visible, local churches of such cities as Philippi, Corinth, Ephesus, Colossae, and Thessalonica. The local church is visible in that the community sees people who belong to the Lord Jesus gathering as the church for regular meetings, often called church services. Outsiders also see those in the visible church living the life of Jesus as they disperse into the community.[45]

The differences between the visible and invisible church can be seen in Chart 2.1:[46]

[39]Acts 20:28; Eph. 5:25.
[40]Deut. 4:10; Acts 7:38; Heb. 2:12 cf. Ps. 22:22.
[41]2 Tim. 2:19.
[42]Millard J. Erickson, *Christian Theology* (Grand Rapids, MI: Baker Books, 1985), 1034.
[43]Grudem, *Systematic Theology*, 853.
[44]For example, see Heb. 10:25.
[45]To examine this further see Erickson, *Christian Theology*, 1030–1033.
[46]H. Wayne House, "Local Church Contrasted with the Universal Church" in *Charts of Christian*

CHART 2.1

Visible	Invisible
Membership: saved and lost	Membership: saved only
Only currently living people	Both dead and living in Christ
Many local churches	Only one universal church
Differing denominations	No single denomination
Part of the body of Christ	The entire body of Christ
Differing types of government	Christ is the only head
Ministering the ordinances	Ordinances fulfilled
(or sacraments)	(e.g., 1 Cor. 11:23-26; Rev. 19:9)

In local churches there are invariably people who love Jesus out of regenerated hearts—Christians—and people who do not—non-Christians. Therefore, while members of the invisible church do participate in the visible church, the Reformers rightly stressed that not everyone who is a member of the visible church is a member of the invisible church and that many are wrongly assured that they are saved because they are in the church, even though they are not in Christ.

As a result, the Reformers defined the church in terms of the presence of the gospel of Jesus Christ. Perhaps the most famous Protestant definition of the church is from John Calvin, who said, "Wherever we see the Word of God purely preached and heard, and the sacraments administered according to Christ's institution, there, it is not to be doubted, a church of God exists."[47] The same definition with minor alterations appears in many strands of Protestantism, including the Lutheran Augsburg Confession (1530), the Forty-two Articles of the Church of England (1553), and the Belgic Confession of 1561.

According to Calvin and the Reformers, with whom we agree, the church is what happens because God the Holy Spirit works in power through the gospel of Jesus Christ and is not a static institution resting its hopes on apostolic succession. This gospel message of Jesus is to be heard by rightly teaching the Scriptures and rightly guarded with baptism, the Lord's Supper, regenerated church membership, and ensuing church discipline as needed.

The result of these definitions was that the Protestant church

---

Theology and Doctrine (Grand Rapids, MI: Zondervan, 1992), 116.
[47]John Calvin, *The Institutes of the Christian Religion*, ed. J. McNeill, trans. F. L. Battles, vol. 2 (Louisville, KY: Westminster John Knox, 1960), 1023.

was continually reforming itself by the Scriptures, in contrast to the Catholic Church. On this point Mark Dever writes, "At the time of the Reformation the Roman Catholic Church had a Latin phrase that became something of a motto: *semper idem*. It means 'always the same.' Well, the Reformed churches, too, had a 'semper' motto: *ecclesia reformata, semper reformanda secundum verbum Dei*. 'The church reformed, always being reformed according to the Word of God.'"[48]

The reforming of the church by the Word of God can be accomplished only by continually returning to the truth of the gospel of Jesus Christ. The great Protestant reformer Martin Luther rightly defined the visible church as a community holding common faith in the gospel of Jesus Christ.

Wayne Grudem writes that the Protestant Reformers, including Calvin and Luther,

> said that the Roman Catholic Church had the outward form, the organization, but it was just a shell. Calvin argued that just as Caiaphas (the high priest at the time of Christ) was descended from Aaron but was no true priest, so the Roman Catholic bishops had "descended" from the apostles in a line of succession but they were not true bishops in Christ's church. Because they had departed from the true preaching of the gospel, their visible organization was not the true church. Calvin said, "This pretense of succession is vain unless their descendants conserve safe and uncorrupted the truth of Christ which they have received at their fathers' hands, and abide in it. . . . See what value this succession has, unless it also include [*sic*] a true and uninterrupted emulation on the part of the successors!"[49]

Because a right definition of the church is so important for both the being of the church and well-being of its members, Protestants have commonly defined the true church as a breakdown of the Nicene Creed, which says, "We believe in one holy catholic and apostolic church."

"One" church means that ultimately all denominations and traditions are one in Jesus Christ and, while not uniform, are unified. This is because they confess Jesus, live for Jesus, serve Jesus, love Jesus, and follow Jesus according to the gospel by the Spirit. "Holy" church means that because of Jesus his people are set apart, changed, and through

---

[48]Mark Dever, *Nine Marks of a Healthy Church* (Wheaton, IL: Crossway Books, 2004), 51.
[49]Grudem, *Systematic Theology*, 856.

sanctification able to become more and more like Jesus in character through the Holy Spirit. "Catholic" church means that the church is without the limitations of time and space so that the church is made up of people from varying tribes, tongues, races, genders, incomes, educations, generations, times, and places. "Apostolic" church means that it is founded on the teaching and preaching of the apostles as recorded in Scripture. This does not equate to apostolic succession as the Roman Catholic tradition defines it; rather, the true church follows the teaching and life example of the apostles appointed by Jesus to proclaim the gospel in word and deed.

In addition, various Protestant theologians and theological traditions have added to these four marks. Examples include church discipline to preserve the distinction between the church and the world, fellowship between God's people who love one another, and God's people on a mission to evangelize lost people and plant churches in the world with the gospel of Jesus Christ.

STREAMS OF THE PROTESTANT REFORMATION

Where Calvinists, Lutherans, and Anglicans formed denominations and understood the church as a large organization of universal or national scope, the sixteenth-century Anabaptists understood the church primarily in terms of its local expression in specific congregations. This understanding was developed by the pietists and the Puritans and came to be known as congregationalism. Today it is the prevailing definition of the church among such groups as Baptists, Pentecostals, Brethren, and independent churches.

Congregationalism, generally speaking, defines following Jesus in seven ways.

1) The church is a community of followers of Christ committed to Christlikeness; it is not a denomination.

2) Every believer is a priest with equal access to God the Father through Jesus Christ and a responsibility to help other believers connect with God.

3) The Scriptures alone are the final authority for faith and practice, and church leaders are to be followed and obeyed only if their life and doctrine agree with Scripture.

4) Local churches are a complete body of believers with Jesus Christ

as their head in ultimate authority and as such are free from external control but are in partnership with likeminded churches for the cause of evangelizing the world.

5) Local churches should make decisions in an essentially democratic way with all church members involved in speaking into and implementing decisions made by the church leadership.

6) Only when individuals are old enough to articulate and demonstrate personal saving faith should they be baptized by total immersion and partake in the Lord's Supper.

7) The local church is separate from the state and neither should control or support the other. The church submits to the state only when it does not contradict the Scriptures, and the church calls the state to righteousness and justice.

The Anabaptist definition of the church continued up to and through the modern era of the enlightenment.

THE MODERN ERA

After René Descartes began his defense of God with the word *I*, one of the great hallmarks of the modern era was its radical commitment to the individual. While not a concept in either the Old or New Testament, the idea that people stand alone as isolated individuals wove its way into the modern era, especially the American consciousness where the rugged individual is the hero in virtually all of our great cultural narratives. As a result, during the modern era the focus shifted from the church to the individual. On this point the historian Mark Noll says, "Up to the early 1700s, British Protestants preached on God's plan for the church. From the mid–1700s, however, evangelicals emphasized God's plans for the individual."[50]

From the declaration by God in the garden to our first parents—that it is not good to be alone—to the example of the one true God who himself exists in Trinitarian community as Father, Son, and Spirit, the emphasis of Scripture is that while we are individuals insofar as there is distinction between us, through the reconciling work of Jesus there should not be division but loving relational community as the church. The Bible is clear that every Christian is a part of the larger church body and is expected to participate in the life of a local church with the

---

[50]Mark Noll, "Father of Modern Evangelicals?" *Christian History* 38, vol. 12, no. 2 (1993), 44.

gift(s) God has given him or her. This is so God may be glorified and so his people may be built up through their service to one another.[51] It is therefore a sin for someone who claims to be a Christian not to be actively loving his or her Christian brothers and sisters[52] and seeking to build up the church as faithful members of a church.[53]

Yet, here we see one of the tragic effects of modernism on church life. Many people who claim to be Christians adopted by God the Father have nothing to do with their brothers and sisters in God's family, the church. Such people will excuse themselves by decrying the hypocrisy of the church while conveniently overlooking their own hypocrisy, or even claiming that all they need is Jesus. In refutation of this modern false teaching, 1 John 1:1–3 says,

> That which was from the beginning, which we have heard, which we have seen with our eyes, which we looked upon and have touched with our hands, concerning the word of life—the life was made manifest, and we have seen it, and testify to it and proclaim to you the eternal life, which was with the Father and was made manifest to us—that which we have seen and heard we proclaim also to you, so that you too may have fellowship with us; and indeed our fellowship is with the Father and with his Son Jesus Christ.

John's point is that believers stay in relation with other Christians. He goes on to speak of false believers in 2:19: "They went out from us, but they were not of us; for if they had been of us, they would have continued with us. But they went out, that it might become plain that they all are not of us."

Why is it important that believers stay together in the church? Because that is where we love other believers, the mark of the Christian according to Jesus.[54] John teaches what he learned from Jesus, saying, "By this it is evident who are the children of God, and who are the children of the devil: whoever does not practice righteousness is not of God, nor is the one who does not love his brother."[55] He also says, "He who does not love his brother whom he has seen cannot love God whom he

---

[51]1 Cor. 12:1–31.
[52]1 John 1:7; 3:17–18; 4:21.
[53]1 Cor. 12:7; 14:6, 12, 26b.
[54]John 13:34–35.
[55]1 John 3:10.

has not seen. And *this commandment we have from him: whoever loves God must also love his brother.*"[56]

Denying the possibility of isolated individual Christians who have no desire to be in the fellowship of a local church, John Calvin said that every member of the invisible church belongs to the visible church.[57] If his words are true, then many people are either in sin, or worse still wrongly believe they are saved when they are not. If they were, it would be evidenced in part by their loving their brothers and sisters, which means getting to know them to serve them and learn from them in love.

Building on the modern devotion to the individual, modern Christianity in practice defined the entire purpose of the church in terms of the individual over and above the glory of God and benefit of the community of people. As a result, the modern church in its various forms defined the church as a place where individual spiritual needs are met. What developed was a view of individual Christians as consumers with felt needs and the church as the dispenser of religious goods and services.

Consequently, the gospel came to be seen as—and in many churches still is—a product to be marketed in an attractive manner so as to draw as many customers to the church as possible to consume religious goods and services. Because in this business model the customer is always right, the church tends to sand off any theological edges that consumers find too rough (e.g., sin, God's wrath, hell). While not denying them, the church hides them so as not to deter or offend the individual customer who is shopping for pop psychology, self-help, and general spirituality.

An entire church-growth industry has arisen to resource this modern, individualistic, consumer definition of church. Furthermore, an entire industry outside of the church has come into existence for people who have forsaken church to instead only read Christian books, listen to Christian radio, watch Christian television, and download Christian vodcasts and podcasts for their personal benefit. While none of these things is bad, they are often abused by modern individual "Christians" with no intent of ever participating in a church or giving to or serving anyone but themselves.

---

[56]1 John 4:20–21.
[57]Calvin, *Institutes of the Christian Religion*, 1021–22.

THE POSTMODERN ERA

The definition of *church* for the postmodern era is still being formulated by those in the broad category of the emerging church, which is not to be confused with the Emergent Village led by Brian McLaren.

In my multiple personal conversations over the past decade with some well-known leaders of the more left-leaning fringe of the emerging church, they have explained that they find their definition of the church more in what we do rather than in what Jesus has done. They talk about how two guys drinking beer are "church" if in their hearts their time at the pub is spiritual. One well-known international missiologist told me that his friends stopped going to church and instead water-ski together every Sunday, and he told them that was fine because being together in the boat was a kingdom activity and therefore qualified as church.

When pressed for any biblical basis for such incredibly thin definitions of the church, Jesus' words in Matthew 18:19 about where two or more are gathered are commonly quoted. At that point I usually chuckle, because the context is church discipline in which multiple witnesses are to be on hand to verify an alleged unrepentant sin. Their use of this verse is ironic because they themselves are in sin regarding their definition of the church and need to repent or face church discipline—something their buddy at the pub or driver of their water-ski boat simply will not be able to do for the very reason that they are not part of a biblical church.

Some churches have opened Internet campuses. They broadcast their entire church service, including music and preaching, on the Internet. With Internet campus pastors overseeing the digital congregations, individuals log on and watch the service and then participate in prayer and discussion boards online, where they can also give their offering via debit or credit card. But we have to wonder: how can it be a biblical church, looking at a Web site alone at home, unable to partake in the sacraments, or participate in the full-person, relational life of the church? It is too much like a persona in a virtual world, an avatar in Second Life.

In today's Facebook world, electronic meeting can be a precursor or supplement to an actual gathering, so it seems a reasonable way for seekers to check out a church. The face-to-face interaction in the service and the home groups can be profitably extended in a social networking environment. But those cannot be a substitute for personal gathering if we follow God's command in Hebrews 10:24–25: "And let us consider how to stir up one another to love and good works, not neglecting to meet together, as is the habit of some, but encouraging one another." This can be a ministry of a church, but cannot be the fullness of church.

Equally concerning is the proliferation of what are loosely called *emergent* churches. These informal communities often lack any spiritual leader, any clear doctrinal convictions, or any Bible preaching and teaching, but they do have discussions, singing, and the sacraments. They meet everywhere from homes to coffee shops and art studios. Often attracted to these avant-garde, neo-church forms are younger people who were raised in Christian homes but have become disillusioned with their parents' megachurch or simply bored after years of consuming seemingly every kind of Christian product and ministry experience. Some retain Christian belief while others are more embittered and critical of Christian truth and authority, including the Scriptures. Are such communities actually churches?

After spending five years interviewing participants in the "emergent conversation," Eddie Gibbs and Ryan Bolger wrote the book *Emerging Churches: Creating Christian Community in Postmodern Cultures*.[58] The book is not from inside the movement; rather, it is an attempt at an objective, outside assessment, and it has been warmly received by many emerging church leaders. Gibbs and Bolger rightly, I believe, do not define many emerging churches by their beliefs (e.g., Trinity, deity of Jesus, cross, resurrection), their view of authority (e.g., parental in the home and pastoral in the church), sacramental practice of baptism and Communion, or practice of church discipline for unrepentant Christian conduct. Rather, they define many emerging churches as those faith communities that share up to nine common practices—three core practices and six derivative practices. At the core, emerging churches are those which (1) take the life of Jesus as a model way to live and (2) transform the secular realm (3) as they live highly communal lives. Derivatively, emerging churches (4) welcome those who are outside, (5) share generously, (6) participate, (7) create, (8) lead without control, and (9) function together in spiritual activities.

In response, none of these things is necessarily bad when practiced

---

[58]Eddie Gibbs and Ryan Bolger, *Emerging Churches* (Grand Rapids: Baker Academic, 2005), 43–45.

as a missional way of life for a church that meets the biblical criteria. However, if used as a new definition of what the church is rather than what the church does, it is dangerous because of what is missing. Missing is any working definition of gospel regeneration as the starting point for Christian life. Also missing is Jesus as anything more than a really good example of how to live a moral life, which is the classic error of liberal Christianity from a previous generation, a view of Jesus that even the Hindu Gandhi held, believing that Jesus was a great man but in no way God.

The result is that some emerging churches are nothing short of a complete redefinition of what constitutes a Christian church. If widely embraced, the postmodern world could have an entirely new definition of church, one in which church is understood as a community of Christians and non-Christians who live together without distinction, without leadership or discipline or doctrine, trying to emulate the character of Jesus without stressing the gospel requirements of repentance of sin and faith in Jesus that enable the life of Jesus to be lived by the power of the Holy Spirit. At best, we may be on the cusp of a new kind of church for a new kind of Christian. At worst, the proliferation of many small sects and cults under the banner of the emerging church may already be well underway.

What is additionally concerning to me, as someone who loves the church and pastors a church, is that so few Christians seem to care or pay much—if any—attention. Perhaps the incessant focus on best practices and innovation in the name of fruitfulness at the expense of doctrinal rooting has led us to forsake any definition of the church. So long as a few people are doing something spiritual we can call it a church.

My friend D. A. Carson made an interesting observation in a personal conversation we had. He said that one generation believes a truth, the next generation assumes a truth, and the third generation denies a truth. Practically speaking, this means that every Christian family, church, and network or denomination is always a few generations, at most, away from death or heresy. There was a great generation of evangelicalism that, although imperfect, was launched roughly fifty years ago under the leadership of men such as Billy Graham, J. I. Packer, John Stott, and Francis Schaeffer. By God's grace there were many people who believed the truths of the Christian church and its head, Jesus Christ.

The next generation of overly emphasized felt-needs, seeker Christianity sanded off the rough edges of theology such as sin, wrath, the cross, and hell along with what constitutes the church and why the preaching of God's Word and practice of God's sacraments by godly leaders was necessary to keep reminding people of the person and work of Jesus. While the truths of the Christian church were not denied, they were often hidden, because they did not sell well to spiritual consumers.

In short, much of a generation of Christians and their churches assumed a great number of truths and are still reaping the consequences. When traveling to speak in churches like this, I have repeatedly asked pastors if they believe particular essential doctrines, and they have each assured me that they do. When I asked why they stress such things as "steps to a more successful life" rather than their essential beliefs, often they said that they simply assume their people believe them.

Tragically, with the encouragement of the postmodern mood that rejects truth and authority beyond oneself and one's buddies who agree with you, children of seeker churches are now denying truths that their grandparents' generation held dear. Furthermore, the seeker generation is completely oblivious to their children's departure from the core beliefs of the historic Christian church and lack the theological discernment to be anything other than encouraged that so many young people are spiritual and are finding cool new ways to reinvent the church to suit their own felt postmodern needs. Tony Jones, national coordinator of Emergent Village, admits exactly this:

> Many of them [Emergents] were nurtured in these seeker-sensitive environments. Some even served on the staffs of these churches. But as the complexities of a globalized world have encroached on their psyches, the emergents have pursued a faith that spurns easy answers. . . . The emergent church movement is a counterreaction.[59]

Protection from these dangers will come by a return to confessing the biblical Jesus as Immanuel, God with us, in word and deed by the fresh preaching of the Word and by Spirit-empowered community on mission to the world for God's glory and their joy, led by godly pastors who passionately follow Jesus.

---

[59]Tony Jones, *The New Christians: Dispatches from the Emergent Frontier* (San Francisco: Jossey-Bass, 2008), 109.

ANSWERS TO COMMON QUESTIONS ABOUT THE CHRISTIAN CHURCH

WHAT IS THE CHURCH NOT?

1) The church is not a building. That's the first definition in any dictionary: "A building for public, especially Christian, worship." Some churches meet in a building and many times that is a home or a multipurpose building. Some churches around the world also gather under a tree or in a field.

2) The church is not any one denomination. The universal church consists of all people who are connected to the living Lord Jesus Christ by the Holy Spirit and have been justified by grace alone through faith alone in Christ alone. There are true Christians in the Orthodox Church, the Catholic Church, and in Anglican, Baptist, Pentecostal, Reformed, and Lutheran churches, to mention only a few. The church is a collection of people from literally hundreds of denominations, networks, and independent churches. There are even occasionally true Christians in heretical groups that falsely claim the name Christian. Conversely, there are people who belong to biblical churches who do not have a relationship with Jesus (Matt. 7:21–29). Only Jesus knows exactly which people are truly his.

3) The church is not a eucharistic society, or a vending machine whereby God hands out grace to those who show up to Mass and partake of the sacraments.

4) The church is not a business. While the church must do business, be organized, and handle money, its mission is quite different from a business. A business exists to deliver goods and services in order to turn a profit. It is driven by the bottom line. In many instances the church is a legal entity recognized by the government but not always, as in the case of the underground church in China and others like it. The church must account for its resources by stewarding them even better than a business

does. Laziness in finance or organization is sin. The church does not exist for profit but for God's glory, which includes good stewardship of its resources.

WHAT IS THE RELATIONSHIP BETWEEN ISRAEL AND THE CHURCH?

The church is not Israel. Israel is an ethnicity, a nation, and a religious system. The church is none of these. When the Bible—Old and New Testaments—uses the term *Israel*, it always means a group of Jewish people, not the "ransomed people for God from every tribe and language and people and nation" (Rev. 5:9), which is the church.

Some Reformed theologians see Israel as having been replaced by the church so that it is defined as *spiritual* Israel; the church in the new covenant occupies the place that Israel occupied in the old. But that would mean God reneges on his promises to the ethnic children of Abraham (Gen. 12:1–4; Deut. 30:1–5; Isaiah 11; Zech. 10:8–12).

Older, dispensational theologians in the vein of Lewis Sperry Chafer see Israel and the church as essentially two different peoples with whom God works separately throughout eternity. Their defining hermeneutic, which means method of interpretation, is never to blur the distinction between Israel and church. But that negates the statements of God breaking down the dividing wall to form one new humanity (Eph. 2:11–16).

It seems best to say there is one people of God saved by grace alone through faith alone in the promised Messiah alone who are organized in different administering institutions of God's one-kingdom purpose. The physical and spiritual descendants of Abraham—Jewish people and especially Jewish believers—are the "first born" of God's working. With the establishment of the new covenant in Acts 2, the people from every tribe and language and people and nation join in the body of Christ, sharing in the inaugurated promises of the new covenant, but not in the Mosaic religion and national structure of Israel. The Old Testament prophecies of a national restoration of Israel (Ezek. 36:22–38; Acts 1:5–7) will be fulfilled by racially Jewish Christians in the millennium who finally "shall be my treasured possession among all peoples, for all the earth is mine; and you shall be to me a kingdom of priests and a holy nation" (Ex. 19:5–6).

WHAT IS THE RELATIONSHIP BETWEEN THE STATE AND THE CHURCH?

The church is not the state. It is neither an instrument of the state nor the ordaining authority for the state's ruler nor an agency to provide moral fiber for the state. In many cases the church has sought to fill these roles, but it has always been at the cost of the mission Jesus gave it. The relationship between the realms is complex, with a lot of tension. Some, like the so-called Religious Right, want to take back America for Jesus while others, like the Amish, do their best to live completely separate from the state. Many Christians try to ease the tension by oversimplifying the nuanced relationship. For example, some say you must always submit to the government. They quote Peter, who tells believers to "be subject for the Lord's sake to every human institution, whether it be to the emperor as supreme, or to governors" (1 Pet. 2:13–14), but ignore the fact that Peter also refused the magistrates' command to stop preaching Jesus, saying, "We must obey God rather than men" (Acts 4:19–20; 5:29). Others oversimplify by referencing Romans 13:1–8, where Paul tells believers to be subject to governing authorities, but miss the fact that Paul also refused the order of governing magistrates to leave town quietly (Acts 16:36–39).

Believers in Jesus Christ seek the welfare of the city where God has sent them to live (Jer. 29:7), and pray to the Lord on behalf of its rulers (Ezra 6:10; 1 Tim. 2:1–2). They live as good citizens of the state while recognizing that they are first citizens of the heavenly kingdom (Phil. 3:20). As the church proclaims the gospel and seeks to win people to Christ, it proclaims righteousness in the culture by deed and word and exposes its evils in a context of grace.

For further study, the following give a good breadth of Christian thinking on this issue: Stanley Hauerwas, *Resident Aliens* (Abingdon, 1989); John Howard Yoder, *The Politics of Jesus* (Eerdmans, 1994); Chuck Colson, *God & Government* (Zondervan, 2007); Greg Boyd, *The Myth of a Christian Nation* (Zondervan, 2007); and D. A. Carson, *Christ and Culture Revisited* (Eerdmans, 2008).

WHAT IS THE RELATIONSHIP BETWEEN THE KINGDOM OF GOD AND THE CHURCH?

The church is not the kingdom. In recent years many theologians have come to a consensus that the kingdom is to be thought of as the reign of God and the exercise of his authority. The church, by contrast, is a realm of God, the people who are under his rule. George Eldon Ladd, a leader in forging the consensus, says, "The church is the community of the Kingdom but never the Kingdom itself."[60] This consensus is called *inaugurated eschatology*, the idea that the kingdom is both here now in some senses and still to come in its fullness.

Some connect church and kingdom too closely, believing the kingdom is here in its fullness now. This is called an *overrealized eschatology*, which virtually identifies kingdom with church, as many Roman Catholics and some amillennialists do. Others see the kingdom exclusively future, as something Jesus will establish when he returns. This is an *underrealized eschatology*, which disconnects kingdom and church completely, as in older dispensational premillennialism.

God's kingdom work is the dynamic activity of the sovereign, triune God manifesting his authority in his sin-alienated creation by redeeming it from the domain of evil, judging all enemies, and bestowing the blessings of his reign on and through his people to the praise of his glory. The relation between kingdom and church can be summarized in seven basic points:

1) Jesus, who came as king, inaugurated his kingdom in the new covenant (Acts 2:16–21) and in the church (Acts 2:41–47).

2) Jesus spoke of a coming kingdom (Mark 13; Luke 19:12–27; 21:5–38; Acts 1:6–7).

3) Jesus is now in heaven as anointed king; he will appear as reigning king (Acts 3:20–21; 13:33–41).

4) Believers are faithful members of the present and coming kingdom (John 14:14–16; Rom. 8:19–21; 1 Cor. 7:29–31; Phil. 3:20; 1 Pet. 2:11).

5) The church witnesses to the present and coming kingdom (Acts 1:3–8; 8:12; 19:8; 28:23, 31).

6) Church is an outpost, a parable, a forerunner, the first fruit of the coming kingdom.

7) The church does battle against the kingdom of darkness using the weapons of light (Rom. 13:12; 2 Cor. 6:7; 10:4–5; Eph. 6:10–20; 1 Thess. 5:8).

Practically, this world still has sin, sinners, the devil, and demons but does not yet have Jesus ruling on the earth with a rod of iron (Ps.

[60]George Eldon Ladd, *A Theology of the New Testament*, rev. ed. (Grand Rapids, MI: Eerdmans, 1993), 109.

2:9; Rev. 2:26; 12:5; 19:15). Subsequently, a naïvely optimistic overrealized eschatology that thinks we can fix all the world's problems and usher in utopia is an extreme error. Conversely, a gloomy, pessimistic underrealized eschatology that thinks we can't make a difference in the world as the church by the power of the gospel is also an extreme error. This tension of the kingdom being already present in the church but not yet fully unveiled until the return of Jesus allows us to labor in hope until he returns by working on both the spiritual and physical needs of people, caring for the whole person including their food, water, shelter, education, and clothing.

CHAPTER THREE

WHO IS SUPPOSED TO LEAD A CHURCH?

Remember your leaders, those who spoke to you the word of God. Consider the outcome of their way of life, and imitate their faith.

HEBREWS 13:7

✝

The neighborhood in which I grew up during the first ten years of my life was near my elementary school. I remember a lot of boys my age with whom I rode bikes in the street, made forts in the woods, caught frogs in the pond, and played sports in a field. We were a ragtag bunch of misfits who generally got along well . . . until we started playing sports.

We would get together and vote on which sport we wanted to play, choosing between basketball, baseball, football, and soccer most of the time. The one thing that remained true no matter what sport we played was the fight that broke out, bringing our game to a grinding halt.

At the time I was not very reflective, and rather than contemplating why fights broke out I exerted my energy by joining in and pounding some kid like a drum. Reflecting on our mini-riots, it now dawns on me that our fights were over authority. We fought over which game to play, the choice of team captains, and the rules for the game, and when a play was made we fought over who had the right to decide such things as balls and strikes, safe and out, traveling and dribbling. Because we had no authorities such as coaches or referees, I am not sure we ever finished a game; we invariably ended up beating on one another.

Many years later, while in my mid-twenties and planting a church, I started to see that my church plant was pretty much the same as my old neighborhood, with a lot of fighting minus the balls. The people who showed up were generally non-Christians, new Christians, legalistic Christians, anti-Christians, and bitter, burned-out, de-churched maybe-Christians who all wanted to be in authority over themselves and do whatever they wanted in the name of community, which was code for mini-riot anarchy.

This included a worship band member at one point stopping the service to read texts from other religions in the name of pluralistic diversity, young guys in their twenties asking on their first visit when it was their turn to preach, singles sleeping together and unwilling to stop because Jesus told them it was okay in his eyes (which were apparently closed), and some guy who threw a bicycle at me in the church because I asked him to park it outside.

Before long I was ready to resign as the pastor and instead volunteer in the nursery with the toddlers to enjoy the company of some more mature people. Instead, I started studying the two least exciting words in the history of the English language—church government. For both of you who did not fall asleep while reading those words, we will now do the same, and start by examining the role of Jesus in the church.[1]

JESUS THE SENIOR PASTOR

Jesus Christ is the head of the church,[2] the apostle who plants a church,[3] the leader who builds the church,[4] and the senior pastor and Chief Shepherd who rules the church.[5] It is ultimately Jesus who closes down churches when they have become faithless or fruitless.[6] Therefore, it is absolutely vital that a church loves Jesus, obeys Jesus, imitates Jesus, and follows Jesus at all times and in all ways, according to the teaching of his Word.[7]

---

[1] Much of this chapter is condensed from my book *On Church Leadership* (Wheaton, IL: Crossway Books, 2008), which is a more thorough examination of church government.
[2] Eph. 1:9, 22–23; 4:15; 5:23.
[3] Heb. 3:1.
[4] Matt. 16:18.
[5] 1 Pet. 5:4.
[6] Rev. 2:5.
[7] Col. 3:16.

Human leadership in the church is little more than qualified Christians who are following Jesus and encouraging other people to follow them as they follow Jesus. Because of this, church leaders must be good sheep who follow their Chief Shepherd Jesus well before they are fit to be shepherds leading any of his sheep. This is in large part what Paul meant when he told Christians in various local churches to "be imitators of me, as I am of Christ."[8]

Serving under Jesus in formal church offices are elders, deacons, and church members. Philippians 1:1 illustrates this church leadership structure: "Paul and Timothy, servants of Christ Jesus, To all the saints [church members] in Christ Jesus who are at Philippi, with the overseers [elders-pastors] and deacons." Packed in this verse we discover the three kinds of leaders who take responsibility for the health and progress of the local church.

In a conversation over breakfast with my friend John Piper, he made a helpful analogy regarding qualifications for church attendance, membership, deaconship, and eldership. He said that the front door to attend church services and other programming should be as large as possible, the door to membership should then be smaller, the ensuing door to deaconship should again be much smaller, and the door to eldership should be very tiny. In this way, every church can help to ensure its health.

ELDERS

Elders are the male leaders of the church. By *male* we mean not just anatomically male, but manly men. Paul makes it clear that manly men are not those who can punch the hardest, argue the best, or get their own way no matter what. According to the Bible, manly men are those who are known for their prayer lives[9] and for modeling Christlike service[10] and being practically responsible in their homes as well as in the workplace.[11] Stu Weber, in his book *Tender Warrior*, writes that such men fill the roles of king, warrior, mentor, and friend. He says a man "watches out for what lies ahead—like a wagon train scout; keeps his commitments, no matter how painful; has a tender heart beating beneath his armor; understands his responsibility to his wife, children, and friends;

---

[8]1 Cor. 11:1.
[9]1 Tim. 2:8.
[10]Matt. 20:26–28; 1 Pet. 5:2.
[11]1 Tim. 3:4–7.

recognizes that he is 'under orders from higher headquarters.' "[12] By God's humbling grace, these men have a life worthy of imitation by other people in the church who have their own lives to figure out.

Since we are devoting only one chapter to the subject of church leadership, we will briefly discuss why we believe that Scripture teaches that only the best of Jesus' men should serve as elders.[13]

1) God made humanity male and female, which means that men and women are equal yet different.[14]

2) The senior spiritual leadership of God's people in the Old Testament was comprised of male priests.

3) Jesus chose twelve men as his apostles, although he befriended, loved, taught, honored, healed, and included women in his ministry, but not in a senior position of leadership.

4) In 1 Timothy 2:11–3:5 Paul writes:

> Let a woman learn quietly with all submissiveness. I do not permit a woman to teach or to exercise authority over a man; rather, she is to remain quiet. For Adam was formed first, then Eve; and Adam was not deceived, but the woman was deceived and became a transgressor. Yet she will be saved through childbearing—if they continue in faith and love and holiness, with self-control.
>
> The saying is trustworthy: If anyone aspires to the office of overseer, he desires a noble task. Therefore an overseer must be above reproach, the husband of one wife, sober-minded, self-controlled, respectable, hospitable, able to teach, not a drunkard, not violent but gentle, not quarrelsome, not a lover of money. He must manage his own household well, with all dignity keeping his children submissive, for if someone does not know how to manage his own household, how will he care for God's church?

Paul begins by stating something quite controversial and unusual

---

[12]Stu Weber, *Tender Warrior: Every Man's Purpose, Every Woman's Dream, Every Child's Hope* (Sisters, OR: Multnomah, 2006), back matter. He has written several helpful books on biblical manhood, including *Four Pillars of a Man's Heart: Bringing Strength into Balance* (Sisters, OR: Multnomah, 1997); *Spirit Warriors: Strategies for the Battles Christian Men and Women Face Every Day* (Sisters, OR: Multnomah, 2001); and *All the King's Men: Strength in Character through Friendships* (Sisters, OR: Multnomah, 2006).
[13]For further study on male eldership, see my book *On Church Leadership*; John Piper and Wayne Grudem, eds., *Recovering Biblical Manhood and Womanhood* (Wheaton, IL: Crossway Books, 2006); Alexander Strauch, *Biblical Eldership* (Littleton, CO: Lewis and Roth, 1995); and James Beck and Craig Blomberg, eds., *Two Views on Women in Ministry* (Grand Rapids, MI: Zondervan, 2001).
[14]Gen. 1:26–27.

in his day—that women should learn theology. In our day, the application of this principle would mean that both men and women should be taught theology, be permitted to attend Bible college or seminary, and be encouraged to be theologically astute. Apparently, the women in Ephesus were behaving in an unruly and disrespectful fashion during church services. They were much like their Christian sisters in Corinth,[15] whom Paul likewise commanded to be respectful toward church leadership. For married women, Paul also placed the onus for answering their many theological questions on their husbands as the heads of their homes.

Paul added two requirements for the Ephesian women who wanted to learn theology: quietness and submission. Quietness here does not mean total silence but rather a peaceable demeanor, which in 1 Timothy 2:2 is also required of everyone. The matter of women submitting to the pastoral church leaders directly correlates with the frequent command that women also submit to their husbands as the leaders in their homes.[16] Clearly, God's intention is that Christian women will be well-informed theologians, and to do so they must first learn to respect the male pastors whom God has appointed to instruct them.

Paul emphatically commanded that women should not teach or have authority over men in the church. Those who hold a hard complementarian interpretation of Paul's command are prone to keep things tidy by simply telling women to teach only women and children (which is, admittedly, the cleanest place to draw the line). Those who hold a soft complementarian interpretation of Paul's commands (as we do) believe that his pairing of teaching and authority refers to the highest authority in the church. While there is huge controversy about the meaning of the word Paul uses for "authority," we follow the standard Greek lexicon understanding: "To assume a stance of independent authority, give orders to, dictate," which describes well the elder-level authority in the church.[17] This also seems logical in the context, as what immediately follows in the next chapter of 1 Timothy is the requirements for elders-pastors, which include being a mature Christian man and an exemplary husband and father.

---

[15] 1 Cor. 14:33–35.

[16] Eph. 5:21–33; Col. 3:18; Titus 2:3–5; 1 Pet. 3:1–6.

[17] "*Authenteno*," in *A Greek-English Lexicon of the New Testament and Other Early Christian Literature*, 3rd ed. (BDAG), edited and revised by Frederick William Danker (Chicago: University of Chicago Press, 2000).

Correspondingly, Paul forbids women to teach and exercise authority as elders-pastors. Later in his instructions to Timothy, Paul honors elders "who labor in the Word and teaching" (1 Tim. 5:17 literally translated). *Teaching* here likely refers to preaching and teaching as done by the elders, as every other time teaching is spoken of in the remainder of the letter, it is in reference to the teaching of an elder.[18] Only elders preach, enforce formal church discipline, and set doctrinal standards for the church.

By definition, the position we are arguing for is complementarianism. A complementarian church should encourage women to use the spiritual gifts and natural abilities that God has given them to their fullest extent. This includes anything from teaching a class to leading a Bible study, overseeing a ministry, leading as a deacon, speaking in church in a way that is not preaching, leading worship music, serving Communion, entering into full-time paid ministry as a member of the staff, and receiving formal theological education—basically every opportunity in the church except what the Bible and the elders deem elder-only duties. Therefore, the issue is not whether a woman can be in ministry, but rather what ministry a woman can be in and remain faithful to Scripture.

CHART 3.1

Egalitarian (liberal)	Complementarian (moderate)	Hierarchical (conservative)
Men and women are partners together in every area of ministry. All ministries and offices in the church are open to men and women. Gender is not a relevant distinction for excluding any person from any church office.	Men and women are partners in every area of ministry together. Women and men are encouraged and equipped to fulfill all ministries and offices of the church with the singular exception of the office of elder, which the Scriptures require to be a male-only office.	Women and men are created to operate in different spheres of ministry within the church. Women are not permitted to be an elder or deacon, serve Communion, teach men, lead worship, pray or speak in the church service, etc. Women should focus on building ministries for other women and children.

While those who oppose Paul's clear teaching—that only qualified men should be elders-pastors—vary in the nuances of their arguments,

---

[18] 1 Tim. 4:11; 5:7; 6:2.

at the heart of each is an insistence that male leadership in the governments of home and church are rooted in humanly defined culture and not in God-defined creation. Therefore, they will purport that this doctrine should change with culture rather than remaining constant. Again, the only problem with this position is the words of Paul in Scripture, where we find that he argues against female elders-pastors from the Genesis account of creation.[19] The issue is one of creation and not culture.

Before we proceed to examine the duties of male elders, it is worth mentioning that this issue is in many ways like a state line. It may not be visible in the world, but depending upon which side of the line you live, you are in one state or another. Any church that accepts women as elders-pastors is consequently changing the entire order of the family, in which the husbands are to be the loving heads and the wives are to be their helpers. Furthermore, any church that maintains a complementarian position should expect continual questioning and opposition, particularly the closer they are to a major city where the culture is often more liberal, less biblical, and nearly entirely egalitarian. The depth of a church's convictions on this issue will be continually tested, and the line must be humbly but courageously held.

The male elders must focus intently on raising up men, particularly young men, to be responsible, loving leaders in their families and the church like Jesus and unlike Adam. This should not be done at the expense of women and children, but in love for women and children who often suffer at the hands of men who abuse, abandon, or avoid their responsibilities. This is precisely why elders should be only the most exemplary and responsible Christian men.

Male elders are synonymously called *overseers* (also translated "bishops," though the Bible does not use the term for denominational officials as English does) who pastor the flock.[20] In English, elders are typically called pastors. This can be confusing because, with the possible exception of Ephesians 4:11, the Bible does not use "pastor" as an office but as a function. A leader does the work of pastoring or shepherding but is not called *pastor* but *elder* or *overseer*. Simply, the various words are used interchangeably to refer to the same person in the same office, not

---

[19]1 Tim. 2:13, cf. Genesis 2–3.
[20]Acts 20:28; Eph. 4:11; 1 Pet. 5:2.

unlike how Jesus Christ is referred to throughout the New Testament by a variety of titles, such as Son of Man, Son of God, Vine, Lion, Chief Shepherd, and Lamb, which all point to aspects of his role as the head of the church.

The elders are men chosen for their ministry according to clear biblical requirements after a sufficient season of testing in the church.[21] Elders are nearly always spoken of in plurality because God intends for more than one man to lead and rule over the church, as a safeguard for both the church and the man. We also see this when Paul speaks of a council of multiple elders ruling in a local church.[22] The leadership of the church is to follow the Trinitarian pattern of shared leadership that God himself models.

The Bible defines the qualifications of elder in two primary places (1 Tim. 3:1–7 and Titus 1:5–9), and the lists are virtually identical. Three things are noteworthy about this list. First, the list is primarily about men being good Christians, assuming that good Christians will make good pastors. Sadly, not all pastors are good Christians. Second, the qualifications for pastor are in large part tied not to his work at the church, but rather to whether he has been a good pastor in his home with his family and in his world with his neighbors and coworkers. Too many pastors are good pastors at the expense of being good husbands, fathers, neighbors, employees, and the like. Third, establishing whether a man actually meets these criteria requires relational time in the church over a long season because the list is about counting character, which is more difficult than counting rocks, as one pastor has quipped. Take a moment to review the character qualities Paul lists as qualifications for elders in 1 Timothy 3:1–7 and Titus 1:5–9.

According to the Bible, formal theological training is not required for elders, though such training can indeed be very beneficial. A salary is also not required, though elder-pastors are worth an honorable wage.[23] Gerry is an unpaid pastor-elder on the preaching team at Grace Community Church in Gresham, Oregon, where he has served since 1996. He has also given his life to training pastors as professor of theology at Western Seminary in Portland, as well as teaching at seminaries around the world. I (Mark) was the founding elder of Mars Hill Church

---

[21] 1 Tim. 2:11–3:7; Titus 1:5–9.
[22] 1 Tim. 4:14; Titus 1:5.
[23] 1 Tim. 5:17–18.

in 1996, where I remain on paid pastoral staff despite the fact that I did not finish my seminary education until 2008.

Elders are not ultimately nominated by committees or congregational votes but called by God himself. Paul tells elders that "the Holy Spirit has made you overseers."[24] Once called by God, a man must then examine his own life and family to see if he meets the qualifications. If he does not, then an appropriate season of growing, studying, and repentant living and transformation is required before there is any talk of his becoming a pastor. Typically this will be done under the mentoring of the elders as he serves in ministry roles in the church. If and when a man is qualified, he must have a personal desire to accept the work and responsibility of eldership and nominate himself to the other elders as a candidate for eldership consideration. On this point 1 Timothy 3:1 says, "If anyone aspires to the office of overseer, he desires a noble task."

Upon nominating himself as an elder candidate, a formal process of testing his calling must be undertaken. This process should include examining his family, financial giving to the church, performance at work, relationship with people outside the church, service in the church, spiritual gifts, ministry passions, attitude toward authority, work ethic, leadership gifts, humility, and anything and everything else related to his conversion, calling, character, courage, and competency.

The rule of thumb for elders and all other leaders is to appoint slowly and terminate quickly. Too many churches appoint quickly and terminate slowly, which is devastating to church unity and momentum. If the man is unanimously confirmed as a called and qualified elder by the other elders, he should then be brought before the church publicly so that the people in the church have an opportunity to raise any concerns or questions they have about the man's eldership nomination. If there is no disqualifying opposition, then he should be voted in by the elders and installed as an elder by the laying on of hands by the other elders, as Scripture states.[25]

The issue of which men lead the church is of the utmost seriousness, because both the reputation of the gospel in the community and the health of the church are contingent upon godly, qualified men who keep in step with Jesus and who can lead the church to do likewise. The

---

[24]Acts 20:28.
[25]Deut. 1:12–16; Acts 14:23; 1 Tim. 4:14; 5:22; 2 Tim. 2:6–7.

elders function as an accountable team, much like Jesus' first disciples, and they are therefore quite unlike secular notions of a business or non-profit organizational board.

In addition to the qualifications of an elder, the Bible also provides the duties of elders-pastors:

- Praying and studying Scripture[26]
- Ruling/leading the church[27]
- Managing the church[28]
- Caring for people in the church[29]
- Giving account to God for the church[30]
- Living exemplary lives[31]
- Rightly using the authority God has given them[32]
- Teaching the Bible correctly[33]
- Preaching[34]
- Praying for the sick[35]
- Teaching sound doctrine and refuting false teachings[36]
- Working hard[37]
- Rightly using money and power[38]
- Protecting the church from false teachers[39]
- Disciplining unrepentant Christians[40]
- Obeying the secular laws as the legal ruling body of a corporation[41]
- Developing other leaders and teachers.[42]

That final point is often overlooked. An elder is not a helper that does a lot of work for the church, because that is the definition of a deacon. Rather, an elder is a leader who trains other leaders to lead various aspects of the church. Therefore, no man should be an elder unless he

---

[26]Acts 6:4.
[27]1 Tim. 5:17.
[28]1 Tim. 3:4–5.
[29]1 Pet. 5:2–5.
[30]Heb. 13:17.
[31]Heb. 13:7.
[32]Acts 20:28.
[33]Eph. 4:11; 1 Tim. 3:2.
[34]1 Tim. 5:17.
[35]James 5:13–15.
[36]Titus 1:9.
[37]1 Thess. 5:12.
[38]1 Pet. 5:1–3.
[39]Acts 20:17–31.
[40]Matt. 18:15–17.
[41]Rom. 13:1–7.
[42]Eph. 4:11–16; 2 Tim. 2:1–2.

has proven that he can effectively train people to be not only mature Christians but also mature Christian leaders who train other leaders.

FIRST AMONG EQUALS

The specific responsibilities of the team of elders will vary according to gifting and personality. There will almost always be one man who is the leader of the elders, a "first among equals" elder. We see this in the role Peter fulfilled among the apostles.[43] While many resist seeing leadership as a team effort, others resist believing leadership within the elder team is biblical. They see any hierarchy within the elders as demeaning of some elders because they are unequal to the other elders. Alexander Strauch, who has written the most thorough book on biblical eldership, correctly points out:

> Failure to understand the concept of "first among equals" (or 1 Timothy 5:17) has caused some elderships to be tragically ineffective in their pastoral care and leadership. Although elders act jointly as a council and share equal authority and responsibility for the leadership of the church, all are not equal in their giftedness, biblical knowledge, leadership ability, experience, or dedication. Therefore, those among the elders who are particularly gifted leaders and/or teachers will naturally stand out among the other elders as leaders and teachers within the leadership body.[44]

When our church was smaller, the handful of elders and I were buddies who hung out a lot and chatted over items until we came to a common agreement as to what we should do. We did not foresee the complexity our church would face as it grew and expanded, but the concept of having firsts among equals has been vital in helping us organize all our leadership teams that include elders, deacons, and members.

Therefore, for any elder team to function effectively, it must have a called, qualified, gifted, devoted, humble, and competent senior leader who leads the elder team and helps guard the gate for new elders joining the team to ensure unity and success. To do his job, that man must not be offered blind obedience or given complete unaccountable authority. Rather, he must have the freedom, trust, authority, respect, honor,

[43]Acts 1:15–22; 2:14–40, cf. Matt. 16:18.
[44]Alexander Strauch, *Biblical Eldership*, 45.

and support of the elders and other church leaders to actually lead the church. If not, there can be no leadership; leaders will no longer lead the entire church working on behalf of the best interests of the gospel but will become representatives of various agendas, departments, factions, and programs in the church. Without a senior leader, dissention will come as people fight over resources; there will not be decisions but compromises, which are the death of the church.

As a general rule, the best person to hold the position of first among equals is the primary preaching pastor. Indeed, 1 Timothy 5:17 says, "Let the elders who rule well be considered worthy of double honor, especially those who labor in preaching and teaching." While all elders deserve respect and honor, the primary preaching pastor is worthy of double honor. The pulpit is the most visible place of exercised authority in the church and is where most criticism and opposition is focused. As such, only qualified elders should preach, which can include welcoming qualified elders from other churches from time to time as appropriate.

For the record, I am not the lead elder on any of the elder teams at our church. In recent years I have handed off the leadership of every elder team to godly fellow elders in an effort to share power and allow the mission of our church not to bottleneck with me. I do, however, wield great influence as the directional leader and primary preaching pastor, thanks to the respect that the fellow elders give to me while also holding me accountable. In this, I enjoy the benefits of influence while the other elders enjoy the fact that I do not control everything that we do, as they truly hold most of the real power in the church.

DEACONS

Unlike elders, the New Testament says very little about deacons. This has led some people to search the New Testament in an effort to find out exactly what a deacon is and does. This commonly results in a series of assumptions that Acts 6:1–7 is the prototypical New Testament example of doing deacon work. This is an exegetical error that has befallen some great Bible teachers, such as Alexander Strauch, who arguably wrote the finest book on elders but failed to do justice to deacons in his follow-up book. The best way to understand deacons is not to read the books written about deacons by elders, but rather to speak with and learn from godly deacons, which is exactly where much of the content for this chapter was derived.

In Acts 6:1–7 we learn that as the church outgrew the oversight of the apostles, discrimination in their care for widows began to occur. The apostles could have given their time to that need but only if they neglected essential pastoral duties, particularly time for prayer and Bible study. Therefore, it was decided that pastoral assistants were to be appointed by the apostles to care for the widows, thereby enabling the apostles to focus on prayer and Scripture.

While Acts 6:1–7 is not a prescriptive passage on the office of deacon, it gives us a very important principle that does relate to deacons. When senior spiritual leadership is overburdened to the degree that they are unable to simultaneously get time for prayer, Bible study, and the care of needy people, they are free to appoint pastoral assistants or ministry team leaders to help alleviate some of their burden. This is the pattern of the New Testament—elders are continually appointed first in local churches, and once they are overburdened they appoint pastoral assistants to aid them.

Deacons are mentioned on two occasions in the New Testament. Both occasions are in relation to elders because the two groups of leaders work so closely together.[45] Practically, elders and deacons work together like left and right hands, with elders specializing in leading by their words and deacons specializing in leading by their works.

Deacons are the servants of the church who are also appointed for the ministry of overseeing and caring for God's people by qualifications that are nearly identical to the elders—minus the teaching and preaching abilities. They must have theological convictions that are true to Scripture.[46] Deacons are appointed only after they have proven themselves to the elders as faithful and mature church members.[47]

While the duties of elders are clearly articulated throughout the New Testament, the same cannot be said for the duties of deacons. The Greek word for *deacon* simply means "servant," and beyond that title we are given little indication of what a deacon should do. This is because while the duties of an elder are universally constant in every church in every place in every age, the duties of deacons vary according to the needs of local churches and their elders. In this way, the Bible brilliantly establishes a theologically grounded, morally qualified group of senior elder leaders and grants them the freedom to appoint whatever deacons are needed to help them lead the church in whatever areas they deem require a deacon to lead. The primary list of qualifications for the office of deacon is found in 1 Timothy 3:8–13, which you can read before we explore them further.

There is much dispute as to whether a woman can be a deacon. Much of this debate centers on Paul's qualifications for deacons in 1 Timothy 3:11. Paul begins that list by speaking of *"gune."* This Greek word is translated either "wives" or "women," depending on context. Various translations opt for one or the other, usually with a footnote that explains the other option. We believe it is best translated "women," meaning deacons who are women. If the verse were giving qualifications for male deacons' wives, then we would have to ask why there are no requirements for the wives of male elders. It would be absurd to believe male deacons are held to a higher standard than male elders, who hold the highest position of authority in the church. Therefore, the verse cannot logically be accepted as an additional requirement for the wives of male deacons.

If understood this way, the text flows quite nicely as the requirements of 1 Timothy 3:8–10 being for both male and female deacons—indicated by the word "likewise" in the following verse (3:11), which applies those qualifications to women. Verse 11 goes on to list the additional requirements for female deacons, while verses 12–13 list the additional requirements for male deacons.

Further evidence for female deacons is found in Romans 16:1, where Phoebe is greeted first, which denotes honor; she is also called a servant, which is the same word for deacon and likely indicates she was a deacon. Additionally, other women whom Paul honors for their assistance to him may also have been female deacons. Among them are Mary,[48] Tryphaena and Tryphosa,[49] and Euodia and Syntyche.[50]

Lastly, every church does have women in positions of leadership, even if their roles are restricted to administration, women's ministries, and children's ministries. Unless a church calls such women by the bib-

[48]Rom. 16:6.
[49]Rom. 16:12.
[50]Phil. 4:2–3.

lical title of deacon and holds them accountable to the biblical qualifications for their leadership, they are forced to invent titles like director and such. This is problematic because it has no biblical precedent.

Therefore, a church should have only male elders who are the senior leadership in the church but who are free to appoint both male and female deacons as assistant leaders as needed. Indeed, some churches will disagree with us, and our only response would be a loving request that they reconsider the Scriptures on this point.

MEMBERS

In addition to elders and deacons, within the church are non-Christians in the process of sorting out their relationship with God and church members already calling the church their home and taking responsibility to ensure its health and growth. Church members are Christians whose eyes are capable of seeing beyond themselves to the well-being of the whole church. They realize that God died not just for them but also for their church.[51] They also realize that he commands them to selflessly give of their money[52] and abilities in order to build up their church.[53]

Some Christians question whether they need to have a church home in which they participate as official members. But the illustrative imagery of the church throughout the New Testament includes the fact that Christians are to work together as a family[54] or as the parts of a body.[55] The early church had a notion of membership that included numerical record,[56] records of widows,[57] elections,[58] discipline,[59] accountability,[60] and an awareness of who was a church member.[61] At the risk of stating the obvious, obedience to New Testament teaching requires that a Christian be a member of a local church, since most of the epistles open by saying "to the church."[62]

---

[51]Acts 20:28.
[52]2 Corinthians 8–9.
[53]1 Cor. 14:12.
[54]1 Tim. 3:15; 5:1–2.
[55]1 Cor. 12:16–17.
[56]Acts 2:37–47.
[57]1 Tim. 5:3–16.
[58]Acts 6:1–6.
[59]Matt. 18:15–20; 1 Cor. 5; Gal. 6:1.
[60]Heb. 13:17.
[61]Rom. 16:1–16.
[62]1 Cor. 1:2; 2 Cor. 2:1; Gal. 1:2; Eph. 1:2; Phil. 1:1; 1 Thess. 1:1; 2 Thess. 1:1; Rev. 1:4.

Tragically, too many churches treat church membership like membership in a country club or civic organization. When the Bible speaks of church membership, it does so in relational terms; Christians are to work within their particular church for the cause of the gospel. Romans 12:4–5 says, "For as in one body we have many members, and the members do not all have the same function, so we, though many, are one body in Christ, and individually members one of another." Furthermore, Ephesians 2:18–19 says, "For through him we both have access in one Spirit to the Father. So then you are no longer strangers and aliens, but you are fellow citizens with the saints and members of the household of God."

Therefore, church members are, in a sense, leaders of and servants in the church who serve according to their abilities in accordance with Jesus' command to love God and their neighbor; this shows up not just in what they feel but also in what they say and do. The church members must be trained and released to use their spiritual gifts in various ways so that they too are leading the church, behind the elders and deacons, as the priesthood of believers that Scripture speaks of throughout the New Testament. This includes nursery captains working with the little people, home-based Bible study leaders, worship band leaders, usher and greeter captains, technical team leaders, and leaders of various mercy ministries. Many ministries take the mission of the church beyond the fellowship. This includes leading workplace Bible studies, being a chaplain in a local hospice, caring for widows in the neighborhood, or showing hospitality to unbelieving friends so they can see how Jesus is honored in our homes. Those who function as exemplary church members are then qualified to occupy the church leadership positions of deacon and elder, respectively.

To become a member at our church, one must be a Christian who has met the requirements of membership established by our elders. Those include being baptized at some point as a demonstration that Jesus died and rose to wash them from sin. Members must also complete the Doctrine Series, which explains the essential beliefs of Christianity and our church as well as the philosophy of ministry and organizational structure of the church, and sign a written covenant[63] with the elders to serve in the church, pray for the church, give to the church, read their

---

[63]A copy of this covenant is included in the Appendix.

Bible regularly, love their brothers and sisters in Christ in word and deed, respect the authority of church leaders including submitting to discipline if necessary, attend church services, and share the gospel with others in word and deed.

Those who become church members should be formally plugged into the church so they have a place for fellowship and service. Ideally, the new members come with new enthusiasm, new skills, new insights, and new ministry ideas that help to reinvigorate and expand the health and size of the church.

At Mars Hill Church, our members also fill out an annual financial pledge, and we send out quarterly giving updates to each member. Their pledges help us set our annual budget based on a credible estimate of what our income will be for that year. Pledges also help our members to have a plan as faithful stewards. Because Mars Hill Church is growing so quickly, about half the people who attend are not yet members. Many of these are not yet even regenerated followers of Jesus. They help in many ways, but we count on our church members to provide the majority of financial support and volunteer hours; without them we simply could not operate.

Our members are also given some privileges that we do not extend to other people in general. For example, we have an online network called The City created by one of our elders. There, new people move toward church membership, and church members are given greater access to share goods and prayer requests, ask questions, organize events, and build community online regarding issues that are more personal and familial in nature. We also operate an "open books" policy for church members and are happy to answer reasonable questions they may have about financial church matters.

Additionally, only members are allowed to oversee certain areas of ministry as primary leaders. Nonmembers are intentionally encouraged to serve throughout the church as a connecting point for community and for the gospel. This is important so that our church can act missionally by bringing people, including non-Christians, into active participation in the life of the church with the intent of seeing lost people become Christians, and disconnected Christians become vitally connected to the church ministries, and eventually become faithful church members themselves.

As a general rule, a healthy church's total weekly attendance should be notably higher than the church membership. If that number becomes too small, then the leadership pipeline is drying up, the church is not growing, or new people are somehow not becoming members of the church family, and the members who are serving will quickly burn out. Conversely, if membership becomes too large, then there could be a lot of dead weight in the church, and the leaders need to get hold of "members" who do not regularly participate in worship, give, or serve. It is important that the membership list be up-to-date and the people active.

When we maintain the balance between healthy, respected, mature leaders and active, worshiping, serving members, the church excels as the living body of Christ.

ANSWERS TO COMMON QUESTIONS ABOUT CHRISTIAN LEADERSHIP

THIS SOUNDS REALLY HIERARCHICAL. WHAT HAPPENED TO THE PRIESTHOOD OF BELIEVERS?

By priesthood of believers,[64] Scripture means that all believers can have direct access to God.[65] We all perform godly sacrifices,[66] hear confession of sin,[67] announce forgiveness and blessing,[68] and give spiritual guidance to each other.[69] The priesthood of believers was also offered to the nation of Israel,[70] but because of their fear and sin,[71] priesthood in the religious system of Israel was limited to the tribe of Levi.

Leadership is a specific gift and office in the New Testament. It is something a smaller group of mature and gifted people does in their specific areas of responsibility. For example, Paul speaks of elders who are responsible for guiding and guarding the whole church,[72] mature, godly women who are responsible to lead younger women,[73] deacons (both men and women) who lead in serving ministries,[74] and apparently an official leadership for widows in that ministry.[75] Importantly, in all of these cases their leadership is by example rather than authoritarian command.[76]

CAN A DIVORCED PERSON BE AN ELDER OR DEACON?

There are several crucial issues involved in this question, all of which are debated fiercely by Bible-believing Christians. First, one must ask if

---

[64]1 Pet. 2:9; Rev. 1:6.
[65]Heb. 4:16; 7:19; 10:22; James 4:8.
[66]Rom. 12:1; Heb. 13:15–16.
[67]Acts 19:18; James 5:16.
[68]Matt. 18:15–18; John 20:23; 2 Cor. 2:6–10.
[69]Col. 3:16; Heb. 10:24–25.
[70]Ex. 19:6.
[71]Ex. 20:18–21; 32:26–28.
[72]1 Tim. 3:1–7; Titus 1:5–9.
[73]Titus 2:2–5.
[74]1 Tim. 3:8–13.
[75]1 Tim. 5:1–16.
[76]Matt. 20:25–28; 1 Tim. 4:12; Titus 2:7; Heb. 13:7; 1 Pet. 5:2–3.

there are any conditions in which divorce is acceptable. To summarize very complex issues, we believe divorce is always a result of sin. Jesus says, "They are no longer two but one flesh. What therefore God has joined together, let not man separate."[77] But he goes on to recognize that hardness of heart and sexual immorality are conditions in which marriage may die, with divorce as the result.[78] Paul adds abandonment by an unbelieving spouse as a condition for divorce.[79] But these conditions do not make divorce sinless or necessary. Reconciliation is always the goal for shattered marriages. It appears that this is a typical, rather than an extensive, list of conditions of the death of a marriage. Perhaps one could sum these up by saying that marriage is dead when there is irreconcilable abandonment.

So it appears that while divorce always occurs in a context of sin, sometimes when the marriage dies, divorce is the outcome. Because the two are one flesh, divorce is like tearing an arm off. You can live through it, but it is really damaging. A lot of healing is necessary for anything like normal life to resume.

Second, can a divorced person ever remarry with God's blessing? Jesus speaks of a legalistic Pharisee seeking to justify his sin of divorcing his wife by issuing her a certificate of divorce. Jesus expects the wife who has been rejected to be remarried and attributes her "adultery" to the man who divorced her.[80] In this case remarriage occurs with assent from Jesus.

Third, are elders and deacons held to a higher standard than church members? They are. Elders and deacons hold these offices because of their devotion to Christ, his call on their lives, their character, and their skill in leadership and service. They are responsible to conduct their lives in Christ so others may imitate them.[81]

If one takes Paul's qualifications for elder at face value, it would seem that only those with exemplary marriages and well-managed households are fit to serve. But this would exclude from service anyone who is unmarried. Most recognize that these are conditions of the perfect leader, and so churches look for people who are generally there and are continuing to grow. Very godly single men often serve as elders in

---

[77]Matt. 19:6.
[78]Matt. 19:8–9.
[79]1 Cor. 7:15.
[80]Matt. 5:31–32.
[81]Heb. 13:7.

the pattern of Jeremiah, Paul, and Jesus. As with any other serious sin, it is possible that a divorced person who has confessed sin, pursued all reasonable routes of reconciliation, and is living an exemplary life could qualify as a leader. Attempts to put this in a policy statement are very risky since these are never abstractions but unique people who need our wisest shepherding.

At Mars Hill, where Mark is an elder, they will not accept an elder candidate who has left a covenant marriage unless there are extreme mitigating circumstances, as well as confession and repentance of any sin joined with great maturity of life and character proven over many years since. Mars Hill will accept a man who was divorced as an unbeliever if he has met all other biblical criteria for the office, including an exemplary, well-tested marriage if he is remarried.

DOES IT REALLY MATTER WHETHER A CHURCH HAS ONLY MALE ELDERS?

Frankly, it matters exactly to the degree that we take the Bible as our authority. Throughout the Bible, women serve as prophets, disciples, and leaders. But there are always male-only offices: king, priest, apostle, and elder. If you really believe the Bible is God's Word, then why not follow that pattern?

Women should be encouraged to be leaders, deacons, and teachers in non-elder roles. Many churches deny such roles to women, perhaps because they are afraid they might compromise the principle of male eldership. But that fear is akin to Jews who refused to speak the name of God lest they do so irreverently.

On the other hand, attempts to explain away such requirements as elders being the "husband of one wife" diminish the authority of God's Word. This is an area where good and godly people strongly disagree, because it goes to the heart of how we understand God's Word. Those who differ must work to understand each other, listening to each other with open Bibles and peaceable hearts. But we see this as a matter of God's direction, and thus we believe male eldership is essential.

CHAPTER FOUR

WHY IS PREACHING IMPORTANT?

Preach the word.

2 TIMOTHY 4:2

✝

As a boy I was very frustrated with the wooden pews in our church
because getting comfortable on them was incredibly difficult while
trying to sleep during the service. Eventually I learned that if I sat at
the end of the row, I could curl up in the corner of the pew and get some
decent sleep during the Mass.

Conducive to the church nap were the preacher's short sermon,
soothing tone, and monotone voice. Subsequently, I often found church
to be a most effective place for a regular power nap, with one exception. I
really remember only one of the hundreds of church services I attended
as a boy. An African priest was visiting. He was a huge man with a boom-
ing voice and dark skin beneath his white robe. He got up to preach and
did some things I had never seen. He looked us in the eye with a serious
face and a captivating smile. He did not go behind the wooden pulpit to
the side of the stage but instead stood in the middle of the stage at the
very front so as to be close to the people. He did not use any notes but
spoke from his memory on something that was obviously well known
to him. He did not mumble his words in a dour voice but rather raised
his voice, which was filled with deep, captivating passion. He walked
around the stage and up and down the aisle, flailing his arms, and was
absolutely motivating.

He captured and kept my attention. As much as anything he said, it was his presence and passion that kept me from curling up in the corner of the pew to nap. I remember literally sitting on the edge of my seat, hanging on his every word and wondering if I had missed something about God and church that he had learned. That was the first time I remember really enjoying church, being curious about God, and wanting to learn more and to come again.

As we left the church I asked my folks if he would be preaching again, because he had captivated my attention and I wanted to hear him every week. My heart sank when my folks said that he was only visiting and that our normal preacher would be back in the pulpit the following week. I told my folks that I was upset because I wanted the African priest to be our preacher, and they agreed that he seemed to know and love God with an enthusiasm that was infectious. We were all sad, and as we neared the car I decided that I would just try to keep sleeping through church, and I did until my teen years, when I stopped going altogether.

Today, in God's curious irony, I am a preacher. As a preacher, I spend a lot of time considering what the Bible has to say about preaching, beginning with the fact that God himself is a preacher.

The first page of the Bible reveals that God created the world through speaking, or, in other words, the world began with a sermon. In the first chapter of Genesis we read that "God said" ten times. We then read seven times that "God saw" what his sermon accomplished, including revealing God, creating order, creating good things, bringing life, creating an environment in which life can exist, separating things, coming with authority, and accomplishing what God intended in powerful authority.

We then see that Satan the serpent shows up in Genesis 3 also to preach, which he did to our first parents, Adam and Eve. His sermon included twisting God's Word and even boldly declaring that God's sermon was a lie. Our first parents then had to choose which sermon they would believe. Tragically, they believed the serpent's sermon over God's, and sin, death, and chaos have ensued ever since. Furthermore, the serpent has continued preaching through false prophets and teachers every day since. In our own day, songs, movies, advertising, politics, and television are in essence sermons that preach about the important matters of life, such as who God is, who we are, and how we are to live our lives regarding such things as sexuality. Sometimes the serpent's sermons are very subtle and other times they are widely public, with false teachers such as Oprah leading multitudes astray.

In the Old Testament, to counteract the false sermons of false preachers God sent forth a succession of prophets to declare his Word in truth with passion and authority. Those prophets declared, "Thus says the Lord" hundreds of times in the pages of the Old Testament. Generally speaking, their messages centered on commanding people to repent of their sin, turn from false spiritualities, turn to God, and trust in the coming of Jesus. The work of the prophets continued until the coming of John the Baptizer, whom the prophet Malachi, hundreds of years prior, had revealed was coming to prepare the way for Jesus.[1] We read about John's prophetic mission in Matthew 3:1–3:

> In those days John the Baptist came preaching in the wilderness of Judea, "Repent, for the kingdom of heaven is at hand." For this is he who was spoken of by the prophet Isaiah when he said, "The voice of one crying in the wilderness: 'Prepare the way of the Lord; make his paths straight.'"

John baptized Jesus later, in Matthew 3. As Jesus came out of the water, God the Holy Spirit descended upon him like a dove, and God the Father spoke from heaven in one of the most intimate portraits of the Trinity in all of Scripture. In this scene we also witness God's public affirmation that Jesus is the God-man anointed by the Holy Spirit for ministry.

In Matthew 4 we read of the Devil coming to Jesus, tempting him to sin and preaching to him a false gospel as he did to Adam. Unlike our first father, however, Jesus (whom Paul calls "the last Adam"[2]) resisted temptation, rebuked the Devil, and preached his own short but powerful sermon by repeatedly quoting Scripture, which served as an effective sword to defeat the Devil in battle.

In Matthew 4:17 we then read, "From that time Jesus began to preach, saying, 'Repent, for the kingdom of heaven is at hand.'" Indeed,

---

[1]Mal. 3:1.
[2]1 Cor. 15:45.

Jesus' ministry included feeding the hungry, healing the sick, loving the outcast, and befriending the sinner. But we must never forget that Jesus' ministry began with preaching. Thus, preaching is the first priority of ministry that leads God's mission, which is accompanied by various other ministries that support, supplement, and sustain the preaching of God's Word in truth with passion.

Jesus' ministry involved ongoing preaching to crowds large and small until his death, burial, and resurrection. In Acts 1 we read Jesus' final words to his small band of followers. He told them to wait for the coming of the Holy Spirit before attempting to preach the good news of his death, burial, and resurrection because they needed to be anointed with the Spirit's power as he was. Jesus then ascended back into heaven, and in Acts 2 we read that the Holy Spirit descended upon the church similar to the way in which he descended upon Jesus and anointed him for ministry.

In the remainder of Acts 2 we read an amazing sermon that was preached by Peter and anointed by God the Spirit; the result was that many people became Christians and the New Testament church was birthed. The New Testament church continued growing in large part through preaching about Jesus to groups large and small as told in nearly every chapter of the book of Acts.[3] Virtually the only chapters of Acts that do not include preaching are those containing seasons where the preachers were in prison for preaching and therefore were temporarily unable to preach.

The most visible preacher in Acts is Paul, who was a great persecutor of the church before becoming a preacher for the church.[4] Everything changed when Jesus came down from heaven to preach a short but effective sermon to Paul:

> And immediately something like scales fell from [Paul's] eyes, and he regained his sight. Then he rose and was baptized; and taking food, he was strengthened. For some days he was with the disciples at Damascus. And immediately he proclaimed Jesus in the synagogues, saying, "He is the Son of God." . . . So he went in and out among them at Jerusalem, preaching boldly in the name of the Lord.[5]

---

[3]Acts 3–4; 5:42; 6:2–4; 7; 8:3–5, 25, 40; 9–14; 15:35; 16:10; 17–26; 28.
[4]Acts 8:3–5.
[5]Acts 9:18–20, 28–29.

Paul was so devoted to preaching that even when he was stoned for doing it by an angry mob and left for dead, Paul did not take a day off but went right back to preaching—dents, bruises, and all—once he regained consciousness.[6] In the final chapter of the book of Acts we read that Paul spent his final years under house arrest but invited anyone over who wanted to be preached at.[7] Obviously, Christ, Christians, and Christian churches hold preaching in high regard.

In addition to recording the efforts and effects of preaching, the New Testament also speaks about the requirements of those who preach. One of the qualifications of elders is that they be "able to teach."[8] This does not mean that every elder be able to preach on Sundays but that every elder be able to teach in some setting, such as in one-on-one counseling or to a group or a class. James 3:1 warns us, "Not many of you should become teachers, my brothers, for you know that who teach will be judged with greater strictness." At least one of the elders in a church needs to be able to "preach the word," as 2 Timothy 4:2 says.

Paul the preacher has many things to say about preachers in 1 Timothy 5:17–19:

> Let the elders who rule well be considered worthy of double honor, especially those who labor in preaching and teaching. For the Scripture says, "You shall not muzzle an ox when it treads out the grain," and, "The laborer deserves his wages." Do not admit a charge against an elder except on the evidence of two or three witnesses.

First, the elders, as a council or team, are to rule the church and do so well, with the Christian church members giving them double honor. Second, honoring elders includes honoring the preaching pastor(s) who work hard in their studies to preach and teach the Bible well. Third, for those who teach the Bible, in general, and preach, in particular, it is imperative that this honoring includes protecting them from the pain of critics. Indeed, the preaching pastor, along with every other church member, should be held accountable for charges of sin. Nevertheless, a church and its leaders must learn to distinguish between charges and criticisms. Charges of actual sin or false doctrine should be investigated

---

[6] Acts 14:19–23.
[7] Acts 28.
[8] 1 Tim. 3:2.

biblically and thoroughly. Criticisms are to be dismissed and not given the same level of attention as a charge. Every preacher will be criticized, and the pain of criticism is one of the great struggles of every preacher.

I once received some helpful counsel regarding criticism from Pastor Rick Warren of Saddleback Church in California. He graciously called simply to see if there was anything he could do to help. His kindness was humbling and helpful. I asked him how he handled his critics, and he offered a great insight—given today's technology, criticism can be instant, constant, global, and permanent. Warren explained that, as Jesus experienced, the strongest criticism for any Christian leader comes from rigid religious people. When I asked him what someone should do when facing criticism, he gave the following insightful advice:

1) Turn your critics into coaches by hearing what they are saying and humbly considering if there is any truth to their criticism.

2) Never engage the critics on their terms because it only escalates the conflict and is not productive.

3) Be very careful about firing off emails or leaving voicemails and responding out of anger in a way that you will later regret.

4) Shout louder than your critics to define yourself, and do not allow them to define you.

PUTTING PREACHERS IN THEIR PLACE

Not only are preachers being criticized, but now preaching itself is being criticized as well. On this last point, which all of the Reformers considered essential for a Christian church, it has been reported, "A number of emerging church worship services involve little more than a meal and music—no sermon at all."[9]

To make matters worse, some well-known Christians, such as researcher George Barna, are now making outlandish claims that any Christian church that owns a building, meets regularly, has a paid pastor, or any leader who preaches a sermon is pagan. In his book *Pagan Christianity?*[10] Barna says that Christians borrowed the idea of weekly church meetings with a preached sermon from pagan stoicism. What he curiously overlooks is the fact that the early Christians took their cues from the synagogue, where people would meet every Sabbath day

---

[9]Shane Hipps, "Visualcy: But Now I See," *Leadership*, Summer 2007, 22.
[10]Frank Viola and George Barna, *Pagan Christianity? Exploring the Roots of Our Church Practices* (Carol Stream, IL: Tyndale, 2008).

in a designated building at a designated time to worship God, which included listening to a sermon from the Old Testament preached by a qualified leader. In addition, he completely overlooks all the biblical evidence for preaching that we studied earlier in this chapter. God's people have always viewed preaching as something to be done when the church gathers as well as wherever and whenever else the gospel can be proclaimed to people.

In preaching, the authority of God's Word is upheld and God's people are led and taught according to the Scriptures in large groups. This is the basis for people to meet in homes to discuss the sermon every week. These home groups include fellowship, Communion meals, open dialogue about the text or topic of the sermon, praying for one another, serving one another, and singing worship songs. Without godly authority and authoritative Bible preaching, sects and cults of various sorts and kinds are prone to rise up and be led by the serpent under the guise of the Christian name and Christian sacraments.

Knowing this, I not only preach God's Word but also want to encourage all preachers to truly preach. Preaching is not sharing or chatting but rather proclaiming with authority and passion the truth of God's Word about Jesus.

PREACH THE WORD

Preachers are commanded to "preach the Word,"[11] although the Bible does not tell us exactly how this should be done or demonstrate it with a model for the perfect sermon. Therefore, how to preach the Word methodologically includes many faithful options that I have used and will continue to use according to what best serves the principle that I faithfully "preach the Word." These methods include expository preaching, textual preaching, and topical preaching, which I will now explore, knowing that everyone but the preachers have already stopped reading this chapter and have moved on to see if there is a picture, anything about sex, or ideally both somewhere later in this book.

EXPOSITORY PREACHING

Among those who hold the Bible in high regard as they ought, expository preaching is increasingly popular. Expository preaching is simply

---

[11]2 Tim. 4:2.

going through a book of the Bible verse-by-verse. While the Bible never commands or really even illustrates this method, some practical reasons make it popular:

1) Because all Scripture is God-breathed and for our benefit, there is not a page of Scripture that is not helpful to our faith, so we should examine it all.[12]

2) From church history we know that influential preachers such as Justin Martyr preached expository sermons that went through books of the Bible line-by-line.

3) It allows non-Christians and new Christians to follow along more easily than if the preacher jumps around the Bible.

4) It doesn't allow the preacher to avoid difficult texts and issues.

5) It helps teach the congregation to study the Bible for itself.

6) It helps show the importance of context in Scripture.

7) It helps people to read and study along with the sermons each week.

8) It makes it easier for people to refer back to what they have learned in Scripture.

9) It forces the authority to reside in the text and not the teacher.

As a general rule, it is best to include preaching from all genres of biblical literature in both the Old and New Testaments over the course of a preaching ministry. Over the years, most of my preaching has been expositional and has rotated between Old and New Testament books. At the time I am writing this chapter I am in my eleventh year of preaching at Mars Hill Church in Seattle and have preached through Genesis, Exodus, Ruth, Nehemiah, Proverbs, Ecclesiastes, Song of Solomon, Obadiah, Jonah, Habakkuk, John, Romans, 1 Corinthians, Galatians, Ephesians, Philippians, 1–2 Timothy, and 1–3 John. If you look online at our church media library (http://media.marshillchurch.org/), you will notice that the books I preached in the earlier years of the church are not available for download because, frankly, the preaching was not that great. Preaching is like driving a stick: you only get better the more you practice, and the hope is not to kill anyone as you learn, while accepting that a few dents are inevitable. Also understand that it takes at least two to three hundred sermons to become a decent preacher.

There is one noteworthy concern regarding expository preaching. The danger of expository preaching is that it can fall into worshiping

---

[12]2 Tim. 3:16–17.

the words of the Bible and ignoring the God who speaks through them. It can also lead to getting so bogged down in examining every word in such painstaking detail that the big themes and concepts of the book are lost altogether. Some who live for expositional preaching seem to believe sanctification consists solely of filling in blanks in printed outlines. While this form of preaching can be wonderful, we must hear the Spirit who illumines the text if it is to be of any benefit to us personally.[13]

As a general rule, it is wise for the majority of a preacher's preaching to be expository while using other formats as needed.

TEXTUAL PREACHING

Textual preaching falls between expositional and topical preaching. Textual preaching is preaching on one section of Scripture from within a book of the Bible without preaching the entire book, as is done with expository preaching. Some practical reasons make this method popular:

1) It shows the consistency of Scripture by linking sections of Scripture together as a thematic series.

2) It allows the preacher with a revolving church, where people move in and out a lot (e.g., college town, military town, major city), to hit central truths every year so that new people are given a basic theological framework through key sections of Scripture.

3) It allows the preacher to work in smaller chunks of four to eight weeks, providing flexibility to deal with issues as they arise. This is especially helpful if a church is adding new services and campuses and needs to remain nimble to synchronize new preaching series with changes in the church.

4) It allows the preacher to work around the Christian calendar with miniseries on the incarnation around Christmas, crucifixion in the dark winter months, and resurrection around Easter.

Examples of textual preaching in my own ministry include a series I did early in the church that walked through nearly every book of the Old Testament examining each messianic prophecy about Jesus Christ in an effort to convince our young, struggling church plant that Jesus is the centerpiece of both Scripture and history. I also preached on the first two chapters of Luke as a holiday series around Christmastime.

---

[13]Isa. 59:21; John 14:26; 1 Cor. 2:10–13.

Another textual series was on worship from the book of Revelation that looked at the heavenly scenes of Jesus seated upon his throne. The series skipped the earthly scenes replete with "the mark of the beast" and such, which sadly tend to be the focus for many who preach Revelation instead of Jesus; the book opens by clearly saying it is "the revelation of Jesus Christ."

TOPICAL PREACHING

The most common type of preaching is topical preaching. Topical preaching is using several texts from one or more books of the Bible or biblical authors to speak on an issue. When this is done, it is good to have the verses on a handout and/or on PowerPoint so that people do not get lost trying to keep up. While we do not have the full transcripts of the sermons preached in the Bible, the portions we do have tend to show that topical teaching was common. Some practical reasons this method is favorable include:

1) The ability to trace a theme through multiple books of the Bible, showing the consistency of Scripture.

2) The ability to preach with multiple perspectives and avoid the common error of reductionism, which is looking only at what one section of Scripture says on an issue rather than at all that the Bible says about it.

3) The ability to address most thoroughly questions and controversies that arise.

4) The ability to select the most appropriate verses from Scripture on a given topic.

Examples of my own topical preaching include a twelve-week series called "Vintage Jesus," which led to the book by the same name, and a twelve-week series on the cross, which resulted in the book *Death by Love*.[14] The danger of topical preaching is that it is really easy for the preacher to bring his own ideas to the people, supported by a few passages. Topical preaching must always be expositional in the sense that it proclaims the message of the Scripture. When it becomes a place for the preacher's good ideas, then it is not exposition but imposition.

As a general rule, I find it best to have expository preaching be the majority of preaching and to use the other forms as needed. The worst

---

[14]Mark Driscoll and Gerry Breshears, *Vintage Jesus: Timeless Answers to Timely Questions* (Wheaton, IL: Crossway Books, 2008), and *Death by Love: Letters from the Cross* (Wheaton, IL: Crossway Books, 2008).

thing a preacher can do is become a legalist and use only one method of preaching as if that alone were biblical. The ensuing self-righteousness is not fitting for the humility required of a gospel preacher. Perhaps the most peculiar example of this kind of legalism was a buddy of mine who was preaching through Genesis. Rather than taking a break to preach the resurrection of Jesus on Easter Sunday, he stuck with the order of the verses and preached a graphic sermon on the sin of Onan without ever declaring that Jesus is alive. To say the least, it was an odd holiday choice, and the various Christian grandmothers who sat around me wearing Easter bonnets just kept shaking their heads while he tried to convince them that Onan masturbated.

Before moving on to provide some practical tips for preachers and teachers, I want to briefly explore the narrative preaching trend. While it is not a genre of preaching per se, it is treated as one by some.

Narrative Preaching

Many young preachers are attracted to narrative preaching. They are prone to declare that all preaching should be narrative, as if every book of the Bible were a narrative story. Some are (such as Ruth, which is arguably the best little story ever written), but not all books of the Bible are stories. To be fair to narrative preaching we must explore its pros and cons.

Pros:

- A sermon can follow the storyline of a Bible tale from one event or person to the next rather than a systematic theology approach of proposition to proposition.
- The hearer is not given the thesis up front followed by its defense but is taken on a journey through the storyline of the Bible through conflict, tension, and eventual resolution. This is often more gripping and memorable than three points and a poem from some guy in an ill-fitting suit.
- The Bible is *the* story (metanarrative) and preaching always connects to *the* story, which is the story of redemption, or the gospel. This means that every sermon needs to be explained in terms of where it fits in terms of creation, curse, covenant, Christ, church, and consummation. This does not mean that every sermon is a story, but that every sermon fits within the Story, and the genre and style of biblical literature

determine the format of the sermon. Some are narrative and some are not. This also allows us to start in a better place than systematic theology. For example, the five points of Calvinism start with the fall and human depravity and ignore the first two chapters of Genesis, where the story of the Bible begins.

⦿ Not only is the Bible the metanarrative story that moves from creation to new creation, but it also has Jesus as its hero and centerpiece in both his humble incarnation and glorious exaltation.

Cons:

⦿ Its current form is derived from mainline liberal Christianity with a low view of the Bible that sees God's Word as a narrative and not *the* narrative inspired in perfection by God in authority over all other narratives. Thus, Jesus is placed alongside Wicca or Islam, telling a story about the world that is merely an opinion or perspective.

⦿ It can be a move away from propositional truth in favor of relativism and perspectivism, as if transformation were possible without any truth statements, and all we need are good stories without any explanation or interpretation.

⦿ It can mean that books of the Bible that are not narrative are not well taught because a method is imposed on a book without regard for its literary form.

In conclusion, there is a form of narrative preaching that works for narrative passages in the Bible and works to connect all passages in the Bible to the narrative storyline of the Bible. But some books—Proverbs is the most obvious example, although it does have a few brief narratives interspersed—are not narratives, and to preach them as such would be to violate the narrative structure they were written in.

PRACTICAL TIPS FOR PREACHERS AND TEACHERS

Having established various ways to "preach the word," I hope to help others, especially those who preach and teach, to study Scripture more effectively by explaining some of what I do.

1) I take a few days a month outside of town in complete silence and solitude. During that time with God I am refreshed and encouraged as I prayer-walk, canoe, read my Bible, repent of sin, journal thoughts that come to mind as I spend the day with God, and ask God to give me

direction regarding my Bible study, out of which comes my preaching and teaching. And I listen to him attentively. Once I believe God has burdened me with a specific book of the Bible, text, or topic, I then spend time prayerfully considering why and how God would have me study it.

I then bring my conviction to our executive elders for consideration and final decision so as to be in submission to spiritual authority. They ask heart questions such as why I am compelled to preach it and how I intend to present it to our people; their loving counsel is very helpful in checking my motives. Once approved, I then plan to spend months, and sometimes years, studying that book of the Bible or biblical topic in preparation to preach it. This is what Paul meant when he called preaching "labor."

2) I continually pray for the Holy Spirit to teach me his Word as I am studying the Scripture. No amount of theological training can overcome the deficit of a person who is not led by the Holy Spirit to understand and proclaim the very words that he inspired. My pattern for this comes from the fact that the Old Testament prophets often walked out of the silence of the woods to preach, and Jesus spent forty days in silence and solitude before beginning his preaching ministry. My goal is to have the Scriptures so grafted into my heart and mind that I am free to speak of them with passion, clarity, and certainty without really needing many, if any, notes.

3) As I study, I wrestle with tough texts as Jacob wrestled Jesus. I find that studying tough texts on topics such as gender roles, the flood, and hell is much like driving a car into a steep curve. If you hit the brakes in fear, you will lose control, but if you accelerate into the tough turns, gravity actually slingshots you through smoothly. Momentum and authority come through accelerating into tough texts in study and then driving the church through them in the pulpit. As a result, the tougher the text, the harder and faster I go, and I try never to tap the brakes.

4) Only after I have spent considerable time solely in the text of Scripture do I check my studies with trusted teachers to ensure I have not come to erroneous conclusions. I try not to pick up the commentaries until I have had much time in the Scripture I am preaching to ensure I do not get lazy or simply rely on another person's walk with God. I will read the Scripture repeatedly in multiple translations and only then

read every decent commentary from every theological persuasion I can find to examine the book from every angle. I also check my conclusions with faithful preachers of previous generations, such as Athanasius, Augustine, John Calvin, and Martin Luther.

5) I seek by God's empowering grace through his Spirit to live what I learn, teach it to my family through ongoing informal discussions, and spend a lot of time repenting of sin, seeking to obey God's Word by the grace he provides. Much of my sermon is then simply explaining what the Scripture says, how it has changed my life, and how it is transforming my family and those people with whom I live in community. I hope to model coming under Scripture to my church by talking about my own sins and flaws so that they see me struggling through Scripture and not just giving my tidy answers at the end of my studies. I believe that preachers or teachers should speak the text from their life, warts and all, so that the people learn that Jesus is their hero too. I am not saying that Bible teachers with serious sin in their life that could disqualify them should be allowed to continue preaching in the name of authenticity; rather, teachers should be godly people who demonstrate their godliness by a lifestyle of open, humble repentance.

No matter what text or topic I am studying, I always ask six questions that help me.

1) THe BIBLICaL QueSTION: WHaT DOeS SCRIPTURe Say?

To answer this we need to hear the text, giving worshipful attention to the words and listening with full concentration for the message. We check translations, do our word studies, and find out exactly what words best convey the meaning of Scripture. To help in this process a good word-for-word Bible translation is best to preach from, such as the English Standard Version, which is my preference, the New King James Version, the Holman Christian Standard Bible, or the New American Standard Bible. Additionally, good Bible software with language tools such as Logos (www.logos.com) or Bible Works (www.bibleworks.org) can be very helpful in answering this question. One of the elders at our church has put together a free New Testament Greek study program at www.theresurgence.com that may also be helpful. Another very helpful free source for excellent online teaching is www.biblicaltraining.org.

2) THE THEOLOGICAL QUESTION: WHAT DOES SCRIPTURE MEAN?

After finding out what Scripture says, we need then to interpret what is said so that we know what it means. Because the Bible is God's Word for all of God's people, its meaning is for all believers in all times. Meaning resides in the text rather than in our imagination, as postmoderns claim. Meaning is different from personal significance, which is the Spirit-empowered application of meaning to our individual lives. At this point we will study other Scriptures to illuminate our understanding of the text(s) we are planning to preach from, read commentaries, examine cultural background studies, and wrestle through the text with other believers.

At this phase, John Glynn's *Commentary and Reference Survey* is a must-have for every preacher and teacher.[15] He rates all of the best commentaries and other reference material on various books of the Bible and theological topics. D. A. Carson's guide to New Testament commentaries and Tremper Longman III's guide to Old Testament commentaries are also helpful to ensure a preacher does not waste time or money on the wrong books.[16] My friend Daniel Akin updates a similar list, "Building a Theological Library," every two years at www.danielakin.com.

3) THE MEMORABLE QUESTION: WHAT IS MY HOOK?

As I study Scripture, I steep in the verses, phrases, and word-pictures that are hooks on which I can hang my big ideas. Too often the principles of Scripture are preached, when the images and word-pictures are far more impacting and memorable. For this reason other movements have co-opted the biblical images so that a dove now represents peace and not the Holy Spirit, and a rainbow represents gay rights and not the flood in which God killed people for sinning. I find that sermons become memorable if the images in the Scriptures can be drilled into the imaginations of the people. A word, image, concept, doctrine, emotion, or person needs to be the hook that is woven through the sermon similar to a music hook that is woven throughout a song. Without a unifying hook, the sermon will not be memorable for the hearer and will end up as a disjointed number of thoughts.

---

[15]John Glynn, *Commentary and Reference Survey* (Grand Rapids, MI: Kregel, 2007).
[16]D. A. Carson, *New Testament Commentary Survey* (Grand Rapids, MI: Baker, 2007); Tremper Longman III, *Old Testament Commentary Survey* (Grand Rapids, MI: Baker, 2007).

Usually the most difficult aspect of putting together a sermon is the hook. More important than points, acronyms, and goofy acrostics is one good hook on which the ideas that comprise the sermon are all hung together. Examples include a word such as *grace,* a concept such as being born again, a doctrine such as the wrath of God, an emotion such as bitterness in the life of Naomi, and the life of a person such as Joseph which dominates the final eleven chapters of Genesis. Perhaps the master at this was Charles Haddon Spurgeon, who would not just describe a scene of Scripture but could actually put his hearers in it through their imagination. As a result, he remains popular over a hundred years after his death and is my favorite preacher outside of Scripture. In reading edited transcripts of his sermons, I am continually enthralled by his focus on memorable images such as a king's throne, a ruler's scepter, a soldier's sword, and a shepherd's staff.

4) THE APOLOGETICAL QUESTION: WHY DO WE RESIST THIS TRUTH?

Here we are assuming that people will not simply embrace God's truth but fight it with their thoughts and/or actions because they are sinners who, like Romans 1:18 says, suppress the truth. So, we attempt to predict their objections so that we can answer them and remove their resistance to get them to embrace God's truth for their life. This part of the sermon must be confrontational and often results in people walking out, standing up to argue, and sending in nasty emails, all of which indicate you've hit a nerve like God wants you to.

The real fight begins at this point, and a preacher needs to come out from behind his pulpit with his hands up and chin down like a boxer looking for an opening while deflecting jabs sent his way. The issue here is uncovering the idols that people have and breaking their resistance to the truth of the gospel. This is also accomplished by co-opting their cultural hopes and presenting the gospel as the only answer to their deepest longing. Thus, they see their yearning for freedom is found only in Jesus, their yearning for pleasure is found only in holiness, and their yearning for greatness is found only in humility.

Without answering the apologetical question, your people will live in sin, lost people will not get saved in great number, and people may find you funny, clever, nice, or even smart but not compelling. They will become indifferent to your teaching because of their "good" objections that you have failed to demolish. You must follow the example of Moses, who kindly smashed the golden calf, ground it to powder, and made his people drink their god to emphasize the point that resisting the truth is never a good idea.[17]

5) THE MISSIONAL QUESTION: WHY DOES THIS MATTER?

We need to connect all that we have said to the missional purpose for our lives, families, church, city, and ultimately God's glory. Something may be true, but if people do not find it to be important and urgent, they tend not to act on it. This also explains why many churches are orthodox but indifferent. Such churches believe that Satan is at work in the world, that people are ensnared by sin, that culture is becoming increasingly pagan, and that every day someone who lives near them is dying and going to hell but they have no sense of urgency to say or do anything.

For us as missionaries in culture, the tip of the spear for our war against Satan, sin, and death is the sermon, if rightly preached with authority for the purpose of gathering God's people for instruction before sending them out on mission with passion. I like to connect Scripture to the character of God, the nature of the gospel, our mission in our city, and the quality of our lives, both individually and collectively as a city of God within our city. This means, for example, that when single people are sleeping together, I need them to know that they are preaching a false gospel to their lost friends and our city with their life, because Jesus does not sleep with his girlfriend but loves his bride the church as a faithful husband. Subsequently, repeatedly telling our people that they should live in our city, love our city, serve our city, and seek the blessing and prosperity of our whole city, like Jeremiah 29:4–9 extols, means that every Sunday I am teaching them how to worship in the world as missionaries sent to bring the transforming power of Jesus in word and deed so that people and the culture in which they live will be transformed.

6) THE CHRISTOLOGICAL QUESTION: HOW IS JESUS THE HERO-SAVIOR?

The Bible is one story in which Jesus is the hero. Therefore, to properly teach and preach the Bible we have to continually lift him up as the

---

[17]Ex. 32:30.

hero. Any sermon in which the focus is not the person and work of Jesus will lack spiritual authority and power because the Holy Spirit will not bless the teaching of any hero other than Jesus. Jesus himself taught this point repeatedly:

- ⊚ "Do not think that I have come to abolish the Law or the Prophets; I have not come to abolish them but to fulfill them."[18]
- ⊚ "You search the Scriptures because you think that in them you have eternal life; and it is they that bear witness about me."[19]
- ⊚ And beginning with Moses and all the Prophets, he interpreted to them in all the Scriptures the things concerning himself.[20]
- ⊚ "These are my words that I spoke to you while I was still with you, that everything written about me in the Law of Moses and the Prophets and the Psalms must be fulfilled." Then he opened their minds to understand the Scriptures.[21]

There is an ongoing debate as to the purpose of the sermon and whether it should focus on converting the lost or maturing the saved. The apparent conflict between preaching for seekers and preaching for believers is resolved simply by noting that both need to repent of sin and trust in Jesus to live a new life empowered by the Spirit. Therefore, a sermon can and should effectively communicate to both audiences, and it will if the preacher is able to go after the root of sin and explain Christian jargon in order to speak the "tongue" of the hearer. This includes saying the name of Jesus and making him known.

Paul says that "God has highly exalted [Jesus] and bestowed on him the name that is above every name, so that at the name of Jesus every knee should bow, in heaven and on earth and under the earth, and every tongue confess that Jesus Christ is Lord, to the glory of God the Father."[22] Without turning the name of Jesus into a mantra like the pagans do with the names of their false gods, I do want to stress the importance, preeminence, power, and authority that reside in the name of Jesus who is alive today and seated on his throne as King of kings and Lord of lords exalted over every person, every nation, every religion, every sexual preference, every race, every language, every ideology, every political party, every financial status, and every generation.

---

[18]Matt. 5:17.
[19]John 5:39.
[20]Luke 24:27.
[21]Luke 24:44–45.
[22]Phil. 2:9–11.

I would be devastated if my wife rarely uttered my name, and Jesus' bride, the church, is too often guilty of not speaking the name of Jesus with frequent passion from the pulpit.

One of the greatest ways to spur evangelism in a church is for the preacher to speak of Jesus and thus train people to connect every discussion and need to the person and work of Jesus. Speaking of Jesus led to one of the greatest encouragements in my pastoral ministry. A local media outlet was doing a story on our church and asked me why I thought we were growing, whereas most other churches in our area were shrinking. Before answering the question, I asked the non-Christian reporter what answers had been given by the people they had grabbed after Sunday services. The reporter told me that every person they asked said the church was growing because of Jesus. Those questioned went on to speak of what Jesus had done on the cross and how Jesus lived to help sinners live new lives. They shared their own stories of what Jesus had done in their lives, and even asked the reporter if they wanted to know more about Jesus. Other reporters have told me that when hanging around our church they have been invited by our members to go out to dinner with a group of people. They have even invited the reporters into their homes for a meal and to talk about Jesus in hopes that the reporters would get saved. In short, I was thrilled that no matter what the question, our people had learned that the answer is always, only, fully, thoroughly, passionately, clearly, Jesus!

As a preacher, I would be remiss not to close this chapter with a few preachy points. I offer them as tips and quips to fellow Bible teachers.

1) Good preaching and teaching takes time, so short messages may not be the wisest. It is becoming more common for younger and more theologically Reformed preachers to have longer sermons (an hour seems to be the new norm) than most evangelical churches (twenty to thirty minutes). While the Bible does not speak to this issue directly, upon occasion we do see Jesus and Paul preaching very long sermons.[23] So give yourself enough time to explain what you mean, including the Christian lingo and theological terms you use. For what it is worth, the better a preacher and the longer a sermon, the younger and larger the congregation tends to be, because God honors the preaching of his Word, and in

[23]Matt. 15:29–31; Acts 20:7–11.

too many cities too few churches have much preaching. My record is well over an hour and a half, and an hour is usually a brief sermon for me.

2) At some point in every message, speak plainly to the non-Christians. This is as simple as noting that some people in the room are not Christians, and you want to take a few moments to tell them exactly why and how to become Christians. Every message should include a clear gospel invitation to salvation for non-Christians. Too many preachers and teachers assume all their people are saved, when they are not, or assume that the non-Christians will figure it out, which they have not. By presenting the gospel every week, you will make it easy for your people to invite their lost family and friends, because they will be assured that no matter what, the gospel will be presented anytime they can get their friends to attend. They will be confident they can follow up with them over a meal or coffee to unpack the message.

3) Speak to the people in the room. However, if you speak *only* to the people in the room, those are the only people who will attend your ministry. Therefore, it is wise to speak also to the people you want to attend your ministry. This means, for example, if your ministry is filled mainly with women, and you want to reach men, you should start speaking as a man to men. In time those men will show up because their wives, moms, girlfriends, coworkers, sisters, and friends will invite them, since you are speaking to them.

4) Keep the major holiday sermons plain. The key to the holidays is simply to tell people the truth with love and joy, such as the fact that God became a man, died on a cross for our sins, and rose for our salvation. To be honest, I pretty much just preach the same sermon every Easter and Christmas and try to keep it short, sweet, and to the point, and no one seems to mind so long as it's all about Jesus. Similarly, every day when I come home from work, my wife says she loves me, and I have not stopped coming home, because it sounds amazing every time I hear it.

5) Remind your people. The preachers and teachers in the New Testament do this as well, and when they remind their people, it is often about Jesus and his grace. Therefore, all preachers and teachers need to have a list of big truths in their mind that they often weave into their sermons to remind their people. For me this includes such things as the truth and helpfulness of the Bible, the nature of God as Trinity,

creation, sin, the cross and resurrection of Jesus, the power of the Holy Spirit, and the freeing power of repentance.

6) Speak out of your life of ministry. Mercy ministries, such as counseling people and visiting the sick, are all part of God's way of giving the teacher his heart in addition to his mind. Both the heart and mind are needed for good teaching, and good teachers teach out of love for people. In so doing, they will use hard words, because soft words produce hard people and hard words produce soft people. But people welcome their words because they are friends, and as Proverbs 27:6 says, "Faithful are the wounds of a friend; profuse are the kisses of an enemy." I have told our people many times that I love them and that I will give my entire life to their well-being until I preach my own funeral before shutting the lid on my coffin. This means I not only deeply care for them off the stage but also preach to them from the stage as both their pastor and preacher.

7) Read the biographies of great preachers and teachers. It helps to learn how they set up their library, organize their schedule, practice the spiritual disciplines, stay connected to their families, and deal with such things as critics and illness. A good introduction to the Puritans, who elevated the pulpit to a thunderous art, is *Light and Heat: The Puritan View of the Pulpit* by Bruce Bickel.[24] I am also a rabid fan of the Reformed Baptist Charles Haddon Spurgeon and read any biography I can find on his life and ministry.

8) Do not speak anyone else's messages. Doing so amounts to plagiarism, unless you get permission. Worse, it subverts God's work in and through you. You miss your time in Scripture. Also, even an excellent online sermon is not a word for *your* congregation. While it is not wrong to listen to other preachers and teachers to see how they taught on a text or topic, your message must be God's word for you and your congregation. If you use the work of others, you are not a teacher, and you should quit your job and go do anything but speak.

9) Learn from politicians, stand-up comedians, and anyone else who stands on a stage to speak to a crowd for a living. I know the fundamentalists who read this would freak out to think that Dave Chappelle, Carlos Mencia, Chris Rock, or Dane Cook have anything to teach a Bible

---

[24]R. Bruce Bickel, *Light and Heat: The Puritan View of the Pulpit* (Orlando, FL: Soli Deo Gloria, 1999).

teacher, but the fundamentalists fail to recognize that their team begins with the word *fun*, and they are guilty of false advertising because they are no fun at all.

Faithful gospel proclamation, which began with God in Genesis, is to continue by faithful gospel preachers until the gospel is finally proclaimed for the last time by the angel mentioned in Revelation 14:6. Until then, do your best and leave the difference up to God's grace. Once you have preached a message, let it go and sleep like a Calvinist unless you have something obvious to repent of to your people. Don't listen to your messages over and over, beating yourself up. Passion, courage, and boldness are the keys to speaking that simply cannot exist in those who are too analytical or critical of themselves; so lighten up, have fun, and let it fly in Jesus' name. God loves to draw straight lines with crooked sticks, and since our entire job is to make Jesus look good, we should rejoice in our crooked sticks.

ANSWERS TO COMMON QUESTIONS ABOUT PREACHING

WHAT CAN CHURCH MEMBERS AND OTHER LEADERS DO TO HELP A PREACHER?

1) The church can pray often for the preacher and his family.

2) Church members can love the pastor's wife and children so that it is easy for them to love the church and share so much of the preacher with the church. Practical love would include designating a parking space for them on Sundays and, if they have young children, appointing someone to help the pastor's wife get the kids in and out of church, since Dad is likely going to be busy working.

3) You can give the preacher a book and Bible software budget sufficient to purchase the books and software he needs to study well.

4) You can permit him to have a set number of uninterrupted hours a week to study and prepare for preaching and teaching. For this to occur, I (Mark) find it best to have my study at my home.

5) You can relieve him of administrative and other burdens on Sundays so he can focus on preaching while knowing that other aspects of the ministry that day are covered by responsible fellow leaders.

6) You can give him a full day off and have other elders and leaders cover pastoral duties. I (Mark) prefer Saturday off so that I can enjoy my family and be well rested and encouraged entering the pulpit on Sunday.

HOW CAN I GET FEEDBACK ON MY PREACHING AND TEACHING?

This is incredibly important, because without constructive feedback it is difficult to improve in your preaching and teaching.

1) You need to exhibit a humble attitude that really seeks input, especially if it is negative. Remember that the respondent is giving you a great gift. Affirm him or her strongly. Find the element of truth that is present even in the most unfair criticism.

2) Making yourself available after your preaching to talk with and pray for people is one way to get instant feedback.

3) You can set up a section on the public church Web site for questions and discussion about the sermon. It would be better yet to do this on a password-protected, private church members' section of the Web site. If you do it this way, make sure people cannot post anonymously and hide in the weeds like snipers.

4) You can humbly consider the pleas of those who will invariably ask you to reconsider (Acts 21:10–15) or lovingly confront you, thinking you are out of line (1 Tim. 5:19).

5) You can actually appoint preselected people to write feedback reports to the sermon so that they are getting input from a variety of people (e.g., older men, younger women, singles, married, etc.).

6) Encourage leaders to channel feedback from people who never come to you because they are too timid to speak their opinions directly to you.

7) One friend of mine who pastors a large church went so far as to pay a non-Christian neighbor to attend his church and write up a full report of what it was like to find the building, park, be greeted, sit in the service, hear the sermon, and hang out for coffee afterward. He said it was the best money the church ever spent.

can preaching also be done as an interactive dialogue?

Most preaching is just monologue; the preacher preaches and the people listen without interacting during the Sunday service. But there is a growing interest in preaching that includes dialogue and discussion so that the sermon time is more interactive.

This is positive when the pastor not only preaches a monologue but also includes in his sermon some leading questions for his people to consider about what the Scripture says. Dialogue or discussion around those questions can help the people understand biblical truth. An elder can preach with authority and then answer the questions of his people in an effort to bring them along toward a personal commitment to the truths of Scripture. In a small church this might include people asking the preacher(s) questions in a respectful and orderly fashion. In a large church it might include something like allowing people to text-message in questions that are then screened for appropriateness and answered as part of the sermon by the preacher(s).

Some promote removing the preacher in favor of a discussion leader of sorts who hosts a sharing of opinions. This comes about often as the result of a low view of church leadership and of the gifts of preaching and teaching, and of the postmodern addiction to complete egalitarianism. The Bible is just one voice at the conversational table. This gives opportunity for false teachers to rise up, speak with equal authority, and lead many astray.

One well-known pastor, who has written a book on this form of preaching, admitted to me while we were debating this issue on a conference panel that in his church, people from any religion, worldview, or belief system are welcome to stand up and speak their opinions. He said that everyone has the right to their own opinion and no one has the right to say anything is incorrect. Such an environment is ripe for heresy and in practice may actually be a cult rather than a church.

Done rightly, interactive teaching that includes both dialogue and monologue can go a long way toward helping the sermon have greater impact. This is because in responding to the objections of people the elder(s) can labor to remove people's resistance to the truth and help get everyone on mission to bring the gospel to others in confidence. But what is unacceptable is discussion alone. Solely offering discussion means that the church either does not have leadership or the leader(s) are not exercising authority and leading, not ensuring that the truth of the Bible is proclaimed, and not correcting any false teaching. The Bible is very clear: an elder "must hold firm to the trustworthy word as taught, so that he may be able to give instruction in sound doctrine and also to rebuke those who contradict it" (Titus 1:9).

CHAPTER FIVE

WHAT ARE BAPTISM AND COMMUNION?

"The cup that I drink you will drink, and with the baptism with which I am baptized, you will be baptized."

MARK 10:39

✝

As an infant I was baptized. As a young boy of seven, I partook of my First Communion. From that day on I participated in the Eucharist whenever I attended Mass with my Catholic parents. In grades five through seven I served as an altar boy. I assisted the priest in preparing the Eucharist elements and stood alongside the priest when he administered them to the people. Although I enjoyed the mystery and beauty of the Mass, I had no real, personal relationship with Jesus or understanding of his work on the cross for my sin, which is the entire point of the Eucharist. In my teen years I rarely attended church and did not become a Christian until some years later, at the age of nineteen.

On the other hand I, Gerry, grew up in fine Bible-centered churches. I was baptized when I was eight. We went to the river, had a picnic, and then three of us were baptized. Everyone sang "Oh happy day, Oh happy day, When Jesus washed my sins away" with a lot of emotion as we came out of the water. But when I got into the party mood and swam into the river before I came back to the bank, everyone got mad at me. The pastor always did the baptisms. He said it represented new faith in Jesus, but those being baptized were almost always people who had been saved years before, which confused me. It seemed you had to prove you were worthy before you could be baptized.

After baptism, I was allowed to take Communion. We "observed Communion" once a month, always tacked on after the regular church service was finished. It was done quickly with the pastor reciting special words from the Bible while saying we didn't do rituals like Catholics. Then the deacons formally passed trays of broken crackers and tiny glasses of tepid grape juice, which they called bread and wine. The only teaching I remember is that this observance was only a symbol of the completed work of Jesus on the cross. There was no present meaning, which left me wondering why we were doing it. I certainly agreed that it was pretty meaningless.

By virtue of reminding us of our connection to Jesus and his people, baptism and Communion are supposed to be incredibly meaningful. In Christianity, baptism and Communion have been sacred rituals practiced for thousands of years in every culture by people who, by faith, trust in Jesus alone for their salvation. Different words are used to describe these sacred rituals. The most common term is *sacrament*, which refers to an outward, visible sign of an inward, invisible spiritual reality. In this sense, there are many sacraments. But most often the term is applied specifically to rites instituted by Christ for his church.

The idea that the sacraments dispense grace and are necessary for salvation and Christian life is called *sacramentalism*, a theology associated with the Roman Catholic Church. Catholics believe the sacraments are actually efficacious signs of grace, means by which divine life is dispensed to us because they actually give us the grace they signify. They act *ex opere operato* (literally "by the very fact of the actions being performed"). This means that Christ always gives participants grace unless they deliberately block him; simply by participating in the rite, the faithful believer receives grace from God.[1]

Because of the faulty teaching of Catholicism, many evangelicals have rejected the term *sacrament*, believing it irredeemably tainted by sacramentalism, and have adopted the term *ordinances* instead. The King

---

[1]See *The Catechism of the Catholic Church*, para. 1127–1134. Also available online here: http://www.vatican.va/archive/catechism/p2s1c1a2.htm#IV.

James Version of the Bible, for example, uses this term for Passover[2] and the Law of Moses.[3] But, sadly, that term is not entirely pure, as it is tainted with legalism. In American English *ordinance* means a statute or regulation, especially one enacted by a city government, like a parking ordinance that when broken results in getting cited with a parking ticket. Significantly, the English Standard Version of the Bible has largely dropped the term. It uses *statute* rather than *ordinance* when referring to the Passover. We will use the traditional term, *sacrament*, and try to define it biblically so as to recapture its intended and biblical meaning.

We believe the sacraments are not so much dispensers of grace but instead are a means of communing with God as the Word is spoken and made visible. Rather than "means of grace," we adopt the traditional language that the sacraments are "occasions" ordained by Christ for his church when the saving and sanctifying knowledge of the gracious Redeemer is presented to people. On this point the *New Bible Dictionary* says:

> The common definition of a sacrament accepted by the Reformed and Roman Churches is that of an outward and visible sign, ordained by Christ, setting forth and pledging an inward and spiritual blessing.... When they are rightly received the sacraments do convey blessings to the believer. But these blessings are not confined to the use of the sacraments, nor when they are conveyed through the sacraments does their bestowal conflict in any way with the strong, scriptural emphasis on faith and godliness. The sacraments, when administered in accordance with the principles laid down in Scripture, recall us continually to the great ground of our salvation, Christ in his death and resurrection, and remind us of the obligations we have to walk worthily of the calling wherewith we are called.[4]

Our hope in this chapter is to serve those who also would benefit from understanding the sacraments in light of Jesus and Scripture.

BAPTISM

While all Christian traditions practice baptism, there are deep disagreements on what baptism means, who should be baptized, if you must be

---

[2]Ex. 12:14ff.
[3]For example, Ps. 119:91, Heb. 9:1, and many others.
[4]D. R. W. Wood, et al., *New Bible Dictionary* (Downers Grove, IL: InterVarsity, 1996), 1034.

baptized to be saved, and how baptism should be administered. We will look at each issue in turn.

What Does Baptism Mean?

We believe the Bible presents baptism as an outward witness of an inward faith in Jesus Christ alone for salvation.

Christian baptism is an act of obedience to the command of Jesus,[5] declaring the believers' faith in and identification with their crucified, buried, and risen Savior. It is a visible declaration of the gospel of Jesus Christ. The believer being baptized is immersed beneath the waters in the name of the Father, the Son, and the Holy Spirit, which expresses the believers' death to sin and the burial of their old life, and then emersed out of the water, which expresses the believers' resurrection to a new kingdom life in Christ Jesus.[6] Furthermore, baptism identifies a Christian with Jesus,[7] the universal church,[8] and the local church.[9]

Jesus commanded that all Christians be baptized.[10] The apostles commanded that all Christians be baptized, which explains why the book of Acts and records of the early church show that baptism was practiced consistently.[11]

Although there are significant differences in detail, Roman, Anglo, and Orthodox Catholics, as well as Lutherans, all believe that the very act of baptism actually purifies from sin, regenerates, saves, and incorporates one into Christ. While adults must prepare for the sacrament, the saving work is the act of baptism rather than the act of repentance and belief. However, because most recipients of baptism are infants in these Christian traditions, personal repentance and belief are neither the prerequisite for baptism nor the basis of salvation.

Lutherans and Anglicans believe that the baptized infant does have seed faith, though it is unseen, and that the child, while growing up, will show his or her faith by living as a Christian. They have discovered, however, that many of the people who were baptized as newborn infants do not grow up to be Christians with saving faith, so they have

---

[5]Matt. 28:19–20.
[6]Rom. 6:1–10; Col. 2:12.
[7]Acts 10:48; Rom. 6:3; Gal. 3:27.
[8]1 Cor. 12:13.
[9]Acts 2:41.
[10]Matt. 28:19.
[11]Acts 2:38.

also created confirmation, which is their attempt to teach children about the Christian faith and persuade them to live up to their baptism as Christians. This attempt is met with varying degrees of success.

Reformed Christians are those who follow the heritage of John Calvin. They include the many Presbyterian groups along with the various denominations using the name "Reformed Church." They understand baptism to be the sign and seal of membership in the covenant community. Baptism is for all persons as they join the community of the church. This entrance into the community could be by either new birth or physical birth. It is not necessarily an act of repentance. The Westminster Confession of faith says: "Not only those that do actually profess faith in and obedience unto Christ, but also the infants of one, or both, believing parents, are to be baptized."[12] Therefore, the infants who are baptized do not have personal faith nor does baptism save them as in the Catholic understanding, but they are members of the church community and therefore are appropriate candidates for baptism.

WHO SHOULD BE BAPTIZED?

The consistent witness of the New Testament is that someone first believes in Jesus and then is baptized. This is called believers' baptism. This position is sometimes referred to with the term *credobaptism* (*credo* means "I believe" in Latin) to distinguish it from infant baptism, or *paedobaptism* (*paedo* means "child" in Latin). Never do we witness the reverse order where someone, such as an infant, is baptized and then later believes in Jesus.

We see six lines of support for this position in the New Testament. (1) In the precursor to Christian baptism, John the Baptizer required that people repent of sin before being baptized.[13] (2) Every baptism in the New Testament is preceded by repentance of sin and faith in Jesus.[14] (3) Baptism is reserved solely for those people who have put on Christ.[15] (4) Baptism shows personal identification with the death, burial, and resurrection of Jesus. This can only happen when someone has trusted in Christ for salvation.[16] (5) The Bible does record occur-

---

[12]See the Westminster Confession, chap. 28. Available online at http://www.reformed.org/documents/wcf_with_proofs/.
[13]Matt. 3:2, 6; Mark 1:4; Luke 3:3.
[14]Acts 2:38–41; 8:12; 9:18–19; 10:44–48; 16:14–15, 29–36; 18:8; 19:1–7; 22:16.
[15]Gal. 3:27.
[16]Rom. 6:1–10; Col. 2:12.

rences where entire households were baptized.[17] In these cases, the Bible also records that each member of these households believed in Jesus and was saved.[18] (6) Both Jesus[19] and his apostles[20] gave the command for disciples to be baptized as an expression of that discipleship.

We can understand how Catholics can baptize people who do not have personal faith since they believe that participation in the sacramental act of baptism itself saves. However, many evangelicals who believe in salvation by faith also baptize infants. Some try to argue that babies of believing parents have saving faith in seed form, but the realities of life convincingly contradict that argument. Reformed evangelicals often say that baptism is the sign and seal of membership in the covenant community rather than a sign of personal salvation. However, the Westminster Confession says, "Baptism is a sacrament of the New Testament, ordained by Jesus Christ, not only for the solemn admission of the party baptized into the visible Church; but also to be unto him a sign and seal of the covenant of grace, of his ingrafting into Christ, of regeneration, of remission of sins, and of his giving up unto God, through Jesus Christ, to walk in the newness of life."[21]

We simply cannot understand how evangelicals who rightly believe that justification and regeneration are by grace alone through faith alone in Christ alone can hold this understanding of baptism and not see baptism as appropriate for believers only. Their central arguments are (1) baptism replaces circumcision as an initiating act,[22] (2) whole families are baptized,[23] and (3) 1 Corinthians 7:14 says the unbelieving family members are made holy by a believing husband or wife.

First, it is true that circumcision is the initiation into the ethnic aspect of the covenant of Abraham.[24] It is the biblically commanded marker that one is Jewish.[25] However, the rest of the Old Testament gives consistent witness that circumcision does not in itself mark one as saved. While circumcision and baptism are initiating rituals, circumcision is different from baptism. They initiate into different covenants.

---

[17]Acts 10:33, 44–48; 11:14; 16:15, 23; 1 Cor. 1:16.
[18]John 4:53; Acts 18:8; 1 Cor. 16:15.
[19]Matt. 28:19.
[20]Acts 2:38.
[21]See the Westminster Confession, chap. 28.
[22]Acts 2:39; Rom. 4:13–18; Gal. 3:13–18; Heb. 6:13–18; Col. 2:11–12.
[23]Acts 16:15, 33; 18:19.
[24]Gen. 17:10–27.
[25]Gen. 34:14–24.

Circumcision is associated with membership in the ethnic community, while baptism is associated with new-covenant salvation in Jesus.[26]

Second, what of passages where whole households are baptized? The simple answer is that all who were baptized were also believers.

Some people argue for infant baptism from Acts 2:39: "For the promise is for you and for your children and for all who are far off, everyone whom the Lord our God calls to himself." However, the entire section of Acts 2:38–41 explains simply that everyone present was old enough to hear the gospel preached and to be told that they needed to repent of their sin before being baptized. Then they were promised that the Holy Spirit would be given to them. The promise of salvation in its fullness was valid not only for the children who repented of sin and believed in Jesus that day, but also for all subsequent children who repent of sin and believe in Jesus.

It is also argued that when the Bible says an entire household was baptized it can be inferred that those households included children too young to have personal faith.[27] But the Bible is careful to explain that each member of the households that were baptized also believed in Jesus, was filled with the Holy Spirit, and served God.[28] Therefore, the Bible rules out the possibility that the people in these households who were baptized included infants.

Third, those purporting the baptism of infants who have a believing parent lean heavily on 1 Corinthians 7:14, which says, "For the unbelieving husband is made holy because of his wife, and the unbelieving wife is made holy because of her husband. Otherwise your children would be unclean, but as it is, they are holy."[29] However, those who support infant baptism go further than the text itself and wrongly use this passage to argue that the faith of the believing spouse is sufficient to cover the children, therefore enabling them to be baptized. But the verse says nothing about baptism or salvation; it simply guarantees God's grace upon faithful Christians and their children who have a spouse or parent that is unsaved.

---

[26]This argument is developed in Paul King Jewett, *Infant Baptism and the Covenant of Grace: An Appraisal of the Argument That As Infants Were Once Circumcised, So They Should Now Be Baptized* (Grand Rapids, MI: Eerdmans, 1978). Jewett was a covenantal theologian and an ordained Presbyterian minister.

[27]Acts 10:33, 44–48; 11:14; 16:15, 23; 1 Cor. 1:16.

[28]John 4:53; Acts 18:8; 1 Cor. 16:15.

[29]For a good statement of this view, see J. I. Packer, *Concise Theology: A Guide to Historic Christian Beliefs* (Carol Stream, IL: Tyndale, 1993), 214–15.

If we are going to use 1 Corinthians 7:14 to argue that children of a believing parent should be baptized because they are under the covenant of their mother or father, then we must be consistent and baptize the adult spouse who is not a Christian because the spouse too is part of the same believing household. The verse clearly teaches that the unbelieving spouse is in the same position as the children. While proponents of infant baptism understandably refuse to baptize unbelieving spouses of Christians, they are willing to manipulate 1 Corinthians 7:14 for their child but are unwilling to do so for the unbelieving parent of such children, conveniently overlooking their inconsistency.

If all of this sounds indefensible from Scripture, we would merely say that, indeed, it is. In the Old Testament there was an emphasis on one's birth because God does often work through families and generations, as even a cursory reading of the Old Testament proves. Yet some Jews erred in thinking that having Abraham as their physical father gave them privileged status with God. Subsequently, they were quite infuriated in their smugness when Jesus informed some that their real father was the devil.[30] Jesus also taught that he could make stones into children of Abraham, meaning that God saves and brings into his family whomever he pleases, regardless of their last name.[31] Paul further taught that one is a descendant of Abraham solely by faith in Jesus Christ, not by birth.[32]

Therefore, whereas newborn or infant baptism and the theology that promotes it is highly concerned with someone's blood and birth, the New Testament is primarily concerned with the blood of Jesus and new birth. This is exactly what Jesus was referring to when he commanded the Jewish Nicodemus to be "born again."[33]

DO YOU HAVE TO BE BAPTIZED TO BE SAVED?

Salvation is solely a gift given to people whose faith rests in the grace of God to forgive their sins through the death and resurrection of Jesus.[34] For example, when the Philippian jailer asked what was required of him to be saved, Paul did not mention baptism but simply said, "Believe in

---

[30]John 8:37–48.
[31]Matt. 3:9.
[32]Rom. 2:29; 9:6–8; Gal. 3:7.
[33]John 3:3.
[34]Eph. 2:8–9.

the Lord Jesus."[35] Likewise, the thief who died on the cross next to Jesus was promised by our Lord that "today you will be with me in Paradise," though he had not been baptized.[36] Someone can be unbaptized and yet be a Christian who is destined for heaven.

Nonetheless, even though one can be a Christian without being baptized, a Christian should be baptized. If nothing else, Jesus commanded baptism to show in outward sign the inward covenant relationship we have with him. Similarly, married people are married regardless of whether they wear their wedding ring, which is the outward symbol of their inward covenant relationship. But I, for one, am glad that my wife wears her wedding ring.

Sadly, the church has substituted all sorts of things for baptism: "Stand up if you have decided to follow Jesus." "Come down the aisle and meet me here in front." "Pray this prayer with me." "Sign this pledge card." Or perhaps worst of all: "Every head bowed and every eye closed. If you have accepted Jesus as your savior, just look up at me. I'll see that and know that you are going to spend eternity in heaven."

Baptism is the biblical way in which we show that by the power of the Spirit, we died to our old way of life through the death of Jesus, and live a new life through the resurrection of Jesus, cleansed from our sin in the same way that water cleanses us from filth. Therefore, being baptized does not make someone a Christian. Not being baptized does not cause someone to stop being a Christian. But a Christian should be baptized.

HOW SHOULD BAPTISM BE ADMINISTERED?

All agree that water is the element of baptism. But the debate ensues regarding how water should be applied. Some prefer to sprinkle with water in light of a handful of biblical texts that mention being sprinkled with clean water.[37] Others prefer pouring, to symbolize the Spirit poured out in new-covenant blessing.[38] Still others prefer to immerse in water. We believe that the Bible clearly teaches baptism by immersion. It is the only mode associated with baptism in the Bible and the only mode that expresses the meaning of baptism as shown

---

[35]Acts 16:31.
[36]Luke 23:43.
[37]Ezek. 36:25; Titus 3:5–6; Heb. 9:13–14, 19; 10:22.
[38]Joel 2:28–29; Acts 2:17–18, 33; 10:45; Rom. 5:5.

in passages such as Romans 6:1–10 and seven other lines of biblical reasoning.

1) The Greek word used for baptism in the New Testament means to plunge, dip, or immerse in water. In secular ancient Greek, this word was used to explain such things as the sinking of ships that had been submerged in water. It is curious that even the great theologians John Calvin and Martin Luther who practiced and strenuously advocated the baptism of newborn infants agree that this is indeed the meaning of the word *baptism*. Catholics also agree: "This sacrament is called Baptism, after the central rite by which it is carried out: to baptize (Greek *baptizein*) means to plunge or immerse; the plunge into the water symbolizes the catechumen's burial into Christ's death, from which he rises up by resurrection with him, as a new creature."[39] Orthodox Christians show they agree since they baptize babies by immersion.

The early translators of the Bible into English ran into the dilemma that translating *baptizein* as "immerse" would confuse people. So rather than translating the word, they merely transliterated it, changing the Greek characters into Roman letters. However, the Dutch Bible actually translates the word so that the man who appears in Matthew 3:1 is *Johannes de Doper*, John the Dipper!

2) According to Mark 1:5 John the Baptizer immersed people in the river. John also selected the Jordan River as the place for conducting his baptisms because "water was plentiful there."[40]

3) When Jesus was baptized it seems he was immersed in water since he came out of the water as the dove descended on him.[41]

4) Philip took the Ethiopian eunuch down into the water to baptize him, indicating it was by immersing him in water.[42]

5) Baptism is in a very real sense the remembrance of and identification with Jesus' death, burial, and resurrection.[43] It would be inconceivable to understand Jesus' brutal murder as something that was sprinkled upon him rather than as a total burial into death and the grave. Only immersion accurately shows Jesus' death and descent into burial, followed by emersion out of the water into resurrection.

---

[39]See *The Catechism of the Catholic Church*, para. 1214. Also available online here: http://www.vatican.va/archive/ENG0015/_P3H.HTM.
[40]John 3:23.
[41]Mark 1:10.
[42]Acts 8:34–39.
[43]Mark 10:38; Rom. 6:1–10; Col. 2:12.

6) When someone who was not racially Jewish converted to Judaism in the Old Testament (and in the present day), they underwent a Jewish proselyte baptism to show that God had cleansed them from their sin. The mode of this baptism was (and is) immersion.

7) The Bible does speak of our salvation in terms of being cleansed from sin,[44] sprinkled by Jesus,[45] and having the Holy Spirit poured out upon us.[46] However, it is important to note that none of the occurrences of sprinkling or pouring in the Bible are in any way related to baptism.

In conclusion, Christians should be baptized in the same manner as Jesus, immersed in water and then brought forth. In so doing, they are identifying with the death, burial, and resurrection of Jesus.

COMMUNION

The second sacrament that constitutes the Christian church has several names. When calling it "Communion," we emphasize the fellowship (or communion) we have with God the Father and each other through Jesus. Calling it "the Lord's Table" emphasizes that we follow the example Jesus set at the Last Supper Passover meal he had with his disciples. The name Eucharist (meaning thanksgiving) emphasizes thanksgiving and the joyful celebration of God's work for us, in us, through us, and in spite of us.

The debates about which name is theologically correct are too often filled with anger, charges of heresy, and threats of excommunication. When controversies come into the evangelical church, they are most ugly when they are little more than cultural and political-control quarrels over "words, which produce envy, dissension, slander, evil suspicions, and constant friction among people who are depraved in mind and deprived of the truth, imagining that godliness is a means of gain."[47] Subsequently, we choose to use any or all three terms depending on the emphasis that is most suitable for the context.

The real issue is the meaning of the sacrament itself. (1) It reminds us in a dramatic manner of the death of Jesus Christ in our place for our sins. (2) It calls Christians to put their sin to death in light of the fact that

[44]Titus 3:5.
[45]Lev. 16:14–15, 19; Ezek. 36:25; Heb. 10:22; 1 Pet. 1:2.
[46]Joel 2:28–29; Acts 2:17–18, 33; 10:45.
[47]1 Tim. 6:4–5.

Jesus died for our sins and compels us to examine ourselves and repent of sin before partaking. (3) It shows the unity of God's people around the person and work of Jesus. (4) It anticipates our participation in the marriage supper of the Lamb when his kingdom comes in its fullness.

Practically speaking, Communion is to be considered as participation in a family around a table rather than as a sacrifice upon an altar. Furthermore, it should be an occasion when God's loving grace impacts us deeply so that the gospel takes deeper and deeper root in our lives. Understood biblically, grace is the unmerited favor or God's goodwill,[48] his helpful enablement for life and service,[49] and a transformational power from the Spirit that brings blessing to us.[50] Each of these aspects of God's grace is inextricably connected to the partaking of Communion.

In the early days of Mars Hill Church we partook of Communion infrequently. All of that changed when I preached through the book of Exodus to our struggling little church plant. As a result of my study of the Passover meal, my view of Communion changed, and we began including it in every church service with wine and juice to accommodate people's conscience. As I studied that meal, it took me on a study that encompassed the entire storyline of the Bible and resulted in our partaking of Communion every week in each of our church services and encouraging Communion meals in homes led by our church members.

MEAL 1: FORBIDDEN FRUIT

In Genesis 3 our first parents, Adam and Eve, committed the original sin when they ate a meal without God in disobedience to him. Sin, the fall, and the curse came upon us all through the tragic decision of our first parents to eat in friendship with Satan rather than God.

MEAL 2: PASSOVER

Exodus tells the story of God redeeming his people from slavery to the tyrannical pharaoh in Egypt to allow them to worship him freely. God poured out ten plagues on Egypt, with the final plague being the slaughter of the firstborn.

---

[48]John 1:16, 17; Eph. 2:8.
[49]Rom. 12:6; 1 Cor. 15:10; 2 Cor. 9:8.
[50]Rom. 6:1, 14–17; 2 Cor. 6:1ff.; Eph. 1:7; 2:5–8.

In Exodus 12 God commanded the entire congregation of Israel to take a young, healthy lamb without defect for sacrifice. This lamb pointed to Jesus, who was also young, healthy, and without defect (or sin) and died for the community of his people. John the Baptizer later cried out that Jesus was "the Lamb of God, who takes away the sin of the world!"[51] And, John the disciple also writes, "Worthy is the Lamb [Jesus] who was slain."[52]

The blood (the symbol of life)[53] of the slaughtered lamb was to be put on the sides and tops of the doorframes of the Israelites' homes. The blood of the lamb, denoting their repentance of sin and faith in God, would be their salvation so that God's just wrath would literally pass over them.

In fulfillment of the Passover, Jesus was slaughtered for our sin.[54] Our salvation was purchased "with the precious blood of Christ, like that of a lamb without blemish or spot."[55] Indeed, Jesus earned our redemption with his own blood as an unblemished sacrifice.[56] Lastly, God commanded the Passover festival be continued every year, which it was until it was eaten by Jesus, whom Paul calls, "Christ, our Passover lamb."[57]

MEAL 3: THE LAST SUPPER

Like all Jewish people, Jesus celebrated the Passover meal. Echoing the great themes of the exodus and Passover, Jesus the firstborn Son and sinless Lamb of God sat down with his friends to remember the killing of the firstborn sons, judgment of false gods, shedding of blood for sin, and deliverance from bondage and sin in Egypt. However, in startling alteration of a thousand-year tradition, as they ate the unleavened bread, Jesus announced that the bread was his body.[58] The disciples had to be stunned.

As a historical aside, it is amazing to note that for a very long time Jewish people have used matzo as the Passover bread. This special bread is not only unleavened but also striped and pierced. It reminds

---

[51]John 1:29.
[52]Rev. 5:12.
[53]Lev. 17:11, 14; Deut. 12:23; Ps. 72:14.
[54]2 Cor. 5:21.
[55]1 Pet. 1:19.
[56]Heb. 9:12–14.
[57]1 Cor. 5:7.
[58]Matt. 26:26.

us of Isaiah's words: "He was wounded for our transgressions; he was crushed for our iniquities; upon him was the chastisement that brought us peace, and with his stripes we are healed."[59]

Returning to Jesus' Passover meal, as they took the third cup, the cup of redemption, Jesus identified the wine as his blood to be shed for the new covenant, or forgiveness of sins.[60] When the time came for the fourth cup, Jesus told the disciples he would not drink this cup with them until the coming of the kingdom. Then Jesus commanded his people to do the same continually in remembrance of him. Next, Jesus went out to be crucified. Jesus was clearly teaching that the ancient prophecies contained in the Passover meal were being fulfilled in his death.

Meal 4: Communion

Immediately following Pentecost, Christians began following Jesus' command to eat and drink in his memory.[61] The Bible gives us a picture of such a meal in 1 Corinthians 10:15–22 and 11:17–34. Paul says that Communion is a meal about Jesus and to be partaken of only by Christians who are singularly devoted to God, repentant of sin, and not partaking in any other religions or spiritualities. He goes on to say that they partook of bread to remember Jesus' broken body and wine to remember Jesus' shed blood in their place for their sins. He also states that at Communion all of God's people are to be treated with equal dignity, and that anyone who does not partake of Communion according to these commands brings God's judgment upon themselves, which may include death. Ever since, it is to be eaten by God's people until we are seated at the fifth and final meal.

Meal 5: Wedding Supper of the Lamb

Because human history began with a meal eaten without God, it is only fitting that history will end with God's church, typified as a bride, eating a glorious meal with Jesus Christ, her groom.[62] Isaiah 25:6 speaks of this feast, which includes the finest cuts of meats and the choicest wines laid out in honor of Jesus and to be enjoyed by those who have lovingly responded to his love.

---

[59]Isa. 53:5.
[60]Matt. 26:28, cf. Jer. 31:31–34.
[61]Acts 2:42.
[62]Rev. 19:6–9.

At the wedding supper, the effects of sin wrought by the first meal eaten apart from God will be completely eradicated from all creation. Those who through faith in Jesus partook of the second, third, and fourth meals will participate in this meal together as the church. Together forever with Jesus we will eat, drink, laugh, and rejoice as friends reconciled to God and one another through Jesus.

Real Presence

Most Christians affirm that Jesus is present in Communion. But the debate about how he is present is one of the deepest divisions in Christianity. For example, disagreement over the presence of Christ in the Eucharist was the central point of division between Martin Luther and John Calvin. I once preached at a conference for three kinds of Lutheran pastors who refused to partake of Communion together. And Roman Catholics and Eastern Orthodox Christians have earnestly pursued ecumenical agreement in recent decades. Although they are close in many ways, they still cannot share Eucharist, as official Catholic teaching states: "With the Orthodox Churches, this communion is so profound 'that it lacks little to attain the fullness that would permit a common celebration of the Lord's Eucharist.'"[63]

Roman Catholic and Orthodox Christians teach that real presence means transubstantiation of the essence of the elements into the essence of the body and blood of Jesus, though the attributes are unchanged. So if a chemist were to test the elements, he would find only bread and wine. Anglicans argue for real presence but are content to leave the mode of that presence a mystery. Lutherans believe the real presence is in, with, and under the forms of the bread and wine. No Lutherans use the term *consubstantiation* for their position, though many others do define it with that word. Reformed Protestants teach a real presence where the Spirit makes Christ present in the service but not especially in the elements.

Many Christians have overreacted to this sacramental understanding, and have reduced Communion to a mere remembrance of something that happened a long time ago. These people follow the teachings of Ulrich Zwingli (1484–1531). They understand Communion as a memorial commemoration of the wonderful gift of Jesus' death in our place

---

[63]*The Catechism of the Catholic Church*, 838, quoting Pope Paul VI. Also available online here: http://www.vatican.va/archive/catechism/p123a9p3.htm.

for our sins. They insist that Jesus is not present in the elements literally, as taught by Catholicism, or spiritually, as taught by Lutheranism. In such cases the Communion service itself is often nothing more than a graceless ceremony tacked on to the normal church service. It is done quickly to point out that the work of Jesus is completely finished and that he is not present in any way.

We stand more in the Reformed tradition and the teaching of John Calvin. Jesus is not literally present in the elements of Communion but is spiritually present in relationship with the Christian partaking of the elements through the indwelling Holy Spirit. As John Calvin said, "There is no need to draw Christ to earth that he may be joined to us."[64] Instead, he rightly argues that we do not need physical elements to unite us to God, since "the Spirit truly unites things separated in space."[65]

In a sense, saying there is spiritual benefit in Communion is similar to saying there is spiritual benefit in being a member of a church. There is great controversy here, but we believe the Bible teaches that the church is the locus of divine life, the very body of Christ and the community of the Spirit.

The followers of Zwingli overlook Paul's teaching in 1 Corinthians 10:16–17: "The cup of blessing that we bless, is it not a participation in the blood of Christ? The bread that we break, is it not a participation in the body of Christ? Because there is one bread, we who are many are one body, for we all partake of the one bread." Paul teaches explicitly what is implicit in Acts 2:42, 46; 20:7, 11. Partaking in Communion involves a recognition that for Christians the benefits of Jesus' sacrifice include communion with both God and one another. And in faith Christians are to partake of Communion until one day they see Jesus and sit to eat with him as friends in his kingdom.

THE SACRAMENTS AND THE CHURCH

What was the Protestant Reformers' understanding of the church in its inclusion of the administration of these sacraments? This point may seem trivial to some, but it is anything but.

In our day there is an escalating proliferation of churches. There are

---

[64]John Calvin, *The Institutes of the Christian Religion*, ed. J. McNeill, trans. F. L. Battles, vol. 2 (Louisville, KY: Westminster John Knox, 1960), 1403.
[65]Ibid., 1370.

house churches, parachurch ministries of all sorts and kinds, church-within-a-church services targeting particular groups of people, informal gatherings of Christians for regular meetings, and quasi-churches that define themselves as new monastic communities and simple churches. *U. S. News and World Report* reported on these new forms of "churches":

> Put simply, the development is a return to tradition and orthodoxy, to past practices, observances, and customary ways of worshiping. But it is not simply a return to the past—at least not in all cases. Even while drawing on deep traditional resources, many participants are creating something new within the old forms. They are engaging in what Penn State sociologist of religion Roger Finke calls "innovative returns to tradition."
>
> You see this at work quite clearly in the so-called emergent communities, new, largely self-organizing groups of young Christian adults who meet in private homes, church basements, or coffee-houses around the country. So free-form that many don't even have pastors, these groups nevertheless engage in some ancient liturgical practices, including creedal declarations, public confession, and Communion. They may use a piece of a bagel as the body of Christ, but the liturgy is a traditional anchor in services that may include films, skits, or group discussions of a biblical topic. . . . It is a means of moving beyond fundamentalist literalism, troubling authority figures, and highly politicized religious positions (say on gay marriage and contraception or abortion) while retaining a hold on spiritual truths.[66]

What is particularly concerning about the longing for the sacred, which both this article and my experience confirm, is that many Christians' longing for sacred ritual is not always an appetite for Jesus. What I mean is that a craving for Jesus includes a craving for biblical truth, repentance of sin, transformed living, and respect for godly spiritual authority. The appetite for sacred ritual is meaningful and purposeful only when it is connected to a proper understanding of the person and work of Jesus.

The question persists: are these really churches or simply Christian ministries that operate in addition to the church; or worse yet, are some sects and cults masquerading as churches to seduce the naïve? On this point theologian Wayne Grudem has said, "Once an organization begins

---

[66]Jay Tolson, "A Return to Tradition," *U.S. News & World Report*, December 24, 2007, 44–46.

to practice baptism and the Lord's Supper, it is a continuing organization and is *attempting to function as a church*."[67] The church can function in many forms. The problem comes when groups add Christian ritual without the Savior. It's heretically deceptive to act like the church of Jesus but leave him out.

In light of the proliferation of Christian ministries and various self-appointed church forms, it is incredibly important for churches and their leaders to have a biblical and practical working definition of what a church is and is not. The church will stay on mission as it reflects deeply on the sacraments as gospel dramas where the Word is spoken and made visible, and where the blessings of life with the triune God brought to us through the Word made flesh, who died for our sin and rose for our new life, are lived out faithfully in the sacramental community of the Spirit to the glory of God the Father.

An illustration of this point seems fitting as the conclusion to this chapter. The week before writing this chapter we had a live baptismal service on Easter Sunday at most of our campuses. I was present at one of the campuses, preaching live, while my sermon was broadcast to the other locations, so I did not witness every one of the roughly two hundred baptisms that took place that day. Yet, what I did see at the one campus was the most amazing gospel experience of my life. After the preaching, at each service we brought up a few new converts to give their testimony and then invited people to repent of sin and trust in Jesus to become Christians. We asked those who responded to come forward and briefly meet with a pastor to confirm their conversion and be baptized. Meanwhile, the rest of the church sang worship songs to Jesus and partook of Communion. We had video cameras set up on the baptismal (bapto-cams) to show people being baptized on all the screens, and the congregation erupted with enthusiasm that did not wane for the entire service.

The few hundred people baptized were from different races, genders, life stages, and incomes. We had men in Easter suits getting saved and baptized in their suits. We had older women in their Easter dresses complete with bonnets get saved and dunked in their dresses and bonnets. As each one came out of the water, the entire room erupted with

---

[67]Wayne Grudem, *Systematic Theology: An Introduction to Biblical Doctrine* (Grand Rapids, MI: Zondervan, 1994), 865; emphasis in original.

cheering and applause. The band kept repeating the songs because people kept coming forward to give their lives to Jesus and be baptized. The elders were up front sharing the gospel with people and laying hands on them in prayer. I stood in the room off to the side just to watch what God was doing and wept through each of the services. Multiple people walked up to me and asked how they could be saved, so I had the great joy of personally introducing them to Jesus and then sending them up on the stage to be baptized. Afterward they came off the stage to take Communion as Christians.

My tears completely overtook me at the final baptism of one service in particular. My dear friend Pastor Tim Smith, who is our worship pastor, was so busy worshiping God and holding back tears while leading us in song that he failed to see that his oldest daughter, a kindergartner named Trinity, had come forward to be baptized. I was amazed to see her before a packed room of over a thousand people, because she is usually very shy. The pastor who confirmed her testimony walked on the stage and pulled Tim over to the baptismal to baptize his daughter. Taking off his guitar and stepping away from the microphone, he was shocked and overjoyed to see his little girl, and as every Christian daddy should, he wept uncontrollably while kissing his daughter as he picked her up to baptize her. Looking around the room, every father I saw, myself included, was weeping uncontrollably and cheering. Following baptism, the new converts were served Communion while the band played on and people kept cheering.

The conversion of a sinner followed by baptism and Communion should make the Super Bowl pale in comparison, because Jesus is alive and nothing is worth cheering more than his grace.

ANSWERS TO COMMON QUESTIONS ABOUT BAPTISM AND COMMUNION

WHO CAN ADMINISTER BAPTISM AND COMMUNION?

The best way to approach the question is to examine what the Bible teaches. We believe that what it teaches by prescription is truth from God and must be followed. As a general rule, the practices that are described there should be followed as closely as possible. Where the Bible is silent, God did not make a mistake and forget to say something. Rather, he was purposely silent to give us freedom to follow wisdom and the leading of the Spirit and develop our own practices to meet the varying needs of different churches and cultures.

Most baptisms in the Scriptures are like those found in Acts 2, where the Bible doesn't say who conducted the baptisms. In Acts 8 Philip baptized the Ethiopian eunuch as a deacon and not as an elder or pastor. And Paul is clear that he didn't baptize many in Corinth and seems not to be overly concerned with the fact that he is unable to remember exactly who he baptized (1 Cor. 1:14–16).

Regarding Communion, Paul describes the event (1 Cor. 10:16–21; 11:23–34) but gives no hint of who led it. The Bible also speaks of "breaking of bread" (Acts 2:42; 20:7–11), which may refer to Communion but says nothing about how it was done or by whom. So the Bible is silent on this question. Subsequently, it should be administered according to the wisdom of the local church and its leaders. It seems reasonable that the person who was instrumental in bringing a person to Christ be the one who baptizes or assists in baptism. And, although any leader in the church could lead Communion, as is the case at Mars Hill, we can understand why many churches relegate it to the role of elder. We respect that belief; since elders are the ones proclaiming the Word, it is natural that they would also administer the sacraments. Whoever administers must be godly and well prepared so the sacrament is done in a God-honoring way.

ISN'T THERE SOME WAY TO INDICATE THE SPECIAL STATUS OF BABIES BORN TO CHRISTIAN PARENTS?

As a newborn child, Jesus was dedicated to the Lord by his parents (Luke 2:21–23). While this action was done under the religious system of Israel rather than within the church, it does give a biblical pattern for us to follow. It is good for us to dedicate the children born into our church in an effort to rejoice with the parents as members of our spiritual family, to welcome the child into the church, and to commit ourselves to supporting the family and child prayerfully in hopes that the child will grow to love and serve the Lord. There is hope for and effort made toward the child's future baptism after coming to personal faith in Jesus.

WHEN SHOULD A BELIEVING CHILD BE BAPTIZED?

A perplexing question is when to baptize children who have grown up in Christian homes with the teaching of their godly parents and the church. They can say the words of faith well. But when are they actually saved? This is a most difficult question. Some prefer to delay baptism until children have been through the tumultuous season of adolescence, a time at which many abandon their parents' faith. Those who prefer such delay think it best to wait until children can express their faith as adults. But don't many others lose faith in the turmoil of midlife crisis? Should we wait until that crisis passes? If we waited out the crisis periods, we'd have to wait until death!

It seems wise to baptize based not on age but on the ability to make a credible profession of faith. So when a child can express his or her own faith and commitment to follow Jesus, baptizing that child seems appropriate.

HOW SOON AFTER CONVERSION SHOULD SOMEONE BE BAPTIZED?

The Bible shows that someone is immediately baptized upon conversion. Most churches delay baptism until converts undergo a baptismal class to be sure they understand what they are doing. This pattern avoids impulsive decisions in the excitement of the moment. So they wait a while to be sure the conversion is real. One problem with this is that baptism becomes an indicator of discipleship rather than conversion. The bigger problem is that it strays from the biblical pattern.

We prefer to have baptismal services where the gospel is presented very clearly in word and in the drama of baptism itself. Afterward an invitation is given for anyone who has repented and believed to be baptized. Those who respond should be interviewed by an elder to see that their confession is their own, and that they agree to the discipleship process. The elder then collects their contact information, if they are unknown, to ensure we follow up with discipleship. As a general rule it is respectful for believers under eighteen to have parental permission before they are joyfully baptized to express their new faith.

Can someone who was previously baptized be rebaptized?

Many Christians ask to be baptized after a deep renewal of their faith, perhaps in a parallel to couples who renew their wedding vows. However, the Bible is clear that there is no need for someone who has been baptized ever to be baptized again. There is only one baptism (Eph. 4:5). Furthermore, baptism is the sign of initial conversion (Rom. 6:3–4; Gal. 3:26–28), not growth in faith.

However, many have been through something called *baptism* that was not a profession of personal faith in Jesus. In such cases they are not baptized in the biblical sense. Following the example of Acts 19:1–5, we encourage them to be baptized in reality of their faith in Jesus. This includes those who were baptized in cults and heretical churches as well as those who were baptized as infants at the request of their parents or who underwent baptism to please parents.

Bible-believing churches differ on what to do with those who went through infant baptism. Grace Community Church (Gerry's church) teaches that people should be baptized as believers and requires them to do so to be members of the church. Mars Hill (Mark's church) does not require but does strongly encourage that those people who were baptized as infants be rebaptized as believing adults, leaving this decision to the conscience of each Christian. However, Mars Hill strongly encourages anyone who was baptized as an infant but did not walk with the Lord as a Christian until after a later conversion to be baptized.

How should Communion be administered?

The Bible gives no direction on how to administer Communion. Following our understanding of biblical authority, God's silence is his encouragement to develop our own practice, guided by wisdom and the leading of the Spirit. It is wise to examine the practices of churches from different traditions and cultures to see what will make the work of the Spirit most effective in each church.

While the New Testament gives no mandate for a service order for a worship service, or even an example of a service order, at Mars Hill Church, Communion is done as the centerpiece of the service each week so that the person and work of Jesus on the cross dying in our place for our sins is made clear.

At Mars Hill the theology of worship is that God initiates and we respond. The services generally open with a word of welcome from the campus pastor, which is followed by a corporate reading from Scripture and congregational singing of a song or two of repentance in preparation for the preaching of God's Word. The sermon always includes an explanation of the sinless life, substitutionary death, and bodily resurrection of Jesus as God and Savior with an invitation for people to turn from sin and trust in Jesus for new life.

Then the service transitions to give people opportunity to respond to God. There is time for people to linger in a mood of reflective repentance, to confess sin and pray silently. When they are ready, they stand to join in prayer, testimony, and singing. At this time people also leave their seats to come forward for Communion. They dip bread into a cup of either wine or juice depending upon their conscience. Children take Communion according to their parents' discretion. It is a joyful time; people are singing, partaking of Communion, and giving their tithes and offerings at the baskets in celebration.

CHAPTER SIX

HOW CAN A CHURCH BE UNIFIED?

I appeal to you, brothers, by the name of our Lord Jesus Christ, that all of you agree, and that there be no divisions among you, but that you be united in the same mind and the same judgment.

1 CORINTHIANS 1:10

✝

Leonardo da Vinci's painting of the Last Supper is among the most well-known works of art in the history of the world. It litters our cultural landscape, appearing everywhere in pop culture.

I had seen the painting so often that it had become inconspicuous to me until one day I was struck by a copy of it on, of all things, a tin of breath mints. Standing in line at a store, I noticed the mints on the display rack near the cash register, and it hit me in a way it never had.

Sitting with Jesus among the disciples was Judas Iscariot. Judas spent three years being trained personally by Jesus. Furthermore, Judas got to sit and eat regularly with Jesus as a friend. While the disciples were unified as a team, Judas in his heart was never unified with them because he was stealing money from them and plotting against them for a long time. Yet, in the painting it appeared that Jesus and the disciples were unified, including Judas. Together they worked on various ministry projects, ate, and traveled for three years. To everyone who saw them, the perception had to be one of unity. Nevertheless, their hearts were not unified. Judas was on his own mission for his own glory. Indeed, Scripture records that before betraying Jesus he opened himself to be possessed by Satan.

While standing in line at the store, I felt a sinking remorse for the other disciples, which I had never felt before. It pained me to think how much it must have grieved and angered them that Judas was never truly in unity with them. Did they feel betrayed? Did they feel lied to? Did they feel used? Did they feel foolish for entrusting themselves to an enemy? Did the subtle signs of his divisiveness start to make sense in retrospect as they reconsidered their years together with him? Did people bombard them with questions about Judas until they were simply tired of talking about him and ready to move on with their ministry? Did gossiping people who liked Judas spread vicious rumors and lies about the other disciples, trying to make them responsible for Judas's suicidal demise?

The source of my questions is my experience, and the source of my sympathy is my pain. Every church and every church leader knows the painful cost they must pay when there is disunity. While a lack of unity does not always rise to the level of betrayal that Judas demonstrated, every breach in unity costs the leaders time, energy, emotion, and momentum. Division is often the cause of the greatest stress, pain, conflict, and despair in any church. I hope in writing this chapter to help churches and Christians define and defend unity.

Theologically, unity is to be pursued by churches and among churches for five reasons. (1) Jesus prayed for it often. (2) As the leadership goes, so goes the rest of the church. (3) Without unity spiritual health and growth cannot be maintained because the church gets diverted from Jesus and his mission for them. (4) Unity is fragile because it is gained slowly and lost quickly, which requires that it never be assumed or taken for granted. (5) Paul repeatedly commands unity in churches.[1]

Practically, unity is something that requires much skill to achieve and maintain. As we examine unity in this chapter, I will include helpful and practical insights gleaned from conversations I have had over the years with a fellow pastor named Larry Osborne, who also wrote the helpful book *The Unity Factor*.[2]

---

[1] Cor. 1:10; 2 Cor. 13:11; Eph. 4:3; Phil. 1:27.
[2] Larry W. Osborne, *The Unity Factor* (Vista, CA: Owl's Nest, 2006).

DEFINING UNITY

Since unity is so important, it must be carefully defined so that it can be effectively pursued in five areas.

1) THEOLOGICAL UNITY

There must be theological unity. This means that the leaders and members of the church agree on what they will and will not fight over. In our church our closed hand of nonnegotiables are those beliefs connected most closely to the gospel of Jesus Christ, outlined in such places as 1 Corinthians 15:1–4. As a result, we will fight for the death, burial, and resurrection of Jesus Christ as our sinless God who became a man to die in our place for our sins according to the inspired Scriptures to save us from hell and grant us salvation by grace alone through faith alone in him alone. But we don't have to fight for every issue with a fundamentalistic spirit.[3] There are many issues we approach with an open hand, where we agree to disagree in an agreeable way.

A reading of the letters that address the conflicts that arose over various issues in the days of the New Testament reveals that legalism (adding rules and doctrines to the Bible) and libertinism (removing moral limits from the Bible) are usually the great enemies of the truth of Jesus Christ that the church needs to defend against. Jesus himself faced this with the Pharisees and Sadducees in his own day.

An example of legalism is found in the church at Galatia. Those people were "Jesus plus" people, and for them it was Jesus plus circumcision. Paul's scathing letter of rebuke was written to remind them that Jesus plus anything ruins everything, because when it comes to salvation Jesus alone is everything. Sadly, they had taken what was supposed to remain in the open hand of belief and sought to force it into the closed hand. Modern-day legalisms come into play with worship styles; mode of children's education (e.g., home school, private school, public school); church service times; method of Christian counseling; tongues; physical location of the church building; alcohol; mode of dress at church (especially the dress of the pastor); political party affiliation; church size; number of services; Bible translation; eschatological fine points; raising hands or swaying or dancing in worship; baptism

---

[3] 2 Tim. 2:14–16, 23; 6:4–5; Titus 3:9.

in relation to Communion; and the age of the earth, as if it came with a "born on" date like a can of Budweiser.

An example of libertinism is found in the church at Corinth. A reading of 1 Corinthians reveals that this church, like so many liberal churches in our day, condoned sin in the name of loving tolerance, which was curiously unloving and intolerant to God. They were "Jesus minus" people. They embraced alternative lifestyles, including sexual perversion and perverts of literally every sort such as "friends with benefits," incest, strippers, cross-dressing transvestites, and cohabitating singles; drunkenness; and a haughty spirit that disrespected spiritual authority and disliked the teachings of Paul on everything from gender roles to homosexuality. People in the small church of perhaps fifty people denied the resurrection of Jesus, turned the Sunday church services into freak shows; got naked and had sex; sued each other for money; and even got drunk at Communion. Furthermore, the Jews and Gentiles were fighting, as were the rich and poor, the feminists and the male church leaders, the tongue speakers and non-tongue speakers, the single and the married, and those who ate certain kinds of meat and those who did not.

Nonetheless, every church must clarify what it considers to be primary, closed-hand doctrines, which require agreement among Christians in the church, and secondary, open-hand doctrines, which permit a range of beliefs providing they fall within a spectrum of evangelical orthodoxy and are held with a humble and teachable spirit. Sadly, single-issue voters are slow to learn this distinction and as a result can wreak havoc by seeking to press their open-handed issue into a closed hand, or vice versa. Practically, I have found it helpful over the years to write position papers and keep electronic copies of articles that clarify where we stand on the most often debated issues to send to people who inquire.

I found that by having a simple statement that explains our open- and closed-hand approach to theology, along with position papers and recommended resources, I could simply email them to people who can then study for themselves. This saved me from a great number of hours arguing with people and saying the same thing over and over. If someone completed the work I gave them, I was willing to meet with them to answer any questions they had. Thankfully, our church has now expanded so that we have a volunteer theological answer team that fields people's questions and does in far greater numbers what I used to do. Nonetheless, the key is to meet with and invest in only those who are humble and teachable and want to do more than waste time arguing, because Paul says we are to have nothing to do with foolish and stupid arguments,[4] and, sadly, they abound.

2) RELATIONAL UNITY

There must be relational unity.[5] This does not mean that every person has matching sweatshirts and takes turns riding on a tandem bike. Neither does it mean that everyone even likes one another. But it does mean that people love one another and demonstrate it by being cordial, respectful, friendly, and kind in their interpersonal interactions, especially as they relate in areas where they differ.

3) PHILOSOPHICAL UNITY

There must be philosophical unity around ministry methods and style. Two people may love Jesus, but if one wants a high church liturgy complete with a pastor in a non-Jedi robe accompanied by a handbell choir, and the other wants three chords for the Lord and to sing one song for a few hours while various people speak in tongues, someone will likely get the right fist of fellowship. In addition to Bible rules, the church family, like all families, also has house rules about how they do things. We call this a ministry philosophy, and it in many ways is the cause of a particular and primary cultural style in a church.

While it could be and has been argued that some ministry methods are more faithful to Scripture than others, the key is to have agreement in the church about how things are done, such as baptism, Communion, service order, church building furnishings, preaching format, worship music, discipleship, and evangelism. Without common agreement, a church quickly divides into factions that criticize one another and unify only in the cause of killing the church.

4) MISSIONAL UNITY

There must be missional unity around what the objective of the church is. Ultimately, the goal of everyone in the church must be to glorify God

[4] 1 Tim. 6:4–5; 2 Tim. 2:14, 23; Titus 3:9–10.
[5] 1 Cor. 1:10; 2 Cor. 13:11; Eph. 4:2–3.

according to Scripture in all they say and do.[6] Sadly, even churches that give lip service to this truth are often in practice more committed to honoring their denominational traditions, glorious heritage, founding pastor, majority vote, or critics than to honoring Jesus by introducing people to him and helping others grow in him.

5) ORGANIZATIONAL UNITY

There must be organizational unity around how things are done in the church. At Mars Hill this includes job descriptions, performance reviews, and policies regarding how money is spent and decisions are made.

REASONS FOR DIVISION

There are many reasons why unity does not exist in so many churches.

HERETICS DIVIDE CHURCHES

Sadly, the word *heretic* gets thrown around too little or too much, and the result is that seemingly no one is sure what or who a heretic is. Heresy is the opposite of orthodoxy, and heretics do exist. The church is to fight against heresy and heretics, not give them an authoritative voice in the church in the name of polite postmodern conversation.

The Bible refers to itself as a sword for good reason: we need it to battle false-teaching heretics.[7] Since the battle in the garden of Eden with our first parents, the serpent, whom Jesus called the father of all lies,[8] and his demon servants have been continually at work seeking to promulgate heretical lies. Joining them is a legion of false apostles[9] and false teachers[10] inspired by demons[11] and taken captive by Satan to serve his cause,[12] who promote false teaching that includes a demonic false gospel[13] about a false Jesus.[14]

In his sobering farewell address to the Ephesian elders, Paul warned them:

---

[6]For example, 1 Cor. 10:31.
[7]Eph. 6:17; Heb. 4:12.
[8]John 8:44.
[9]2 Cor. 11:5–13; 12:11–12.
[10]1 Tim. 4:1–7; 2 Pet. 2:1.
[11]1 Tim. 4:1–8.
[12]2 Cor. 11:13–15; 2 Tim. 2:14–26.
[13]Gal. 1:6–9.
[14]2 Cor. 11:1–4.

Pay careful attention to yourselves and to all the flock, in which the Holy Spirit has made you overseers, to care for the church of God, which he obtained with his own blood. I know that after my departure fierce wolves will come in among you, not sparing the flock; and from among your own selves will arise men speaking twisted things, to draw away the disciples after them.[15]

Echoing our Chief Shepherd Jesus' language of God's people being like sheep, false teachers being like savage wolves, and church leaders being like shepherds entrusted with the care and protection of a flock for which Jesus died, Paul warns us that wolves not only attack a church from the outside, but also rise up from within, disguised as either sheep or shepherds.

After his departure, Paul's prophecy came true, and false teachers became very popular in the church (they were possibly even elders). Thus, Paul commissioned his assistant Timothy to fight the heretics and command them to stop teaching false doctrines.[16] Paul commanded Timothy not only to quell this uprising but also to replace it with "sound doctrine,"[17] which means doctrine that is healthy and would cause the church and its members to be spiritually healthy and fruitful.

Regarding this work of shepherding, Paul tells the young pastor:

I charge you in the presence of God and of Christ Jesus, who is to judge the living and the dead, and by his appearing and his kingdom: preach the word; be ready in season and out of season; reprove, rebuke, and exhort, with complete patience and teaching. For the time is coming when people will not endure sound teaching, but having itching ears they will accumulate for themselves teachers to suit their own passions, and will turn away from listening to the truth and wander off into myths. As for you, always be sober-minded, endure suffering, do the work of an evangelist, fulfill your ministry.[18]

Elsewhere, Paul tells Timothy he must preach and teach the Bible with the strength and fortitude of an ox,[19] fight like a tough soldier,[20]

[15] Acts 20:28–31.
[16] 1 Tim. 1:3–7, 18–20; 6:12, 20–21.
[17] 1 Tim. 1:10.
[18] 2 Tim. 4:1–5.
[19] 1 Tim. 5:17–18.
[20] 2 Tim. 2:3–4.

train and compete with the precision of a skilled athlete,[21] and sweat at his labor like a farmer.[22] When done rightly, ministry is work. Ministry work includes not only teaching what is true but also refuting what is false. Paul instructs Titus that an elder "must hold firm to the trustworthy word as taught, so that he may be able to give instruction in sound doctrine and also to rebuke those who contradict it."[23] Many respond with horror when leaders rebuke people, declaring "It is not nice!" But Paul models exactly this in 2 Corinthians 10:5, saying, "We destroy arguments and every lofty opinion raised against the knowledge of God, and take every thought captive to obey Christ." Furthermore, the New Testament calls heretics dogs and evildoers,[24] empty and deceitful,[25] puffed up without reason,[26] given to mythical speculation and vanity without understanding,[27] products of a shipwrecked faith,[28] demonic liars with a seared conscience,[29] peddlers of silly myths,[30] arrogant fools with depraved minds,[31] the spiritual equivalent of gangrene,[32] foolish and ignorant,[33] chatty deceivers,[34] destructive blasphemers,[35] ignorantly unstable,[36] and antichrists.[37]

The problem with some churches and their leaders is that they won't fight, and the problem with others is that they won't stop fighting. The key is to fight for what pertains most essentially to the person and work of Jesus with the humbly loving courage that the gospel requires.

PRIDE DIVIDES CHURCHES

The Bible mentions a man named Diotrephes only once, tragically, as the man who always wanted to be first.[38] Proud people think they are

[21]2 Tim. 2:5.
[22]2 Tim. 2:6.
[23]Titus 1:9.
[24]Phil. 3:2.
[25]Col. 2:8.
[26]Col. 2:18.
[27]1 Tim. 1:3–7.
[28]1 Tim. 1:19.
[29]1 Tim. 4:1–2.
[30]1 Tim. 4:7.
[31]1 Tim. 6:3–5.
[32]2 Tim. 2:14–18.
[33]2 Tim. 2:23.
[34]Titus 1:10–14.
[35]2 Pet. 2:1–3.
[36]2 Pet. 3:16.
[37]1 John 2:18.
[38]3 John 9.

very important and delight in airing their opinions, expect to be consulted regarding their opinions, and get very angry when they are not obeyed. Proud people love the church because in it they are prone to find nice polite people who are easy to take advantage of and push around. Proud people act like leaders whether they are or not. Proud people like to say things such as "God told me," as if they are the mediator between God and people instead of Jesus and as if God prefers to communicate to his people through them. Proud people only think about themselves and their family and conveniently overlook the fact that the earth has other people, some of whom even have different last names than theirs. Lastly, proud people love to tell others what to do, but when confronted for their own sin of pride, they welcome correction as warmly as a cat does water. The most special kind of proud people talk about how you hurt their feelings, and they get really sad, sometimes even cry, so that you will talk about their feelings instead of their pride.

Pride is an ugly sin that we are all guilty of to varying degrees. Pride invariably leads to division. The only way that a church can get on and stay on Jesus' mission is by practicing Jesus' humility, beginning with the elders. Proud people who want to be first and are unwilling to do whatever is best for the mission of the gospel and the whole church because they are primarily concerned about their own glory over Jesus' are sinners who need to be called to repentance, not coddled to ruinous division.

In addition to personal pride, organizational pride divides some churches. Organizational pride includes "not invented here" syndrome, which means we only sing songs and do things that we created, and "that's not how we do it here" syndrome, which means that past success is used to resist future change for the sake of the mission. A humble organization is willing to learn from those outside its church, network, denomination, and tradition. But this requires discernment to decide what to implement and what to ignore.

LEGALISM DIVIDES CHURCHES

Legalists love to act like God by making rules. Legalists love rules about the rules. Legalists love rules about who gets to make the rules about the rules. Legalists love rules about who gets to enforce the rules made by the people whom the rules appointed to make the rules about the rules.

Legalists really love rules about who gets to interpret the rules that rule. Legalists get perfectly euphoric when they get to enact the rules by punishing people who break the rules as interpreted by those appointed by the rules. In the end, legalists want to rule through rules and wield their rules like weapons to divide the church body into bloodied parts.

DISTRUST DIVIDES CHURCHES

When there is distrust among people in the church, especially among leaders, division is certain. The larger a church gets, the more vital trust is. Without trust, distrust, mistrust, suspicion, gossip, and harsh systems of accountability that avoid relationship become weeds that grow up to choke the life and joy out of a church. The ligaments that hold together the various parts of the church body are relationships, and without trust there can be no relationships or even a biblical church. Unfortunately, our postmodern pop culture specializes in practicing the hermeneutics of suspicion that causes distrust.

Leaders have the God-ordained responsibility to be trustworthy and above reproach;[39] meanwhile, people have a God-ordained duty to honor and submit to their leaders.[40] However, this is always a two-way street where each side must be the initiator in seeking trust and unity. For example, sometimes church members will have reasons they distrust a church leader but unless they bring that concern to the leader in an appropriate manner, the leader is completely unaware and unable to rebuild trust and unity. The worst thing that can happen is that someone has distrust, and rather than pursuing resolution with the person they distrust in the church, they gossip about it, thereby creating greater distrust and division.

TRADITIONALISM DIVIDES CHURCHES

Jesus had some pretty nasty things to say to people who loved their man-made traditions. Yet, such people in our day apparently read really fast when they get to those parts of the Bible because they remain guilty of traditionalism themselves. By *tradition*, I am referring to anything done in a church three times in a row. If you disbelieve me, have something visible change in your church next Sunday, and do it three weeks

---

[39] 1 Tim. 3:2, 10; Titus 1:6.
[40] 1 Thess. 5:12–13; 1 Tim. 5:17; Heb. 13:7, 17.

in a row. Then try to change it, and you will find someone complaining because you have broken a tradition.

I found this out as a young church planter who, for three weeks in a row, set up the drum kit on the center of the stage, only to move it to the left on the fourth week. Curiously, a chain-smoking, tattooed indie rocker essentially rebuked me for putting the drum kit in the wrong place, as if I had forgotten to consult the Indie Rock Book of Church Order. Traditions are not a bad thing necessarily. However, they become bad when a method is elevated above its intended function and basically worshiped so that its function is sacrificed for the sake of the mummified method. I once visited a church that gave me a free copy of the pastor's sermon—on tape—even though I have not seen a tape player since the days when Michael Jackson was male. Looking around the room at the obvious lack of anyone younger than Methuselah, it seemed obvious that their traditionalism had run off emerging generations, thereby dividing their church into the two groups of BT (before tapes) and AT (after tapes).

TOO LITTLE and TOO MUCH ORGANIZATION DIVIDES CHURCHES

Extremes in organizational informality and formality divide a church. Some churches are organized too informally, and, as a result, such things as decision making, record keeping, communication, and related policies and procedures need to be formalized, written down, and enforced so that there can be efficiency. Conversely, some churches are organized too formally with such tight systems and policies that innovation is constrained; order overtakes results and creativity is squelched in the name of due process as defined by a guy with a clipboard and no hobbies or friends.

There is a fine balance that a church needs to maintain regarding organizational formality. Simply, a church needs to be as formally organized as is necessary to get on and stay on mission, and no more. As a church grows, it is imperative that the level of organizational formality increase if there is to be any hope of staying on mission.

In my experience, it is more common for churches to be too disorganized to have any unity. Without job descriptions or performance reviews for leaders, no one is sure who is supposed to do what and how. Without any clearly communicated mission, unity is impossible, because no one is sure what they are unifying to accomplish. Without organizational structure, no one is even sure who they report to or who is responsible to fix problems that arise, and division ensues.

FOUNDER DYSFUNCTION DIVIDES CHURCHES

It is not uncommon for the human founder(s) and leader(s) of the church to become the impediment to the unity of the church. They do so by wielding power wrongly and not empowering other leaders to lead, to make changes, and to disagree with them in a respectful and healthy manner that benefits the gospel. The founder can become popish, resulting in other leaders wasting energy trying to work around the leader who is not leading well but remains in place out of a sense of obligation and entitlement. The result is always painful division.

MISSION LOSS DIVIDES CHURCHES

Mission loss occurs when the entire point of the church is lost and the church gets off mission; the original vision or mission that sustained the movement is lost. For example, one church planter I know started off with the declared mission of reaching his community for Jesus Christ. When he did not see any conversions, rather than getting back on mission, he cast a new vision to disciple Christians. When that did not happen, he adopted the very vague mission of blessing people, because he could not fail at a mission that could not be measured in any way. He eventually shut down the church because he lost sight of his mission and as a result had no great cause to call his people to, and they became divided over what their church even existed to accomplish.

DOING TOO MUCH DIVIDES CHURCHES

Pursuing potential rather than calling gets a church off mission. Too many churches do too much. This is because their mission is too big, or they accommodate too many people in the church who have their own various missions. A local church needs to prayerfully and carefully define what God has called it to be and do and then excel at that. Good leaders do not pursue every opportunity, but only those few that are most strategic for the forward progress of Jesus' mission for their church. Bluntly stated, most churches are doing too much and doing it all poorly. To get and stay unified, church leaders must focus their resources (e.g., people, dollars, facilities, emotion, technology) on accomplishing a few things if they hope to accomplish anything. If not, there will be division as people jockey for resources for their various missions.

In summary, to continually pursue unity a church must continually pursue change. A living church must change in the same way that a living person grows and changes, hopefully toward maturity. Any church that does not change is more like a museum than a people on a mission. In the past, the big ate the small. Today, the fast eat the slow. The key is not so much the size of a church but its speed and ability to remain nimble and adaptable to make changes quickly so that the mission momentum and unity are not lost. This is only possible as the church is broken into smaller, unified, working teams that remain nimble with delegated authority and power. Without this, informal and inefficient leadership systems are birthed by virtue of necessity to get things done, and division ensues.

It is true that some churches and church leaders make changes too quickly. However, I would argue that for the vast majority of churches and church leaders, the mistake is to make changes too slowly. Change needs to happen. Yet, the pursuit of change often causes conflict in the church, which is the cost of growth.

CONFLICT IS THE PRICE OF GROWTH

When a church grows, it changes, and that change causes conflict. Importantly, conflict is not always a bad thing in a church. Conflict, if handled in love and humility according to the principles of Scripture, can and should be the impetus for a more mature church that is more unified than ever. By way of analogy, every married couple knows that there is inevitably conflict in any loving relationship. The question is not will we ever have conflict, but rather how will we deal with our conflict. Having been with my high school sweetheart for many years, I can attest to the fact that learning to work through our conflict has allowed us not to fear conflict but to use it as an occasion to build our loving unity by God's grace, and the same is true for my eleven years of service in our church.

The price of your church growing so that more people are worshiping Jesus is conflict. I am convinced that many churches refuse to grow, even building theological justifications for not growing, because they are afraid of conflict, which means that rather than worshiping Christ, they are worshiping comfort. Simply, the desire to grow in numbers and maturity requires change, and change causes conflict. Therefore, growing churches are the ones that are prone to experience the greatest seasons of division, as the following process illustrates:

1) Growth causes change.

2) Change causes complexity.

3) Complexity causes chaos.

4) Chaos causes concern.

5) Concern causes conflict.

This conflict comes in eight different forms. With each form, a person or a faction of people want something that they perceive they lost due to change. They fight to preserve what they lost and in so doing oppose change. Their efforts focus on gaining or regaining one of eight forms of church currency that they value.

The first church currency is power, and attempts to grasp it cause conflict. Change requires that some people lose power (e.g., job title, prominence, proximity to the top leaders, and the right to make key decisions) when responsibilities must be divided. Power conflict particularly rises up when people have a change of title that they cling to as a source of power, righteousness, and identity rather than cling to Jesus Christ. When told they do not meet the qualifications to become an elder or deacon, for example, or are placed under the leadership of someone they perceive to be less qualified than they, such people can be very insulted. They forget that Jesus took the title "servant" for himself as our model of humility, and they are not to act like the power-grabbing heathens he warned about. Power illicitly motivates some people and when they lose power they fight to retain it.

Second, people value remuneration, and, therefore, there is remuneration conflict. Change requires that tangible compensation such as salaries and benefits be reallocated to other priorities. Practically, this means that some people don't get raises commensurate with their self-assessment, and some even lose their job at the church. Money motivates some people, and when their pay does not meet their expectations, there is conflict over their compensation.

Third is the currency of preference, and where this is fought for, there is preference conflict. Change requires that long-standing leaders be reassigned in roles and responsibilities, sometimes further from the center of influence and the senior leader, so that new leaders can be raised up and those who have been faithful can be promoted to higher levels of leadership. Preference motivates some people, and when they lose a position of preference close to or as the senior leader(s), there is conflict over their role. Church leaders who change their email address or phone number to get a bit of privacy experience the pressure some people impose to retain preferential access to them.

Fourth, there is the currency of information, and trying to get it causes conflict. Change requires that new people have access to certain information, which means that some people will feel out of the information loop. This is because as a church grows, the lines of communication increase exponentially:

- A church of 50 people = 2,450 lines of communication
- A church of 100 people = 9,900 lines of communication
- A church of 200 people = 39,800 lines of communication
- A church of 300 people = 89,700 lines of communication
- A church of 400 people = 159,600 lines of communication
- A church of 1,000 people = 999,000 lines of communication
- A church of 6,000 people = 35,994,000 lines of communication.

While it is important to make every effort to keep people appropriately informed, those who are motivated by information will fight to be "in the know" and incite conflict over who is allowed to know what in the church.

The key to unity is that both the people and the leaders have the right information in a timely manner. For example, when a church is smaller, the senior leader(s) can have a general sense of how things are going by trusting their gut and simply being present at the church and in peoples' homes. However, as a church becomes too large for the senior leader(s) to know what is going on, it must rely on five to seven key reports of information to keep them abreast of health metrics, with year-to-year and month-to-month comparisons to evaluate progress or regress. Possible variables include the numbers of adults and children attending services, visitors, people giving financially and the average giving per attendee, conversions and baptisms, people pursuing membership, people actively serving both in and out of the church, people in a class or group, weddings, and babies born. Likewise, there must be effective ways for the leaders to communicate openly and accurately to the church members, such as emails, a password-protected members' Web site for open dialogue, and a church blog.

Fifth, there is the currency of visibility. Change requires that new people become more prominently visible, while others who used to be prominently visible become less so. Some people love to be seen and known in the church, and those motivated by visibility will cause conflict if their visibility is reduced. In some churches, this means that the guy who used to fill the pulpit when the pastor was out, the person who used to give the announcements, and the lady who used to play in the band no longer do because the church now has more capable people to do those visible jobs. Sadly, by causing conflict over their loss of visibility, such people tend to forget that Jesus is still watching their behavior and is quite disappointed.

Sixth, there is the currency of personal energy, and a shift in who has it causes conflict. Change requires more physical, emotional, and spiritual energy than might have been needed in a prior season of ministry. Practically, as the pace picks up, some church leaders can no longer keep up and are overtaken by stronger, healthier leaders who can keep up and take the church to the next level of fruitfulness. Some who gain their sense of well-being and identity from being a leader, or some who feel that because they served well in a previous season have the right to retain their leadership position, cause conflict over the pace of growth. Such people complain about things changing too fast and might even sabotage the ministry in an effort to slow things down rather than to humbly accept their limits and find a place to serve that best suits their energy levels.

Seventh, there is the currency of expedient pace. Obstructions and delay cause conflict. Change requires that decisions be made at an expedient pace so the church can mature and grow. Some people value their ability to control the pace of church decision making and change because it is for them a method of power and rule. While it is true that churches can make overly hasty decisions, what I am speaking of here are people who obstruct decision making and delay change by essentially pulling the emergency brake all the time. Such people tend to be in the minority, if not alone, and cause great conflict by set-ting themselves up against the will of the vast majority of leaders and people. Their tactics include various kinds of stalling, such as delay-ing votes, missing meetings, demanding an unreasonable number of meetings and an unreasonable amount of information, nitpicking over fine details that are truly unimportant, and even sharing confidential information with others in the church in an effort to gain enough of a following to slow down change.

Eighth, there is the currency of control. Church change results in less control over everything, especially as it grows. Some who inordi-nately value control try to control growth and change in the name of order and accountability. The truth is that the Holy Spirit, who indwells the Christians, ultimately directs a church. People in the church, partic-ularly leaders, are to influence the church through exemplary doctrine and character that is contagious in a way that is more like laughter than herpes.

At its best, a church is like a river that can be channeled and influ-enced for progress and power. However, every attempt to control a church kills either the church or the person seeking to control the church with stress-related illness. Therefore, churches must accept that change is messy and cannot be controlled but can be influenced through such things as systems, leaders, training, preaching, publishing, and getting good resources (e.g., books, sermons) into the hands and ears of its people.

In summary, for a church to grow it must accept the pain that accompanies change. Because we want more people to worship Jesus as God, we must be willing to accept the inevitable conflict that change brings. Such change can be perceived by some as a loss of power, remu-neration, preference, information, visibility, role, sustainable pacing, or control. Or, it can be viewed as an opportunity to share those things with others for the sake of Jesus' gospel and his church.

In closing, I, Gerry, asked Mark to share with you a personal picture of how this has played out in his own life and ministry. Mark hesitated to share it with you for fear of appearing proud. But we both want this book to be a real book from real pastors about real ministry in real churches with real people. For that to happen we need to include some real snapshots into the messiness of church. So

I asked Mark to share a letter that he wrote to the members of Mars Hill Church as an act of his repentance and instruction. It is a letter about some incredibly painful issues in his life as pastor of a church experiencing explosive growth amidst the greatest season of division the church had ever faced. We have edited it slightly in a few places because a few details aren't appropriate to share with nonmembers. My intent in asking Mark to share it is to show that not only do sinners and heretics ruin churches, but sometimes well-meaning, overworked pastors do as well. We need not only preach repentance to others but also to ourselves, and practice it for their example, according to Peter's instruction to the elders in 1 Peter 5:1–5.[41]

> November 8, 2007
> Dear Mars Hill Church Members,
> I grew up in Seattle not knowing Jesus. Thankfully, Jesus saved me when I was nineteen years of age while a college freshman. Shortly thereafter he led me to my first church, where a humble and godly pastor was used of God to change my life by teaching me about Jesus from the Bible. While attending my first men's retreat with that church, God spoke to me for the first time in my life. He told me to marry Grace, preach the Bible, train men, and plant churches. It was then, at the age of nineteen, that I began preparing to devote my life to obeying his call for me.
> I studied speech in my undergraduate work to prepare for preaching. I joined as many as six Bible studies a quarter to learn Scripture. I began reading nearly a book a day, which continued for many years. I married Grace while still in college. In addition, I began recruiting college friends to one day be part of the core group for Mars Hill Church, which I intended to see planted in Seattle. Following graduation from college, Grace and I moved back to Seattle where we got jobs and started settling in as a broke young couple trying to figure out how and where to plant Mars Hill Church.
> By the age of twenty-four we were gathering the core group for the church plant while I was working part-time....
> At the age of twenty-five I had the privilege of preaching the opening sermon at Mars Hill Church, and I have remained the primary preaching pastor ever since. I have learned a lot over the years. Much

[41]You can download Mark's sermon confessing his arrogance by going to http://www.marshillchurch.org/sermonseries/philippians/ and selecting "The Rebel's Guide to Joy in Humility, Phil. 2:1–11."

of that learning has been through mistakes, failure, and pain. The early years of the church, chronicled in my book *Confessions,* were very difficult in every way. In more recent years, our fast growth has been a wonderful blessing but also fraught with difficulties.

For me, personally, everything culminated at the end of 2006. Despite rapid growth, the church was not healthy and neither was I. My workload was simply overwhelming. I was preaching five times a Sunday, the senior leader in Mars Hill responsible to some degree for literally everything in the church, president of the Acts 29 Church Planting Network which had exploded, president of The Resurgence, an author writing books, a conference speaker traveling, a media representative doing interviews, a student attending graduate school, a father with five young children, and a husband to a wife whom I have adored since the first day I met her and who needed my focus more than ever. I was working far too many hours and neglecting my own physical and spiritual well-being, and then I hit the proverbial wall. For many weeks I simply could not sleep more than two or three hours a night. I had been running on adrenaline for so many years that my adrenal glands fatigued, and the stress of my responsibilities caused me to be stuck "on" physically and unable to rest or sleep. After a few months I had black circles under my eyes, was seeing a fog, and was constantly beyond exhausted.

Nonetheless, the demands on me continued to grow as the church grew. We added more campuses, gathered more critics, saw more media attention, planted more churches, purchased more real estate, raised more money, and hired more staff. It was at this time that I seriously pondered leaving Mars Hill Church for the first time ever. I still loved our Jesus, loved our mission, loved our city, and loved our people. However, I sunk into a deep season of despair as I considered spending the rest of my life serving at Mars Hill Church. I simply could not fathom living the rest of my life with the pace of ministry and amount of responsibility that was on me. Furthermore, the relational demands of the church and its leaders depleted me entirely. In short, I had lost my joy and wanted to lose my job before I lost my life. Tucking my children in bed at night became a deeply sorrowful experience for me; I truly feared I would either die early from a heart attack or burn out and be left unable to best care for my children in the coming years. I have met many pastors who have simply crossed the line of burnout and never returned to health and sanity, and that was my frightful but seemingly inevitable future.

One of the problems was that Mars Hill had essentially outgrown the wisdom of our team and needed outside counsel. The church had grown so fast that some of our elders and other leaders were simply falling behind and having trouble keeping up. . . .

At the same time I began receiving other lucrative job offers that would allow me to study, preach, and write without all of the administrative duties and burdens for which I am not sufficiently gifted. For the first time in my life, the thought of leaving Mars Hill sounded very relieving. Since I had given ten years of my life to the church and love the people desperately, it was obvious to me that something was deeply wrong that such offers would even be intriguing.

So, I began pursuing counsel from godly men outside the church that I respected. . . . On top of that, I pursued counsel from a Christian doctor regarding my health and what needed to change in my diet, exercise, and schedule. In short, I sought wise outside counsel about whether I should stay at Mars Hill and make changes in my life and our church, or simply move on to another church and start over.

The consensus was that Mars Hill was poorly architected to be a multi-campus, multi-elder, multi-thousand-person church. My administrative gifts had simply reached their capacity, and the church needed to be reorganized so that campuses could be led by elder teams to ensure that our people were best cared for, our doctrine best taught, and our mission best led. This meant that I needed to give up a great deal of power and trust other elders, deacons, and members to care for the church with the same passionate affection that I have for our people.

To begin this process I had to go first and divest myself of a great deal of power. In the history of our church I have held the three positions of greatest authority. Legally, I was the president of the Mars Hill Church organization. Practically, I was the preaching pastor and primary voice of Mars Hill Church. Administratively, I was the president of the elder board and highest authority on the staff. So I resigned as the legal president, the president of the elder board, and the highest authority over the staff. I have retained the position of primary preaching pastor but have also started a preaching cadre to train many other elders in preaching so as to begin sharing that load roughly twelve times a year with other gifted men.

Having shared power, I was then able to establish a new executive elder board to architect the future of Mars Hill. I remained one of the men on that team to help lead the church but came under Pastor

Jamie Munson, the team leader. In our church I have seen Pastor Jamie saved, baptized, married, produce four children, and rise up from an intern to the lead pastor with great skill and humility that includes surrounding himself with godly gifted older men who complement his gifts. I simply did not have the giftedness to architect something as complex as our church, which intended to grow to multiple campuses, possibly even stretching out of state or out of country. Yet, I wanted to ensure that our church remained theologically precise and committed not just to growing but also to caring for our people. So the new executive elder team sought outside counsel from bigger churches that we respect. . . .

The newly formed executive elder team began working on new bylaws that would serve as the architecting document for a better Mars Hill. The big issue was empowering our campus pastors to lead elder teams. This would ensure the best care for the people at each campus by being accessible and able to make decisions quickly. We could not care for our people across multiple campuses with one large and fast-growing elder team that had to meet to make decisions across campuses many of us had never even attended. So the bylaws had to be rewritten to break the elders into teams with campus areas of oversight as well as accountability. . . .

Today, I am thrilled that what is best for Jesus and all of Mars Hill has been unanimously approved by our entire elder team, because I do love Jesus and the people of Mars Hill. Furthermore, my physical, mental, and spiritual health are at the best levels in all of my life. Now having joy and working in my gifting, I am beginning to see what a dark and bitter place I once was in and deeply grieve having lived there for so long without clearly seeing my need for life change. My wife and I are closer than ever, and she is the greatest woman in the world for me. I delight in her, enjoy her, and praise God for the gift that she is. She recently brought me to tears by sweetly saying, "It's nice to have you back," as apparently I had been somewhat gone for many years. Our five children are wonderful blessings. I love being a daddy and am closer to my children with greater joy in them than ever. In short, I was not taking good care of myself, and out of love for our church I was willing to kill myself to try and keep up with all that Jesus is doing. But, as always, Jesus has reminded me that he is our Senior Pastor and has other godly pastors whom I need to empower and trust while doing my job well for his glory, my joy, and your good.

The past year has been the most difficult of my entire life. . . . Furthermore, sin in my life has been exposed through this season, and I have also benefited from learning to repent of such things as bitterness, unrighteous anger, control, and pride. As a result, I believe we have a pruned elder team that God intends to use to bear more fruit than ever. This team of battle-tested, humble, and repentant men is now both easy to enjoy and entrust.

Emotionally, I told our board of directors recently that I felt like I walked Mars Hill down the aisle and married her off so that she could be best cared for and loved in the next season of her life. I remain her father who loves and cares for her and is vitally involved in her growth and well-being, but I now trust the elders to take good care of her, thanks in part to a structure that enables her to be loved well. Subsequently, for the first time in my tenure at Mars Hill I am able to work in my area of gifting with men I trust on a mission I believe in with church members I love and a Jesus I worship. That harmony is priceless.

Today I write this letter after finishing my studies for my upcoming sermon on Philippians 2:12–30. In God's providence it is incredibly timely. Paul said that the people in the church were "grumbling" against and "questioning" the church leadership. . . . He tells the church not to nitpick over details but to be "blameless" and "innocent" and to work for unity so that the world will not think less of Jesus. To remedy things Paul sent a letter to the church he planted and cared for, which prompted me to write this letter to you. . . .

I have stayed to grow in my own repentance and not abandon the work Jesus called me to nearly half my life ago, because I love you. Today, I am weary but elated and confident that Jesus who began this work will see it through to completion. I am confident that I will be able to remain with you for every step of that journey serving as my gifts permit. Subsequently, I am rejoicing.

For Jesus' Fame,
Pastor Mark Driscoll

ANSWERS TO COMMON QUESTIONS ABOUT CHURCH UNITY

IF UNITY IS SO IMPORTANT, WHY START NEW CHURCHES?

A church plant is an expression of unity. It is quite different from a church split. A church plant should be done in cooperation with local churches that share common beliefs and a passion to reach unchurched people. They collaborate to reach the community for Christ. The existing churches may contribute people and finances to aid the new church. The church-planting pastor seeks the advice and assistance of local pastors so he can supplement the work they are doing while receiving the benefit of their wisdom.

Missional churches know that church planting is one of the most effective means of reaching the unchurched. And, rather than robbing members from existing churches, a church plant is intended to reach those people that existing churches are not reaching. Wise pastors see a new church as a member of God's team for extending the kingdom, not as competition or as a danger to their own ministry.

I DON'T SEE HOW WE CAN HAVE UNITY. THERE ARE A LOT OF THINGS WE DISAGREE ON.

Of course you can't agree on everything! In passages such as Romans 14, the Bible gives a very realistic perspective of godly disagreement. It tells us to remember that "the kingdom of God is not a matter of eating and drinking but of righteousness and peace and joy in the Holy Spirit" (Rom. 14:17).

Leaders know that the main thing is to keep the main thing the main thing. They have a nose for significance, creating a climate of unity around central issues while moderating and directing discussion over secondary issues. They see how seemingly insignificant matters may undercut the central points of the gospel even as they appear so benign, so cultured, so loving. They sense that other issues that appear so fundamental are actually seeds of division planted by the enemy of our souls.

IS THERE A WAY TO DIFFERENTIATE BETWEEN WOLVES IN SHEEP'S CLOTHING AND SHEEP IN WOLVES' CLOTHING?

One way is to distinguish levels of certainty.[42] Then you can differentiate what's really essential from that which is merely controversial. The first level of certainty covers truths we should be willing to *die for*. If you knowingly deny these, you show that you are outside the realm of evangelicalism and perhaps excluded from salvation in Christ. An example of such a truth is that Jesus is God uniquely come in the flesh. If we are vigilant about such essentials, we are less likely to fall for the cultural accommodations of Christianity, which lead to liberalism. Being vigilant also helps us keep secondary issues in perspective and avoid the divisions they create. Standing for these things does not make us fundamentalists. It does make us biblical.

Second are things we would *divide for*. We are Christians, fellow members of the body of Christ, but we can't be in the same local fellowship with everyone in clear conscience. The meaning of the sacraments and women serving as elders are typical division points. Such differences are legitimate so long as the unity of the body of Jesus Christ is affirmed and the dividing points are truly central issues. They become problematic when the dividing walls are so high that there is little contact between different groups and when arguments between the groups drain significant energy from our worship of God and hinder building godliness and proclaiming the gospel. Instead of blogging about them, talking trash, or sending hate mail condemning them to hell, we should love them and emphasize our unity in the essentials.

Third are things we would *debate for*. In the midst of ministering and laughing together, issues such as style of worship or political involvement come up and emotions may flare; we end up growling at each other. The wrestling may be prolonged or painful, but we do it while maintaining regular fellowship, joining together in worship and proclamation.

---

[42]Gerry Breshears, "Learning to Distinguish between Degrees of Certainty," in *Lessons in Leadership*, ed. Randal Roberts (Grand Rapids, MI: Kregel, 1999), 48–53.

Finally are things we *decide for*. The differences over such issues spring from little more than personal opinion. In our churches, *decide fors* include issues like having a glass of wine with supper, raising hands in worship, or eating a vegan-only diet.

Divisive people are ones who elevate lower-level issues to *divide fors*. False teachers treat *die for* issues as questions open for humble discussion. As we utilize these levels as a community of believers, we can avoid the trap of being unnecessarily divisive on one hand and compromising the faith on the other.

HOW DO I PICK A CHURCH?

1) Is it in agreement with your *die for* and *divide for* issues? Don't be afraid to ask. Good churches will know where they stand on these issues. Their leaders will be glad to discuss them with you. If that is not so, pass on the church and seek another option.

2) Does the preacher proclaim the Word clearly from the pulpit? Do his sermons speak to life? If a church does not take preaching seriously, find one that does.

3) Is it a place where your gifts can be developed and utilized in ministry? Do you feel a connection with the people leading that ministry?

4) Do you connect with the worship style, the personality and culture of the church? If the music makes you flinch, you won't want to invite your unsaved friends. You won't do well in a church where not tucking your shirt in gets frowns from the deacons. If you like wearing a dress to church but no one else does, you might want to keep looking if they judge you negatively.

5) What is its reputation in the community? If it were to close its doors, would community people be relieved or grieved?

6) Are there people there whom you know from other venues of your life? If so, then you are more likely to make deep friendships.

7) Is Jesus the person everyone wants to please? It seems a little elusive, but after all, it is all about him!

WHAT ARE LEGITIMATE REASONS FOR SOMEONE TO LEAVE A CHURCH?

The bottom line is that when the membership covenant is broken irreparably, then it is time to move on. First, if a church begins to compromise the biblical essentials, conceding *die for* matters, then members should follow the pattern of Acts 15 and bring a complaint to the leaders. If they refuse to return to biblical teaching, the complaining member must leave.

Such was the case with J. I. Packer's decision to leave the Canadian arm of the global Anglican Communion. He could no longer stay because Bishop Michael Ingham had sanctioned blessing same-sex unions in the church. The central issue was the authority of inspired Scripture. Ingham persisted in teaching that the church needs to allow people room to come to a new understanding of the Bible. Packer correctly believes "the Bible is the 'absolute' authority on divine truth, which clearly describes homosexuality as a grave sin."[43]

A second reason is when differences in belief or practice become so serious that cooperation in ministry is gravely hindered. Differences in ministry philosophy can differ to the point that conflict overshadows partnership. When persistent, gracious efforts to resolve the differences fail, it is time to part company. This is what happened in the dispute between Paul and Barnabas over taking John Mark with them on their second journey (Acts 15:36–39). The best way to handle a parting is for the parties to speak clearly of their differences and then publicly and prayerfully bless each other as they part.

A third reason to leave a church is when legitimate needs are not being met. We said good-bye to a good family that moved to another church as their son emerged into varsity basketball and wanted to go to the church where several team members went. We blessed each other and maintained strong friendship as they went on to serve Jesus elsewhere. This is quite different from those who leave because "our needs are not being met." That statement often comes out of the false belief that the church exists to minister to *me*. Foolish people think that if the church isn't ministering to *me*, then the church has violated its divine commission and that they have every reason to depart in disgust!

A fourth reason to leave is when the leadership becomes abusive, serving themselves at the expense of the members, or tolerating sin that should be disciplined. If a church becomes cultic, members should leave lest they support evil. Jesus' accusations against the Pharisees in Matthew 23 apply to many cultic groups.

---

[43]Quoted in Douglas Todd, "Influential Evangelical Theologian Latest to Split with Anglican Church," *Vancouver Sun*, Saturday, April 26, 2008.

The decision to leave should always be done carefully, prayerfully, and with communication with the church leaders to see if things can be worked out. It is terrible when a family just disappears from a church. The exception to this is when there is true spiritual abuse, rendering communication dangerous.

A fifth reason, one that is incredibly positive, is to serve in another church so that the gospel can flourish. Leaving an established church to help a church plant get started and doing so with the church's blessing is one example.

In summary, Christians need to be committed to the church.

WHAT ARE ILLEGITIMATE REASONS FOR LEAVING A CHURCH?

The only valid reason for leaving a local church is a desire for more effective ministry in and for the body of Christ. One illegitimate reason for leaving a church is that it is not perfect or it does not meet all legitimate needs. Every church has problems and shortcomings. That is the nature of life in this sinful world. Leaving because things are not perfect simply reveals our low level of faithfulness.

It is helpful to realize that we are part of the problem of imperfection. My presence and ministry in the church may be part of what keeps it from being a perfect place for someone else. Paul exhorts us to live "with all humility and gentleness, with patience, bearing with one another in love, eager to maintain the unity of the Spirit in the bond of peace" (Eph. 4:2–3).

A second illegitimate reason for leaving is that the church doesn't have a ministry that you need. It may be that God wants you to minister to the church instead of them ministering to you. God gave you certain gifts, talents, and life experiences that he wants you to use for his glory. Rather than complaining about the church, approach the leadership respectfully and work with them to make a concrete proposal for ministry development. This might be a wonderful gift to everyone.

A third illegitimate reason is leaving to get away from problems. Trouble in relationships often causes people to leave. It may be far better to learn how to draw on the grace of God to overcome those difficulties. We may need to grow in the fruit of the Spirit, gaining more patience, kindness, and love. Running away will derail the very process God uses to conform us to the image of Christ.

A fourth illegitimate reason to leave is that we are being challenged about our doctrine or pattern of life and find it uncomfortable. We should not run because we feel threatened by someone challenging our cherished notions. We ought always to be ready to examine what we believe and what we do in light of the Word of God and the wisdom of the Spirit-led community. How else can we grow? We should be willing to enter into discussion about important questions of life and doctrine.

On the other hand, some pastors make it unnecessarily difficult for people to leave their church. It seems wise to approach members' departure with grace, not guilt. Guilting people not only wounds those who want to leave but also other members of your flock. Consider sending people out with a blessing no matter why they choose to leave, along with an invitation to visit any time. Many who leave for inappropriate reasons return when they discover the grass on the other side is not greener.

CHAPTER SEVEN

WHAT IS CHURCH DISCIPLINE?

**Whoever loves discipline loves knowledge,
but he who hates reproof is stupid.**

PROVERBS 12:1

I was an intern on staff at a large, multicultural, suburban church and will never forget the look of horror on the woman's face. A seasoned pastor and I were standing in the back of the room during a Sunday service, and she was running out of the building leading her small children by the hand. Tears were flowing down her face, and she was visibly distraught.

The seasoned pastor motioned for me to follow him as he sped off to catch up with the woman. I stood quietly by, hoping to learn from his example, and I was not disappointed.

He kindly and calmly asked the woman to please share what was wrong so that he could lovingly serve her. Nearly hysterical, she explained that she was a Christian who had been attending the church for a while and was in the midst of a painful divorce. She said that her husband, a professing Christian, had been committing adultery with another woman who claimed to be a Christian. He had abandoned his wife and children, filed for divorce, and intended to marry the other woman he was living and sleeping with.

As she was sitting in the church service with their children, her husband to whom she was still legally married sat a few rows in front of her . . . with his adulterous girlfriend. Apparently not noticing his wife and children seated behind him, the man proceeded to enjoy the sermon, nodding his head and responding with the occasional "amen" while snuggling with his girlfriend and giving her the occasional romantic glance and kiss on the lips.

The man's wife and young children were watching all of this transpire. Obviously confused, the young children began asking their mommy why Daddy was in the church with another woman.

As I listened to the woman's story, my heart broke for her and the children, and I became furious with her husband. I watched the seasoned pastor to see how he would respond and was impressed. He asked the woman to point out her husband from the back of the room and proceeded to walk up to the man during the sermon, tap him on the shoulder, and motion for him and his girlfriend to follow him out of the auditorium.

They did and were mortified to see the man's wife and children standing in the foyer, wailing uncontrollably. The pastor asked if the man was guilty of adultery and confirmed the facts of the story as told by his wife.

At first, the husband tried to explain himself, which only dug him a deeper grave with the seasoned pastor. Seeing that things were not going well, his girlfriend spoke up and attempted to defend their relationship. The pastor responded by quoting multiple Scriptures from memory about adultery and rebuked them both for saying they were Christians and living in unrepentant, gross sin.

The pastor kept his cool but was as firm and direct as I had ever seen anyone in such a tense situation. The pastor then asked the wife what she wanted. She said that she wanted her husband to repent of sin, end his adulterous relationship, and meet with her and a pastor to try to save their marriage. The pastor then told the man that he would meet with him and his wife to seek to reconcile their marriage and family, but if the man was unwilling, he was never to set foot in the church again. His reasoning was that although the wife and children had intended to leave the church, they should not have to because they were the victims of gross sin and needed the loving support of the church. On the other hand, the man and his whorish girlfriend would be welcome in the church only if they repented of their sin and lived as Christians. If they did not, they should be the ones to leave.

I do not know what transpired in that family. But I do know that pastoral ministry involves dealing with human sin in the midst of intense emotion. Furthermore, because church leaders love the reputation of Jesus, love the entire church in which they serve, and love the sinner, dealing with sin is an art form that takes great courage, discernment, and wisdom.

All of the individual and corporate shortcomings of God's perfect intentions for creation, whether intentional or unintentional or through omission or commission, qualify as sin or the effects of sin. Satan committed the first sin.[1] He led a rebellion against God.[2] After Satan and demons were cast out of heaven, Satan tempted our first parents, Adam and Eve, to join his sinful rebellion against God. Adam was the representative and father of humankind, and when he sinned and fell out of favor with God, so did every person who would ever live.[3]

Every person since Adam is a sinner, both by nature and choice.[4] Everyone (except Jesus Christ) is, from conception, sinful by nature and corrupted to the very core of his or her being and therefore incapable of doing anything that pleases God.[5] Thus everyone, except Jesus Christ,[6] sins[7] by breaking God's holy laws,[8] because they are sinners in their hearts.[9] Therefore, the question is not whether people will sin against one another, but rather how they will deal with that sin. The following process should normally occur when a Christian sins.[10]

---

[1] Isa. 14:11–23; Ezek. 28:1–19.
[2] 2 Pet. 2:4; Rev. 9:1; 12:3–4, 7–10.
[3] Hos. 6:7; Rom. 5:12–21; 1 Cor. 15:21–22, 45–50.
[4] Pss. 51:5; 58:3; Rom. 3:23; see also Ps. 53:3; Isa. 53:6; 64:6; 1 John 1:18.
[5] Ps. 51:5; Rom. 3:10–18; 8:7–8.
[6] Heb. 4:15.
[7] 1 John 1:8.
[8] Ps. 14:1–3; Isa. 53:6; Rom. 3:10, 23; 1 John 3:4.
[9] Prov. 4:23; 17:19; 20:9; Matt. 6:21; Luke 6:45.
[10] This chapter is adapted from a document written by our elders to clarify and explain the Bible's teaching on church discipline for our church members. While I, Mark, did participate in its drafting, the content was collected and edited from among our elders by Pastor Scott Thomas, who also directs our Acts 29 Church Planting Network (www.Acts29Network.org). Therefore, this part of the book, like many others, is simply the product of the elders and me, which we are sharing with you in hopes of being helpful.

STEP 1: CONVICTION

God made us with a conscience to guide our decision making through life and to make us feel convicted when we do wrong. God the Holy Spirit shines the light of grace on our sin, exposing it for what it is, calling us and helping us move to repentance. This is the convicting work the Bible frequently speaks of.[11] He often does his convicting work through other Christians who love us enough to ask about junk they see in our lives.

We naturally avoid conviction because it hurts to feel the pain of guilt and the shame of our sin. But working through conviction takes us to the motivations behind the behavior, the sinful desires of our flesh,[12] and the corrupt passions[13] that will continue to drive us until we identify them and put them to death.[14] In Jesus we have been delivered from the Adamic heritage[15] and the dominion of darkness[16] so we are no longer under the authority of sin or the power of the devil. Romans 6:6 says, "We know that our old self [our membership in the family of Adam] was crucified with him in order that the body of sin might be brought to nothing, so that we would no longer be enslaved to sin." Conviction is an essential step to exposing sin for what it is so we can be free from enslavement to sin.

STEP 2: CONFESSION

As the Holy Spirit convicts us of sin and renews our mind, we must then name our sin as God does and accept the truth that we have sinned. Confession means agreeing with God and telling the truth about who we are and what we have done. Confession includes naming our sin to Jesus and anyone else we have sinned against or is directly affected by our sin. James 5:16 teaches us it is best to confess the sin to faithful Christians who will pray for us and help us grow in holiness. We must do this without blaming anyone else for our sin, excusing it, minimizing it, or only partially confessing it. While conviction is a gift God gives to us, confession is our response, which then prepares us for a life of repentance, restitution, and reconciliation.

---

[11]John 16:8–11; 1 Thess. 1:5; Jude 1:15.
[12]Gal. 5:19.
[13]1 Pet. 4:2.
[14]Col. 3:5.
[15]Rom. 5:12–21.
[16]Col. 1:13.

STEP 3: REPENTANCE

The heart of repentance is changing your mind about who is god in your life. When we sin, we are worshiping someone or something else as a false god and functional savior. In repentance we turn from those false gods back to the true and living God of the Bible, who alone loved us enough to die for our sin and freedom. This means that a deep change of values occurs, and we change our mind about what we deem important. Then there will be a heart-sourced change of behavior. We must learn to repent continually by turning our face to Jesus and turning our back on sin. Repentance is not trying to manage our sin, but rather putting it to death before it puts us to death. Colossians 3:5 says it perfectly: "Put to death therefore what is earthly in you: sexual immorality, impurity, passion, evil desire, and covetousness, which is idolatry."

It is important to note that false repentance takes many forms, none of which can be accepted as true repentance. Some forms of false repentance are explained below. [17]

MERE CONFESSION

When God's people confess their sins without truly repenting, they are agreeing that they are guilty of evil but are not living lives of repentant transformation. This is what often happens in the psychobabble churches where everyone glories in how broken they are but neglect to live out the Spirit's power for new life.

WORLDLY SORROW

In 2 Corinthians 7:10 we are told, "Worldly grief produces death." This is because worldly sorrow feels bad for sin but does not understand that Jesus died for sin as our "man of sorrows"[18] and "carried our sorrows"[19] so that we can move from sorrow to salvation, forgiveness, new life, and joy marked by his salvation and not just our sin. People who exhibit mere worldly sorrow are left in the deadening hopelessness of their guilt and shame.

---

[17]These forms of false repentance are adapted from Tim Keller's paper *All of Life is Repentance*, which is available online here: http://www.greentreewebster.org/Articles/All%20of%20Life%20is%20Repentance. pdf.
[18]Isa. 53:3.
[19]Isa. 53:4.

SELF-RIGHTEOUS REPENTANCE

Proud, self-righteous repentance occurs when we confess the sins of other people while neglecting our own manifestations of depravity. It can also happen when people repent of "acceptable sins" to deflect attention from deeper sins. Perhaps the most legendary example of this is spoken of in Luke 18:9–14, where Jesus delineates between the false repentance of the self-righteous Pharisee who confesses the sins of others rather than his own, and the true repentance of the humble tax collector.

RELIGIOUS REPENTANCE

Religious repentance is the attempt to keep God happy or to get God to bless us. It is going through a ritual of confession but only to manipulate God to like us, not to work change in us. It is feeling sorry for getting caught in sin or feeling sorry for the consequences of sin, but not feeling sorry about the sin itself as a violation against God so severe that Jesus had to die for it.

This one may be the worst of all forms of false repentance. Religious repentance seeks in some way to pay God back by feeling really bad and wallowing in shame, guilt, and condemnation. It is void of the gospel truth that Jesus has taken our shame, guilt, and condemnation so that we are no longer under condemnation.[20] Through the gospel we receive forgiveness, but in religious repentance we grossly seek to earn it by attempting to punish ourselves—often by denying ourselves the pleasure of gifts from God. Religious repentance falsely believes that if we do not punish ourselves for our sin, God will be angry and punish us. The gospel tells us that Jesus was already punished in our place for our sin and that God is just, so he will not demand further retribution by punishing us. Furthermore, religious repentance is rare because religious people believe their righteousness before God resides in their good works and not solely in the cross of Jesus. As a result, religious repentance is filled with pride whereas the gospel brings humility, telling us that we truly are sinners, and joy, telling us that Jesus loves us and died to forgive our sins and take them away.

True repentance is among the greatest gifts given to us because of

---

[20]Rom. 8:1; Heb. 12:1–2.

Jesus' work on the cross for our sins. In it we find our humility, joy, forgiveness, hope, redemption, perspective, identity, and future. Instead of going through killing shame or superficial ritual, true repentance looks deep into the new heart to discover the godly desires that are at the core of our being by virtue of regeneration and actively turns away from anything and everything that hinders our deepest regenerated desires to glorify God. If we pause and take time to think and pray, along with other grace-based believers, and do what will make us most deeply happy, then we will almost always do the right thing. From the base of these godly desires, we can enter into battle with the sinful desires that motivate the sin we are confessing and repenting of.[21]

Through true repentance we will see the transformation of our lives, friendships, marriages, children, churches, cities, nations, and future offspring. Subsequently, it is wise for us not only to repent of sin to God when the Spirit prompts us, but also to humbly ask others we have sinned against to forgive us.

STEP 4: RESTITUTION

When we sin, we are also stealing from other people. This may include actual property or such things as trust, love, and intimacy. The Bible is clear that our redemption is a gift of grace from Jesus alone to be received by us through personal faith in him.[22] The result of this gift of salvation is a new heart that loves Jesus, is humble, and leads to an ongoing life of good works[23]—not so that Jesus will redeem us, but because he has. These good works will include our seeking to make restitution for all that we have done to damage others. Because we love people at a heart level, we want to restore what we took. Parts of the Bible, such as Exodus 22:1–17 and Numbers 5:5–10, speak of this kind of repayment, and men like the rich people in Nehemiah and Zacchaeus in the New Testament[24] modeled it when they repaid the people they had stolen from. One man I know was physically violent with his daughter until he was converted, and as an act of restitution he has very intentionally pursued a loving relationship with her by frequently calling her, taking

---

[21]Col. 3:5–15.
[22]Eph. 2:8–9.
[23]Eph. 2:10.
[24]Luke 19:8.

her out for meals, serving her, praying over her, and making new, loving memories in place of the love and joy he stole from her as a child.

STEP 5: RECONCILIATION

Once the previous steps have been undertaken, the sin that separated people is forgiven and taken away by Jesus with the hope that they can be brought back together in loving and trusting relationship. No matter what, if we commit ourselves to the lifelong pursuit of the above gospel process, then reconciliation with others is possible in this life. However, trust, friendship, and relationship are restored only upon confession of sin and are the fruit of repentance. Confession and repentance involve (1) real acknowledgment of the offense; (2) remorse (beyond "I'm sorry I got caught") for the pain it caused; (3) restitution where appropriate; and (4) renewal of character and lifestyle. Trust is always lessened or destroyed when sin is glossed over or "forgotten" without restoration. Such spiritual denial subverts forgiveness and reconciliation.

It almost goes without saying that this is a very difficult process. Even when all parties involved are working hard to ease the impact of sin, the bruising and pain sometimes make restoration impossible. If one or more fail to work through the process in good faith, restoration is impossible. But by God's grace, even if it does not occur on earth, we have the promise that it will happen in heaven if those involved are Christians.

Sadly, while everyone sins, not everyone deals with it in this kind of manner, and the result is a need for church discipline.

CHURCH DISCIPLINE

Church discipline is one of the most misunderstood and yet most desperately needed ministries within the church. We do not believe that it is an optional ministry of the church but one required of us in Scripture.

There are multiple mandates for church discipline to church leaders and churches throughout the New Testament from both Jesus and Paul.[25] Subsequently, it is imperative that unrepentant sin and false teaching by professing Christians be disciplined by the church through its leaders.

Discipline is the responsibility of the church body, which includes

---

[25]Matt. 18:15–17; Gal. 6:1; 1 Cor. 5:1–13; Titus 3:10–11; 2 Thess. 3:14–16.

Jesus Christ and the elders, deacons, and members of the church. Discipline is intended to bring believers in line with God's standard for his glory, the progress of his kingdom, and the blessedness of the individual as well.

Sadly, what most people think of when they hear "church discipline" is excommunication, the final stage of the biblical process. Excommunication is what happens when discipline fails to result in repentance and reconciliation. This misunderstanding plagues most discussions and most practices, sabotaging the grace of God that can come through church discipline.

Biblical discipline is, first and foremost, training. *Discipline* and *disciple* are from the same root word. Simply, to be a disciple of Jesus means to live a disciplined life and humbly receive discipline as needed. As a result, a wise disciple of Jesus accepts the truth of Proverbs 12:1, which says, "Whoever loves discipline loves knowledge, but he who hates reproof is stupid."

There are two major kinds of biblical discipline: formative and restorative. *Formative discipline* is primarily positive, instructive, and encouraging. It involves preaching, teaching, prayer, personal Bible study, small-group fellowship, and countless other enjoyable activities that challenge and encourage us to love and serve God more wholeheartedly. *Restorative discipline* has a corrective purpose. When we forget or disobey what God has taught us, he corrects us. One of the ways he does this when we fall into sin is to call the church to seek after us and lead us back on the right track. This process is likened to a shepherd seeking after a lost sheep. Thus, corrective or restorative discipline is never to be done in a harsh, vengeful, or self-righteous manner. It is always to be carried out in humility and love, with the goal of restoring someone to a closer walk with Christ. When we speak of "church discipline" in this chapter, we are referring particularly to restorative discipline. Though we put our focus on restorative discipline, especially on its more difficult and controversial aspects, it must never be separated from nor substituted for formative discipline, the process of discipleship and spiritual formation.

In the days of Nehemiah, God's people rebuilt the wall encircling their city with a trowel in one hand and a sword in another.[26] With the

---

[26]Neh. 4:15–23.

trowel they built, and with the sword they defended. The images of the sword and the trowel are incredibly important because they show that anything we build for God (e.g., spiritual life, marriage, children, business, ministry) requires carefully undertaken, painstaking work as typified by the bricklayer's trowel. Yet, building alone is insufficient because what is built can and will be destroyed unless it is also defended and protected. Subsequently, the ability to wield a sword in our other hand is a noble and godly skill to be mastered. In keeping with this analogy, formative discipline is trowel work and restorative discipline is sword work.

There are many reasons why the church must wield this sword.

1) Through church discipline we seek to glorify God by obedience to his instructions in the maintenance of proper church government. God's Word makes it plain that he intends discipline of various types to be a part of church life.[27] It is always glorifying to God when we obey his Word rather than cater to our own ease and expediency. At every church, the first and foremost concern in all we do is God's glory.

2) The value of church discipline is reclaiming offenders. In every type of discipline, whether it is gentle correction, admonition, rebuke, or excommunication, we seek the restoration of the offender.[28] This is in keeping with the mandate to make disciples[29] and present everyone mature in Christ.[30]

3) Discipline is valuable in that it vindicates the integrity and honor of Christ by exhibiting fidelity to his principles.[31] The church that refuses to exercise discipline can command neither the world's respect nor the confidence of its own members.

4) Discipline in the church helps to deter others from sin.[32]

5) Discipline in the church helps to protect the church from false teachers and wolves that cause heresy and divisiveness.[33]

6) Church discipline is valuable to prevent giving God cause to set himself against a continually sinful local church.[34]

---

[27] Matt. 18:15–19; Rom. 16:17; 1 Cor. 5; 1 Thess. 5:14; 2 Thess. 3:6–15; 1 Tim. 5:20; 6:3; Titus 1:14; 2:15; 3:10; Rev. 2:2, 14, 15, 20.
[28] Matt. 18:15; 1 Cor. 5:5; Gal. 6:11.
[29] Matt. 28:18ff.
[30] Eph. 4:11ff.
[31] 2 Cor. 2:9, 17.
[32] 1 Tim. 5:20.
[33] Acts 20:25–31; Titus 1:10–11.
[34] Rev. 2:14–25.

One goal of all church discipline is reconciliation. In the Bible *reconciliation* is the word used to refer to the process by which God changes human beings and adjusts them to the standard of his perfect character. God reconciles us to himself through the death, burial, and resurrection of Jesus Christ.[35] God does not need to be reconciled to man. That has been accomplished in the propitiatory work of the cross, which is the basis and power for the sinner's reconciliation. No reconciliation can be accomplished apart from repentance and personal application of the payment of penalty at the cross that was accomplished through Jesus to us.

We are going to hurt others, and we are going to be hurt by others because we are sinners.[36] The gospel provides a means for reconciliation between God and people and between people and other people. Therefore, when a Christian encounters discipline, it is to prompt him or her to live in accordance with the standard of God so that reconciliation with God and others can occur.

Another obvious goal of discipline is to protect the flock from doctrinal error. The apostle Paul warns the elders,

Pay careful attention to yourselves and to all the flock, in which the Holy Spirit has made you overseers, to care for the church of God, which he obtained with his own blood. I know that after my departure fierce wolves will come in among you, not sparing the flock; and from among your own selves will arise men speaking twisted things, to draw away the disciples after them. Therefore be alert, remembering that for three years I did not cease night or day to admonish everyone with tears.[37]

Lastly, punitive correction is another biblical (though often unpopular) means by which repentance is sought. First Corinthians 5:9–13 talks about punishment for the unrepentant sinner. This correction is not vindictive or joyous punishment. Christians in the Corinthian church were to gather together in order to take action against the offending brother.[38] Paul defines this as "punishment by the majority."[39] As a protective measure, we also find that the whole church in Rome and in Thessalonica

---

[35]2 Cor. 5:21.
[36]James 4:1–2.
[37]Acts 20:28–31.
[38]1 Cor. 5:4–5; Phil. 3:17–19.
[39]2 Cor. 2:6.

were to take action with regard to the unruly and schismatic, not just a few.[40] The goal of these corrective measures is to make every effort for Christians who love their wayward brother or sister to show their overwhelming sorrow and concern in an effort to compel the sinner toward repentance and reconciliation with God and their church.

THE THEOLOGY OF CHURCH DISCIPLINE

Through the natural course of a church community, there are invariably times in which sin and error need to be addressed. Therefore, it is imperative for the people of God to know the various means of resolution God has given in his Word for addressing sins and errors. Sadly, very few churches actually practice church discipline with any degree of consistency. The following are nine guiding principles from Scripture on the matter of church discipline.

1) When sin has come between people, the goal is repentance and reconciliation, along with recompense, if needed.

2) Church leaders must always pursue the protection of the gospel's reputation and the well-being of the entire church, not just the interests of individuals who have sinned. This explains why sometimes individuals must be put out of the church.[41]

3) Such matters in the church are entrusted to Christian leaders who must be careful not to abuse in any way the responsibility to oversee the obedience of its members.[42]

4) Discipline is unpleasant but, in the end, produces a holy people by distinguishing between the world and the church.[43]

5) All matters in the church, including church discipline, are to be done in a fitting and orderly manner.[44]

6) Because the situations leading to church discipline can be incredibly frustrating, it is important that those involved don't let their anger lead them into sin.[45]

7) For the truth to emerge, the elders must hear firsthand reports from all sides of a dispute before a decision is reached.[46]

---

[40]Rom. 16:17–18; 2 Thess. 3:6–15.
[41]Deut. 17:7; 19:19; 21:21; 22:24; 24:7; 1 Cor. 5:13; 2 Cor. 2:7; Rev. 2:2.
[42]1 Pet. 5:1–5.
[43]Heb. 12:11.
[44]1 Cor. 14:40.
[45]Prov. 16:32; 17:27.
[46]Prov. 18:17; Acts 15.

8) When at all possible, multiple witnesses should be required.[47]

9) The fellowship of the church is a regular time appointed by God when his people are to be reminded that unrepentant sin and unnecessary division are unacceptable to a holy God. It is a time to look at sin in light of God's grace and commitment to help us grow.[48]

At Mars Hill Church the issue of church discipline is so important that we have included a statement about it in our membership covenant (see Appendix). Members of Mars Hill Church and all other professing Christians who regularly attend or fellowship there who err in doctrine, or who unrepentantly engage in conduct that violates Scripture as determined by an elder team (e.g., campus, departmental, ad hoc, executive, all-elder council), are subject to church discipline. Church discipline is exercised in cases such as the following, examples of which are found in Scripture:

- When a Christian sins against another Christian, and it cannot be overlooked in love.[49]
- When a Christian who professes faith lives in sin without repentance.[50]
- When a Christian continually blasphemes God.[51]
- When someone encourages or promotes false doctrine.[52]
- When a Christian is a habitual doctrine debater.[53]
- When a Christian will heed only false teachers.[54]
- When a Christian is sincere but deceived.[55]
- When a teacher is in moral sin or doctrinal error.[56]
- When an elder is in moral sin or doctrinal error.[57]
- When a Christian appoints himself or herself to leadership.[58]
- When a Christian is divisive.[59]
- When a Christian is an idle busybody.[60]

---

[47]Deut. 19:15; 2 Cor. 13:1.
[48]1 Cor. 11:17–32.
[49]Prov. 19:11; Matt. 18:15–22.
[50]Gal. 6:1–5; 1 Cor. 5:1–13; 2 Cor. 2:5–11.
[51]1 Tim. 1:18–20.
[52]Acts 20:25–31; Gal. 1:6–9; 1 Tim. 1:4–7; 4:1–8.
[53]2 Tim. 2:14–26.
[54]2 Tim. 4:1–5.
[55]2 Cor. 11:3–4, 13–15.
[56]James 3:1.
[57]1 Tim. 5:19–21.
[58]3 John 9–10.
[59]Titus 3:10–11.
[60]2 Thess. 3:6, 11.

- When a Christian promotes legalism.[61]
- When a Christian refuses to obey civil laws.[62]
- When an alleged offended Christian seeks legal recourse.[63]
- When a Christian has repeatedly rejected counsel by a church elder.[64]
- When a Christian is not consistently in community.[65]
- When a Christian leaves the church to pursue sin or heresy.[66]

Perhaps church discipline is so under-practiced because it is so under-taught. It seems reasonable to expect that if Christians understood how to undertake church discipline practically, they would do so. To that end, the following five steps are offered.

STEP 1: WEIGH THE OFFENSE

The first thing those who have been sinned against should consider is whether they should simply forgive the person(s) involved, overlook the sin, and let it go. Sometimes the issue is so minor and the sin so out of character, or there are extenuating circumstances such that granting some mercy is required. A woman I know, who was generally very respectful and loving toward her husband, became irritable and spoke harshly to him for a few days after the death of her father. He knew she was grieving, stressed out, and sleep deprived, so he continually prayed for her silently and showered her with loving affection. Within a few days she apologized to him for how she had treated him and was back to her old self. Indeed, God himself models "kindness [that] is meant to lead you to repentance."[67] Furthermore, Proverbs 19:11 says, "Good sense makes one slow to anger, and it is his glory to overlook an offense." People are not perfect. As sinners we need to be gracious, patient, and merciful with one another just as God is with us, or the church will spend all of its time doing nothing but having church discipline trials.

It is worth stressing, however, that we cannot simply overlook an offense if doing so is motivated by our cowardice, fear of conflict, and/or lack of concern for someone and their sanctification. In the end, it is the

---

[61]Gal. 5:7–15; Phil. 3:2–3.
[62]Rom. 13:1–7.
[63]1 Cor. 6:1–8.
[64]1 Thess. 5:12–13; 2 Thess. 3:14–15; Heb. 13:17.
[65]Col. 3:16 ; Heb. 10:24–25.
[66]1 John 2:19.
[67]Rom. 2:4.

glory of God, the reputation of Jesus, the well-being of the church, and the holiness of the individual that must outweigh any personal desires for a life of ease that avoids dealing with sin biblically. Sometimes God in his providential love for us allows us to be involved in dealing with another's sin as part of our sanctification and growth. It is good for us and for the sinner, the church, and the reputation of the gospel if we respond willingly to the task God has set before us.

STEP 2: CONSIDER THE CRIME

Sometimes the offense or sin is also a criminal act. In such cases we need to call the police so that we are obeying the governing authorities and their laws as Scripture states.[68] State governments specifically require churches to report any abuse against minors and seniors. Tragically, some Christians and churches rebel, believing they are exempt from government authority. They take the law into their own hands, trying to substitute church discipline for legal process and allow crimes to go unpunished.

Hanging on the wall in my church office is an old black-and-white photo of many young children posing together in front of their church building. I found the picture in a church building many years later, after the church had died and closed. Curious as to what had happened to all the children and why none had remained in the church when they became adults, I interviewed an elderly woman who had attended the church for nearly all of her life. She said that the pastor's brother had allegedly sexually abused some of the children in the church basement, but no one had contacted the police. He was not brought to justice in this life and the families left the church, thereby leading to its death. As a daddy to five children, I fight back tears every time I look at the faces of the kids in that picture and wish someone had called the police to investigate. There is simply no excuse for a church to cover up a crime by seeking to handle it internally rather than notifying the proper authorities. When this happens, it is often women and children who live in harm's way without legal protection and justice, which is a sin.

In addition to contacting the police and allowing them to investigate, a church can and should also do its own investigation and render its own verdict regarding the guilt or innocence of an alleged sinner and

---

[68]Rom. 13:1–7.

then impose its own consequences. Still, church discipline must never be done in isolation when a crime has possibly been committed because not only is the sinner part of the church, but they are also part of greater society and are subject to courts in both realms.

One issue that can complicate the ability of a church leader to notify the authorities if and when a crime has been committed is confidentiality. There is a widespread misunderstanding that the so-called sanctity of the confessional exempts churches from the laws regarding reporting crimes. In fact, failure to report is a crime. While all pastors and counselors must respect people's confidentiality, they must also remember that there are limits to confidentiality. Specifically, it ends where crime begins. We are in no position to give legal counsel in criminal matters, but we encourage church leaders to hire reputable attorneys and have them check the law for specifics. After doing so, the church leaders may choose to include something on the issue in their church bylaws for legal protection. Ours state:

> Members of Mars Hill Church are not guaranteed confidentiality regarding issues of church discipline, and understand that in submitting themselves to the authority of the church, issues of a sensitive or personal nature may become known to others. This includes, but is not limited to, notification of the authorities if a crime has been committed or if a real threat of someone being endangered exists, as well as other violations of scripture that may not result in physical danger.

Furthermore, we do not conduct biblical counseling with someone unless they sign a waiver relinquishing their right to confidentiality. If we refer people to an outside counselor, we likewise have them and their counselor sign a confidentiality waiver so that if we need to know about something, or if we need to notify the police, we can without legal recourse. Without this kind of foresight, sinners corner church leaders between a proverbial rock and a hard place, like the guy who early in my pastoral ministry told me he had cheated on his wife repeatedly and feared he had a venereal disease but did not want to tell her and expected me to cover for him under the guise of confidentiality. I just laughed loudly as I picked up my phone to call his wife while he threatened to sue me.

Paul also has some things to say regarding the involvement of secular courts in disputes between Christians.[69] Ours is an incredibly litigious society. Things were not much different in Paul's day. Greece, home of the world's first democracy, had a bustling court system. Paul seeks to address how a Christian should relate to the secular court.

Paul says that disputes between believers should be decided within the church by appointed impartial people who love God and his justice.[70] This refers to what we call civil law. Criminal matters, which cover such things as treason and murder, are not issues in which believers sue each other but are offenses against the law. Christians are welcome to pursue justice on civil matters if they believe they have been wronged and are to do so within the church if at all possible. A few clarifying points need to be made on this matter, as 1 Corinthians 6:1–11 has been subject to widespread misuse:

- Paul is referring to disputes between believers, not to crimes.
- Paul understands that some things needing judgment are not even considered improper outside of the church (e.g., fornication, adultery, gossip) because they are sins, not crimes.
- Paul is not forbidding Christians and churches from disclosing a crime to secular authorities. Paul is not forbidding a Christian from filing a suit against a non-Christian.
- Paul is not saying that a Christian can never sue another Christian but rather that an effort must be made to resolve it outside of secular court.

Any Christian considering bringing a charge against another Christian must be careful not to harm the reputation of the gospel in the eyes of non-Christians. In some instances it may be preferable to suffer loss than to publicly harm the reputation of Jesus. In addition, Christians must never seek to use litigation as a way to accumulate wealth or power, although it can be used for the just collection of stolen wealth.

While justice is to be pursued in this life, the sad truth is that ultimate and perfect justice will not come until the day of judgment by Jesus at the end of time. On that day those who habitually practice sin will be exposed for what they are—unbelieving non-Christians who got their rewards on earth only to spend their eternity in hell locked outside of God's kingdom.

---

[69] 1 Cor. 6:1–11.
[70] Rom. 13:1–7.

Because of Jesus we do not need to accept ourselves for who we are; rather, we can be transformed into someone else. Subsequently, true Christians are former perverts, homosexuals,[71] adulterers, thieves, addicts, swindlers, and liars. Because of Jesus and the power of the Spirit, Christians can be so transformed that they do not need constant judgment from Christian and secular courts because they do not live a life of habitual sin.

STEP 3: ADMONISH

If a sin seems too serious to overlook, we are to go to our brothers or sisters in private, discover the truth, and, if sin is present, appeal to them with a spirit of reconciliation to repent.[72] In this we are trusting God the Holy Spirit to be faithful to convict their conscience of sin. In this step, those who have been offended must be careful not to ascribe guilt to others without faithfully seeking the truth about what was done or said. Hearsay and secondhand reports from one person do not qualify as a credible charge.[73]

STEP 4: REPROVE

If the one we have confronted does not respond to our repeated appeals, we are to go back again to the erring one with one or two other believers, so that they too can urge the sinning believer to turn back to God and serve as witnesses that we are making every effort to lovingly bring the sinner to repentance.[74]

Philippians 4:2–3 gives a practical illustration of two people who have a personal dispute. There is no hint of immoral sin or doctrinal heresy. For some reason, they just do not get along and are causing tension in the church because of their differences. The apostle Paul deals with this by setting up a mediator to cause them to agree in the Lord and expects them to submit to the mediator. Sometimes there is sin that needs formal discipline, and sometimes there are hurt feelings and strained relationships that need mediation.

If the Christian persists in sin, we may seek the formal involvement of the church, initially from the elders, and, if necessary, the elders may

---

[71]Gen. 19:1–29, cf. Lev. 18:22; 20:13; Rom. 1:26–27; 1 Tim. 1:9–10; Jude 1:7.
[72]Matt. 18:15; Rom. 15:14; 2 Cor. 5:18–21; Col. 3:16; 1 Thess. 5:14; 2 Thess. 3:14–15; Titus 3:10.
[73]Deut. 19:15; 1 Tim. 5:19.
[74]Matt. 18:15; Eph. 5:11; 1 Tim. 5:20; 2 Tim. 4:2; Titus 1:9, 13; 2:15.

inform and invite the prayers and assistance of the entire congregation. As a general rule, the lead pastor appoints a team to adjudicate each discipline case. At this point the member is formally placed under church discipline. At the discretion of the elders, the fact that a member is under discipline may be brought to the attention of the entire church or campus, and the member under discipline may be removed from any leadership roles and fellowship opportunities. To ensure there is no confusion or miscommunication, the member under discipline should be notified in writing of the disciplinary status and any applicable consequences. Furthermore, specific elders must be appointed to investigate the situation and work for repentance and reconciliation.[75]

Mediation and arbitration may be used at this time to help reconcile two opposing parties. Mediation means bringing another person along to help resolve conflict and explore solutions if the conflict cannot be resolved through private peacemaking.[76] Arbitrators can also be appointed to listen to both sides and render a binding decision about substantive issues.[77] In all of this, it is imperative that both sides of the dispute agree to submit to the findings of the mediator or arbitrator if the process is to be a worthwhile use of time and energy.

STEP 5: SEPARATE

If these efforts do not bring a believer to repentance and reconciliation, or if a person refuses to be reconciled, Jesus commands us to treat that one as "a Gentile and a tax collector."[78] This means we no longer have normal, casual fellowship with the believer but instead use any encounters to bring the gospel of reconciliation to him and lovingly urge him to repent and turn back in obedience to God.[79]

Not only must a church have biblically qualified leaders holding biblical offices, there must also be a clear understanding of various courts of leaders that make various decisions so as to avoid confusion and conflict. The offices represent the individual people and their roles, while the courts represent decision-making teams with a defined

---

[75]Gal. 6:1.
[76]Matt. 18:16.
[77]1 Cor. 6:1–9.
[78]Matt. 18:17.
[79]In the vernacular of the time of Christ, "Gentile" and "tax collector" referenced those outside the covenant, and hence those outside the fellowship of the gathered assembly. These terms carry a connotation of betrayal rather than a neutral non-Christian. You don't treat this person merely as a non-Christian, but as someone who is collaborating with the enemy.

authority and responsibility. This point is incredibly important when it comes to the matter of church discipline. The elders and pastors in the church need to define who is officially on the court overseeing the investigation of a church member.

In the early days of our church when we had fewer people and fewer elders, the entire council of elders acted together as a court on all cases of formal church discipline. In time, as the number of church members and the number of elders grew, it became impractical to continue doing so. Today we have thirty-two elders scattered among seven campuses, and the amount of work involved to bring them all up to speed on every discipline case among our 2,200 church members would require them to neglect all of their other pastoral duties. So, for our purposes, we have decided that a church discipline court is defined as two or more elders who follow the process articulated in this chapter. The reason we have chosen two elders is that the Bible uses that number as the minimum requirement for establishing the facts regarding church discipline cases.[80] Practically, having at least two elders also ensures that one elder cannot wield too much power.

In convening a court, the elders involved first meet to confess their sins to one another, seeking to walk together in holiness before God. They also spend considerable time fasting, praying, and studying Scripture alone and together to make every effort to have their hearts and minds open to the leading of God the Holy Spirit. Together they discuss how they will practically work out the details laid forth in this chapter, including the distribution of the workload and a time line. The distribution of work includes but is not limited to determining which questions the elder court will ask the person being investigated, who else will be brought in as a witness, what documents (if any) will be allowed in as evidence, and what Scriptures most clearly speak to the sin being investigated. Once the process is laid out, the elders overseeing the investigation then proceed to follow the steps in this chapter.

If members of our church or those who regularly participate in church activities are found guilty, they may be dismissed from the church by the agreement of the elder court. The dismissal of a church member may be made known to all church members. If the offense is a publicly known matter, the executive elders (our senior team of elders)

---

[80]Matt. 18:16–20; 1 Tim. 5:19.

have the discretion to determine if the member's discipline should be made known to the entire church. The Bible does not support an appeal process by the one being removed from fellowship unless true repentance is demonstrated, and so we do not practice it, in general. To do so could allow an unrepentant sinner to take months or even years of various elders' time and wreak absolute havoc in the church by continually fighting for a different verdict.

An offense may be serious enough to warrant the temporary, immediate removal of a member from the church body for the well-being of the church until a thorough investigation can be completed. Removal does not equate to guilt but allows an opportunity to investigate before other members are affected. If someone is accused of rape, for example, he will be removed from fellowship for the well-being of others in the church until his guilt or innocence can be determined.

Members who resign their membership while under discipline do not terminate the discipline process. It is expected that a member under discipline and the elders will walk together toward repentance until full reconciliation takes place. Until it does, the member may be notified that he or she is not to be present at church-sponsored functions for such a period of time as is deemed necessary for the safety and well-being of others. If someone under discipline begins attending another church, we notify the leaders of that church that they are unrepentant and have been removed from fellowship in our church. We ask that they also deny that person fellowship in their church so that we can continue working to bring the sinning one to repentance in a holy fashion. Admittedly, this is not always the result, but we make every effort to work for repentance and reconciliation so that our conscience is clear before God, and so we can tell our people that we earnestly did all that we could.

TREATMENT OF AN UNREPENTANT BELIEVER

Jesus instructed us to treat one who will not repent as "a Gentile and a tax collector."[81] Although rejection and disassociation may seem harsh, these responses are simply a means by which the individual in question may come to an acknowledgment of his or her sin and repent. The idea is not that we stop caring for them but that when they sin and refuse to

---

[81]Matt. 18:17.

repent, we treat them as if they were enemies of the gospel. We find this sort of response in 1 Timothy 1:20, Titus 3:10, and 1 Corinthians 5:1–7.

Paul admonished church members in 2 Thessalonians 3:6 and 14 to withdraw from the brother that walks disobediently and to have nothing to do with him. First Corinthians 5:9–11 is the strongest of all these biblical admonitions, commanding us not to associate or share a meal with believers who are guilty of sexual immorality, greed, idolatry, revilement, drunkenness, or swindling. Because sharing a meal is symbolic of hospitable and cordial fellowship, it is not to be allowed under the circumstances. When you put a person out of the church, you don't have him over for a meal. You don't treat him like a brother. You don't treat him as an unbeliever. You treat him like an outcast.

Even though we don't have fellowship with unrepentant Christians, we do not regard them as personal enemies but as enemies of the gospel. When we see them, we warn them as brothers that they are acting like enemies. Until they repent, we cannot pretend to be in fellowship with them.[82]

There is a sense in which you never really let the unrepentant sinner go. Though you don't associate with him, you keep calling him back. He is put out for the purity of the church but is always admonished to come back.[83] Practically speaking, it is fine for you to see an unrepentant brother as long as your speech or actions do not dismiss the gravity of the sin or imply that reconciliation has been completed when he has not yet repented. He is a brother, but because of his persistence in sin, he is separating himself from the body.

In closing, the words of Romans 12:18 are important to remember. They instruct us to be at peace with everybody if we are given the chance. We are to be willing to forgive everybody of everything. As soon as the individual repents, we should welcome him or her back into the body of Christ with open arms as a demonstration of the gospel truth that where sin abounds, the grace of God much more abounds![84]

---

[82]2 Thess. 3:15.
[83]2 Cor. 2:5–11.
[84]Rom. 5:15.

ANSWERS TO COMMON QUESTIONS ABOUT CHURCH DISCIPLINE

JESUS SAYS TO TREAT SOMEONE UNDER DISCIPLINE AS "A GENTILE AND A TAX COLLECTOR," THAT IS, LIKE AN OUTCAST. BUT SHOULDN'T WE SOCIALIZE WITH THAT PERSON, SO HE'LL SEE THE LOVE OF JESUS IN US?

Gentiles refused God's revelation. Tax collectors were traitors, Jews who worked for the hated Roman conquerors. They are consciously rebellious against God and his people. Jews would not socialize with them at all because they were to the Jews what Judas was to Jesus.

People who claim to be Christians but refuse to confess sin indicate by their lives that they are rebels against Jesus and his spiritual family. Therefore, they cannot be allowed to enjoy the fellowship of the church body. They receive the compassion and urgency needed to encourage them to repent. They must not receive fellowship of the community that is reserved for fellow disciples and seekers.

IT SEEMS MEAN FOR JESUS TO TEACH US TO TREAT UNREPENTANT CHURCH MEMBERS AS OUTSIDERS. WHY WOULD HE DO THAT?

It's really because Jesus wants us to love them. Love means seeking a person's best for their sake and for the sake of the entire church body. We must realize that they are a danger to themselves and to others. To be "nice" to them enables and encourages the continuation of the danger.

Consider the case of a pedophile. No one says you should be nice and invite him to come to the children's picnic day in the park. Rather, you isolate him and press him to get treatment because of how dangerous he is. If he refuses, you realize that the problem is his persistent sin, even when he's whining about how mean you are. Those who agree with him and support him are joining him in hurting himself and the church body.

Other sins seem less dangerous than pedophilia, and in a sense that's true. Some sins are greater than others in nature and in their impact on people (Lev. 4:1–35; 5:15–19; Matt. 11:20–24; 23:15; Luke 12:48; John 19:11; 1 Tim. 5:8; James 3:1). But all sin is sin and an offense against God and people.

Meanness is dealing with that sin self-righteously and legalistically, delighting in the punishment of the offender we don't like. Love means moving people to righteousness out of love and doing so graciously.

The goal is that they would confess their sin and repent through the deep sorrow of lost fellowship (2 Cor. 2:5–7). We want them to know they are truly loved by a church body (2 Cor. 5:8). We pray that the Holy Spirit will work in their hearts because they miss and long for the normal fellowship of other believers.

PRACTICALLY SPEAKING, HOW CAN WE TREAT AN UNREPENTANT CHURCH MEMBER AS AN OUTSIDER?

When we see the unrepentant member in the store, we are not called to turn away ostentatiously, stick our noses in the air, and start singing "I have decided to follow Jesus." We treat them as outsiders by refusing to have normal social or business relations with them. Where we do connect, we do it cordially, but we always prayerfully admonish and encourage them to confess and repent. If they do confess and repent, then we inform the church.

The church also asks the person not to attend regular worship services and other church activities. This would include refusing them participation in Communion until they repent.

While changing the way we associate with the sinning member, we treat the rest of that person's family as normal as possible insofar as the other family members do not act as facilitators, defenders, or liaisons for the unrepentant family member. The whole family will feel the effects of the sin, even those who are not a participant in the actual transgression.

DON'T WE HAVE TO FORGIVE EVERYONE, EVEN WHEN THEY WON'T REPENT OF THEIR SIN?

It is not this simple. In Luke 17:3–4 Jesus said, "If your brother sins, rebuke him, and if he repents, forgive him, and if he sins against you seven times in the day, and turns to you seven times, saying, 'I repent,' you must forgive him." Matthew omits the "if he repents" phrase, so it sounds as if we must always forgive (Matt. 18:21–22). But Jesus had just told the people, "If your brother sins against you, go and tell him his fault" (Matt.18:15). This is not simply forgiving him and moving on.

Forgiveness means that no matter how much we may have been hurt by others' sin, we give up our right to hurt them back. We love them and seek their best. Forgiveness does not mean that we ignore their sin. Neither does it mean that we act like the sin never happened and go on in trusting relationship with the offender. That happens only after humble confession and honest repentance. But we must keep in mind that repentance is not merely sadness, tears, or behavioral change. In true repentance, there is a change of mind or mindset or values (*metanoia*). This change of mind will always evidence itself in a change of behavior. On this point, John the Baptizer admonished people to produce fruit in keeping with repentance (Luke 3:7), and Paul said that sinners should repent and turn to God, performing deeds in keeping with their repentance (Acts 26:20).

Remember that while God loves the world enough to die for it (John 3:16; Rom. 5:8), and he reaches out to his enemies with love (Rom. 5:10–11; Col. 1:21–22), he does not forgive everyone. His wrath remains on those who refuse the Son (John 3:36; 2 Thess. 1:8–9). There are some whom he forgives but refuses to trust (Num. 14:20–23). But when they confess and repent, God is consistent to forgive and cleanse (1 John 1:9). When they confess and repent, we forgive them and do everything we can to restore trust and relationship. Our forgiveness should be like God's (Eph. 4:32).

HOW SHOULD WE TREAT A REPENTANT CHRISTIAN?

Once godly repentance has been demonstrated, we freely and gladly receive a sinning Christian back into fellowship. A person dismissed from a church for disciplinary reasons will be reinstated to full membership under the leadership of the elder team that oversaw the person's discipline. If the dismissal was public, the restoration must be too. Jesus said, "There is joy before the angels of God over one sinner who repents" (Luke 15:10). We get to join that rejoicing.

HOW DO WE DO CHURCH DISCIPLINE FOR AN ELDER OR PASTOR?

The principles for church discipline that apply to church members also pertain to every church leader, including elders and pastors. Spiritual authority that accompanies the office of elder can in no way be an excuse for overlooking sin or error of any kind. James 3:1 is clear that "Not many of you should become teachers, my brothers, for you know that we who teach will be judged with greater strictness." We hear Paul speaking with gravity in 1 Timothy 5:21: "In the presence of God and of Christ Jesus and of the elect angels I charge you to keep these rules without prejudging, doing nothing from partiality."

First Timothy 5:19 tells us to accept a charge against an elder only on the witness of two or three witnesses, echoing Deuteronomy 19:15–19 and Matthew 18:15–17. Paul recognized the danger in holding to just one disgruntled person's charge against an elder or pastor. When there is corroboration of the charges of sin, everything must be carefully investigated under the supervision of the elders.

When a pastor sins at a personal level, he must be confronted in grace. If he repents, that is the end of it. But if he persists in the personal sin or if he commits a sin against the office of elder, he must be rebuked publicly (1 Tim. 5:19–20) or dismissed from the office (1 Cor. 9:27). His sin disqualifies him from his elder role when he persists in sins against the responsibilities of the office or in ways that destroy his qualifications for elder. If a pastor speaks harshly to his wife, for example, he should be held accountable for the action. He should be admonished for his sin as would any believer. The sin would merit a public rebuke if the conduct was habitual, or impenitent, especially if it were public. It would become disqualifying if it became clear that his marriage ceased to be a model for marriages in the church (1 Pet. 5:3).

To help ensure the Bible's warning against an elder's doing anything out of favoritism or partiality, it may be wise to get external help in assessing the charge. Respected denominational leadership or local godly pastors are best suited to participate in the examination and trial of an elder charged with a disqualifying sin.

Church discipline simply cannot be biblically practiced unless it begins at the top, with the elders. When it is done well at this level, it is more likely to be practiced throughout the church for the good of all and the glory of God.

CHAPTER EIGHT

HOW IS LOVE EXPRESSED IN A CHURCH?

Anyone who does not love does not know God, because God is love.

1   J O H N   4 : 8

✝

As cancer treatment began, he was no longer able to attend church or school and could no longer play outside, which felt like torture. His mom posted pictures of him on the Internet, lying in the hospital bed without any hair, looking thin and weak.

As concerned as I was for the little boy and his single mom, I was simultaneously encouraged by the response of some people in our church. Included in the bedtime routine of my children and many others in the church were prayers for the little boy and his family. Many of the children in the church emptied their piggy banks and brought in their money to buy the boy a video game player and games so that he could have some fun while in cancer treatment. Some women with gifts of caring sought out his mom, built friendships, and listened to her heart, sharing hopes, fears, and tears. When she could say nothing in her overwhelming grief, they sat silently with her.

One Sunday we brought the mom on stage so the church could pray for her. We all joined her hopeful sadness, feeling her little boy's absence deeply. A couple in the church responded with incredible grace as the Spirit made her plight powerfully real to them. Some hours prior to the church service, the couple had purchased a new truck, and though they had never met the mom or her son, they decided to return the truck to the dealer and give the money to her. Their gift enabled the mother to take roughly a year off work to care for her sick son.

God empowered the medical procedures, and her little boy was healed. One of the godly men in the church who came alongside to help them grew to love her. So he married her and adopted her beloved son, and today they are a loving Christian family.

As a pastor I have seen similar acts innumerable times. The number of vehicles given by church members to families in need, meals delivered to those healing from illness or a birth, dollars informally given from those who have to those who need, hours of free child care, discounted homes sold, goods given such as children's clothes and furniture, and hours of service for everything from home repairs to moving assistance are beyond measure. But God knows all that has been done and also named it in the Bible with one word: love.

Love is one of the most important words in the Bible and appears roughly eight hundred times in the Old and New Testaments. In our culture, though, it is one of the most misunderstood words and is used for everything from sexual sin to sloppy sentimentality. In 1 John 4:8 the Bible plainly states that "God is love." Subsequently, to understand love as the Scripture speaks of it, we must begin with the Trinitarian God who is the source and ultimate example of love.

Based upon the teaching of the Bible, Christians believe that in the unity of God's essence there are three persons—the Father, the Son, and the Holy Spirit—who are fully equal in essence, attributes, and eternality, yet eternally relating in fully personal ways. While the word *Trinity* does not appear in Scripture, the concept very clearly does. The church father Tertullian (AD 155–220) was the first to use the word *Trinity*. To say that God exists as a Trinity does not mean there are three Gods, or that one God merely manifests himself as solely Father, Son, or Holy Spirit on various occasions. Rather, the Lord is one,[1] but his oneness, like the oneness of a marriage,[2] contains more than a single person.[3]

---

[1]Deut. 6:4.
[2]Gen. 2:24.
[3]Matt. 28:19–20.

Each person of the Trinity thinks, feels, acts, and speaks in self-consciousness and continuity of identity. Each is able to understand self and creation, to initiate loving relationship with each other and humanity. Father, Son, and Spirit exist and relate in perfect loving harmony in the one divine essence. Christians of all ages and branches affirm that there is no God but the Lord, who is Father, Son, and Spirit.

Inextricably connected to the doctrine of the Trinity is love. In the very nature of God there is a continuous outpouring of love, communication, and oneness. In perfect love, the three persons are characterized by reciprocal self-dedication to the good of the whole Trinity. Because God is a relational community of love, God is the source and model of all that is love. During his earthly life, Jesus frequently spoke about the deep love between him and God the Father. In John 3:35 we read, "The Father loves the Son and has given all things into his hand." In John 5:20 we read, "The Father loves the Son and shows him all that he himself is doing." Also, in John 14:31 we read, "I [Jesus] do as the Father has commanded me, so that the world may know that I love the Father."

God's love compelled him to make us in his image and likeness to be in loving relationship with him and with one another. God did not make us because he was lonely, or because he wanted someone to talk to, and certainly not because he was relationally needy. He has experienced relationship perfectly within the Trinity.

However, God did make us to worship, to pour ourselves out in love to him in a relationship of self-giving adoration and action patterned after the community of the Trinity. Speaking of creation, in general, which also applies to the creation of mankind, in particular, the Orthodox theologian Kallistos Ware says:

> The world was not created unintentionally or out of necessity; it is not an automatic emanation or overflowing from God, but the consequence of divine choice. We should think, not of God the Manufacturer or God the Craftsman, but of God the Lover. By voluntary choice God created the world in "ecstatic" love, so that there might be besides himself other beings to participate in the life and the love that are his.[4]

Furthermore, because men and women are made in God's image

---

[4]Kallistos Ware, *The Orthodox Way* (Crestwood, NY: St. Vladimirs Seminary Press, 1995), 44.

and likeness, we too are created for loving relationship with God and one another. This need for relationship and love explains why, prior to sin even entering the world, the one thing declared to be "not good" was "that the man should be alone; I will make him a helper fit for him."[5]

Tragically, because of sin, our love and worship are marred. As sinners separated from God, we are prone to love people, things, and experiences as gods rather than God. Too many people worship angelic beings who pretend to be god.[6] As worshipers, we pour ourselves out in adoration and action for the demons, people, things, and experiences that we love in place of God.

In love, however, the Trinitarian community of God enacted a plan through which we sinners might be saved from our sin and reconciled to God and one another in loving relationship. The Bible reveals that God's loving plan was that God the Father would send God the Son into human history as Immanuel, God with us in flesh. The God-man, Jesus Christ, lived as a perfectly Spirit-filled human, a perfect example of our life of love for God and others. He died on a cross in the place of sinners and then resurrected to bodily life to bring us newness of life so that God the Spirit would indwell lost sinners, regenerating them and sealing them as God's possession.[7]

Subsequently, the most loving person who has ever walked the earth is Jesus Christ. The most loving act the world has ever seen is Jesus' death on the cross in place of sinners, reconciling them into loving relationship with God. Indeed, Romans 5:8 gloriously declares, "God shows his love for us in that while we were still sinners, Christ died for us." Jesus, who is declared repeatedly to be the Son of God,[8] did this work of salvation in love.

For those who turn from sin and trust in Jesus, the Bible declares that we are now adopted into the family of God; God is our Father and we are sons of God.[9] While the language that both men and women are sons of God may seem curious to modern ears, it was a reflection of God's deep love to those who first heard it. Paul was saying that believers are like sons who have full legal standing in the family with all the inherent blessings of that status, as was the case in ancient culture.

---

[5] Gen. 2:18.
[6] Deut. 12:1–3; 1 Kings 11:1–10; Ps. 106:37–39; 1 Cor. 8:5; 10:20.
[7] Eph. 1:3–14.
[8] Rom. 1:3, 4, cf. Gal. 4:4; John 1:1–14; 5:18–25; 10:30–38.
[9] Rom. 8:14, Gal. 3:26; Heb. 12:7.

Similarly, Christians are blessed to have God as their Father, the church as their family, fellow Christians as their brothers and sisters, God's provision as their sustenance, and God's full inheritance for their eternity. Furthermore, as sons, God's people have a duty to obey God the Father by following the humble example of love set by God the Son by the power of God the Spirit.

In sum, God the Father through God the Son by God the Spirit has made it possible for sinners not only to enter into the loving relational community of the church, but, incredibly, to live in the very life of the Trinity. Jesus prays that believers of all times "may all be one, just as you, Father, are in me, and I in you, that they also may be in us, so that the world may believe that you have sent me."[10] According to Jesus, the incredibly important big idea is that we share in the life of the Trinity itself.

The practical implication of being reconciled to the source of love is that the Christian is not only loved but is also enabled to love. Romans 5:5 says, "God's love has been poured into our hearts through the Holy Spirit who has been given to us." Because the Holy Spirit puts the love of God into the root of our new nature, we can bear fruit that begins with love. As Galatians 5:22 says, "The fruit of the Spirit is love."

In addition to being the source of all love, God has also defined love for us:

> Love is patient and kind; love does not envy or boast; it is not arrogant or rude. It does not insist on its own way; it is not irritable or resentful; it does not rejoice at wrongdoing, but rejoices with the truth. Love bears all things, believes all things, hopes all things, endures all things. Love never ends.[11]

Jesus himself said that this kind of supernatural Trinitarian love would be among the chief marks of a Christian church. In John 13:35 he said, "By this all people will know that you are my disciples, if you have love for one another."

One of Jesus' disciples, John, went on to write at length about the church as a people marked by Trinitarian love that is exemplified at the cross and empowered by the Spirit:

---

[10]John 17:21.
[11]1 Cor. 13:4–8.

Beloved, let us love one another, for love is from God, and whoever loves has been born of God and knows God. . . . In this is love, not that we have loved God but that he loved us and sent his Son to be the propitiation for our sins. Beloved, if God so loved us, we also ought to love one another. No one has ever seen God; if we love one another, God abides in us and his love is perfected in us. By this we know that we abide in him and he in us, because he has given us of his Spirit. . . . Whoever confesses that Jesus is the Son of God, God abides in him, and he in God. So we have come to know and to believe the love that God has for us. God is love, and whoever abides in love abides in God, and God abides in him. . . . We love because he first loved us. If anyone says, "I love God," and hates his brother, he is a liar; for he who does not love his brother whom he has seen cannot love God whom he has not seen. And this commandment we have from him: whoever loves God must also love his brother.[12]

Furthermore, Jesus speaks of the reward of such a Spirit-empowered, Christlike life of love, saying, "If anyone loves me, he will keep my word, and my Father will love him, and we will come to him and make our home with him."[13] Difficult as it is to comprehend, those who love God in word and deed and life will experience the presence of God in a loving intimacy akin to a warm, safe home in which a family lives together.

Earlier in this book we spoke of the characteristics of the church, and perhaps they are best summed up in this chapter under the single word *love*. In many ways, love is the mark of the church that is expressed in other marks of the church. Similarly, Jesus himself compressed the more than six hundred Old Testament laws down to two: "'You shall love the Lord your God with all your heart and with all your soul and with all your mind and with all your strength.' . . . 'You shall love your neighbor as yourself.' There is no other commandment greater than these."[14]

Because God commands us to love, we must acknowledge that while it can and should include our emotional feelings, it is not based solely upon them. Despite our emotions, it is always possible to obey God and love because of the indwelling power of the Holy Spirit, who

---

[12]1 John 4:7–21.
[13]John 14:23.
[14]Mark 12:30–31.

has connected us to the source of all love. Thus, we can love even when we are not feeling loving. That is why the Bible likens love to a fruit of the Spirit's work in our lives.[15]

DEEP TRINITARIAN LOVE

Not only does Scripture command Christians and churches to love, but it also tells us who we are to love. (1) We are to love God.[16] (2) We are to love our family.[17] (3) We are to conduct ourselves in such an honoring and respectful way that our church leaders find it a joy to pastor us, which is a practical way of loving them.[18] (4) We are to love fellow Christians.[19] (5) We are to love our neighbor even if our neighbor is a despicable person.[20] (6) We are to love strangers.[21] (7) We are to love even our enemies.[22] In summary, we are to love everyone with God's love.

The question persists, how should we love? Obviously, since Jesus was Love incarnate, he is the greatest example of love and the model for our own loving life, empowered by the same Holy Spirit as was his.[23] In the remainder of this chapter we will explore some of the ways that deep Trinitarian love is visibly seen in the lives of the Christians who comprise a church.

LOVE IN LEARNING

A loving church practices learning. Out of love for God and his Word, there is both biblically faithful teaching and an earnest desire on behalf of the people to learn as an act of worship so that God is loved with all of one's mind.[24] The goal of such study is to have what Paul called "the mind of Christ" so that we can live the life of Christ by the empowering enablement of the Spirit of Christ.[25] This learning is not just cognitive or intellectual. It also goes to the heart and the conscience and flows out into life.[26] The matter of biblical learning is

---

[15]Gal. 5:22–23; Rom. 5:5; 2 Tim. 1:7.
[16]Matt. 6:24; 22:39.
[17]Eph. 5:25; 6:1–4; Titus 2:4.
[18]1 Tim. 5:17; Heb. 13:17.
[19]1 John 3:14.
[20]Matt. 22:39; Luke 10:30–37; Rom. 13:9–10; Gal. 5:14; James 2:8.
[21]Heb. 13:2.
[22]Matt. 5:43–45; Luke 6:32.
[23]John 13:34; 15:12; Eph. 5:1–2.
[24]Mark 12:31.
[25]1 Cor. 2:16.
[26]Rom. 12:1–2; 2 Tim. 2:15–26.

so important that Jesus prayed that we would study our Bible, saying, "Sanctify them in the truth; your word is truth."[27] To help us learn Scripture we are told to hear God's Word,[28] which means that listening to sermons, lectures, and audio Bibles is very beneficial. We are also told to read God's Word[29] and study God's Word,[30] as Jesus often did. Thankfully, we are also blessed to have resources Jesus did not have, such as good books for reading and reference along with good Bible software and other online Bible study tools. Lastly, we are told to memorize God's Word[31] as Jesus did, which enabled him to freely quote Scripture as needed.[32]

The Scriptures speak of teaching very broadly and in many forms. Elders are to be the senior leaders and teachers in the church.[33] Men and women with the gift of teaching who are approved by the elders can have formal teaching ministries in the church.[34] Parents are also supposed to be teachers and to continually instruct their children in wisdom, as is illustrated throughout Proverbs. Fathers in particular are commanded to be teachers.[35] In some sense, every Christian is to be a teacher who imparts biblical truth to others. Paul tells every Christian to seek the gift of prophecy, by which the Spirit enables believers to speak the Word of God so that it presses deeply into the hearts of people, enabling them to reorient their lives and values in light of God's promises, priorities, and purposes.[36] Those who practice this gift will strengthen, build up, encourage, and comfort people.[37] Paul even commands an entire church, "Let the word of Christ dwell in you richly, teaching and admonishing one another in all wisdom."[38]

In a learning church, people are devoted to availing themselves of the providential opportunities God gives them to share what the Holy Spirit has taught them with others for their strengthening and encouragement. These opportunities include formal ministries, such as teach-

---

[27]John 17:17.
[28]Luke 11:28; Rom. 10:17.
[29]Rev. 1:3.
[30]Ezra 7:10; Acts 17:11.
[31]Ps. 119:11; Prov. 22:17–19.
[32]Matt. 4:1–11.
[33]1 Tim. 3:1–2.
[34]1 Cor. 12:28.
[35]Eph. 6:4.
[36]1 Cor. 14:1.
[37]1 Cor. 14:1–4.
[38]Col. 3:16.

ing a class or leading a group, and informal ministries, such as coffee with a friend. When a loving church learns God's Word, it also discovers why and how to love in other ways.

LOVE IN OBEDIENCE

A loving church practices obedience.[39] Sadly, some Christians believe that information alone will result in transformation. However, the entire point of study is to repent of what grieves the Lord and become increasingly transformed to be more and more like Jesus. Information must lead to transformation or we have nothing but head knowledge, or what Paul called the kind of knowledge that "puffs up" with pride rather than increases our humility and reliance on Jesus.[40]

Jesus foresaw this potential problem, which explains why some of his last words to us included directives not just to teach people but to teach them to obey his Word. In Matthew 28:19–20 Jesus says, "Go therefore and make disciples of all nations, baptizing them in the name of the Father and of the Son and of the Holy Spirit, teaching them to observe all that I have commanded you. And behold, I am with you always, to the end of the age." Elsewhere in Scripture we are likewise told that we should not only study Scripture but also obey what we learn from it. Jesus himself said, "Blessed rather are those who hear the word of God and keep it!"[41]

I am assuming that there will be some degree of resistance to the word *obedience* because it has negative connotations for many people. Yet Jesus repeatedly connects loving him with obeying him.[42] In fact, Jesus is emphatic that obedience to him will flow out of our love for him. What this does not mean is that we must obey Jesus so that he will love us. Rather, he has loved us by grace apart from anything we have done, and as a result we trust him, which is the essence of faith. It is because Jesus is perfectly good and loves us that we should logically obey him as evidence of our trust in him, if we claim to love him. If we really believe that Jesus is wiser, holier, kinder, and more loving than us, and that he is for us, then it would be foolish to disobey him.

Jesus' own brother James says it this way: "But be doers of the word,

---

[39]John 14:15, 21–24.
[40]1 Cor. 8:1.
[41]Luke 11:28.
[42]John 14:15, 21, 23, 24.

and not hearers only, deceiving yourselves."[43] James compares people who only hear the Word to a fool who sees his dirty face in a mirror and just walks away. We have all likely met someone who had a lot of Bible knowledge but lacked a love for Jesus and obedience to the Bible. Such people are deceived and arrogantly consider themselves spiritually mature when in fact they are not. They are by definition hypocrites, because they do not obey what they have learned. Furthermore, such people are like Satan. The Bible records that Satan knows the Bible, but he does not love Jesus or obey him, which explains his unparalleled pride and self-deception.

As we open the Bible to meet with Jesus and repent of sin that causes distance from Jesus, and as we are filled with the same Holy Spirit that empowered Jesus, we are able to gladly obey Scripture so that we may live like Jesus as we live for Jesus because we live with Jesus according to his Word. The result of loving obedience is blessing. As Jesus said, "If you know these things, blessed are you if you do them."[44]

LOVE IN SOLITUDE

A loving church practices solitude. Solitude is fasting from people for a prescribed time to connect with God and replenish the soul. This solitude might take place for a few minutes or a few days. It often includes personal and environmental silence. For most of us, time away from external stimulation, from noise and busyness, people and voices, can be very disorienting. It is this sort of dis-ease that cures spiritual disease. When Elijah hit a spiritual wall, he ran into the desert where he was able to hear the low whisper of the voice of God.[45] Habakkuk's consternation at what God revealed to him led him to a quiet tower in the night to hear what God would say to him.[46] Zephaniah urged people to be silent before the Lord,[47] something Zechariah echoes as he contemplates the reality that the Lord will move in salvation.[48]

Solitude is not punishment like that inflicted on prisoners and is not intended to be indefinite, as practiced by some extremist monks. Instead, solitude is the recognition that just as we need time with those we love to build our relationships, so too we need focused time with

---

[43]James 1:22.
[44]John 13:17.
[45]1 Kings 19.
[46]Hab. 2:1.
[47]Zeph. 1:7.
[48]Zech. 2:13.

Jesus to build our relationship with him. Like all relationships, this includes using the special times we get with him to listen to him as we read Scripture and speak to him in prayer.

Despite the constant pressures upon Jesus' time from family, friends, and fans, his own life was marked by ongoing times of solitude. Many Scriptures speak of how Jesus often practiced the spiritual discipline of solitude,[49] and my personal favorite is Luke 5:16 (NIV), which says, "Jesus often withdrew to lonely places and prayed."

Furthermore, as we study Scripture, we see that Jesus used solitude for a multitude of purposes. After his baptism Jesus spent forty days in solitude preparing for his public ministry.[50] Jesus used solitude as an opportunity to pray and seek the Father's will before choosing the twelve disciples.[51] After the beheading of his cousin John the Baptizer, Jesus spent time alone to mourn.[52] Jesus often used solitude as occasions for intense and focused prayer.[53] He also used solitude to rest after a hard day of work.[54] Knowing he was going to be crucified soon, Jesus spent time alone with a few chosen friends in the garden of Gethsemane, coming to grips with the painful obedience that was required of him.[55]

There are many things you can do during periods of solitude, including nothing, reading Scripture, meditating on Scripture to deeply consider its meaning for your life, resting, worshiping, praying, journaling, reading a good book, and enjoying God's creation. While church services, Bible studies, classes, and service projects are important, a loving church also leaves time and gives permission for people not to be out every night of the week doing church activities but also to get some time for solitude.

LOVE IN FELLOWSHIP

A loving church practices fellowship. Fellowship is living life together with Christian brothers and sisters as the church. In addition to regularly taking time for solitude, we also see in Scripture that Jesus spent considerable amounts of time in community with others. In fact, Jesus spent most

---

[49]Matt. 14:23; Mark 6:31; Luke 4:42.
[50]Matt. 4:1–11.
[51]Luke 6:12.
[52]Matt. 14:12–13.
[53]Matt. 14:23; Mark 1:35; Luke 5:16.
[54]Mark 6:31.
[55]Mark 26:36–46.

of his time in community with his disciples and frequently had dinner in the homes of people he was befriending. Jesus seemed to have particularly close fellowship with the youngest disciple, John,[56] the sisters Mary and Martha, and their brother Lazarus, whom he loved very much.[57]

Following the pattern of Jesus and led by the Holy Spirit, those in the early church "devoted themselves to . . . fellowship."[58] Other New Testament Scriptures likewise stress the importance of Christians living life together in supportive community.[59]

For many people raised in the church, the word *fellowship* brings to mind potluck suppers in the "fellowship hall" where the appetizer is roast pastor, the main course savage gossip with a garnish of slander, followed by a dessert of quarrels over ignorant controversy.[60] Fellowship or community is nothing like that. While it may include getting together to share a meal, watch sports, and swap recipes or advice on raising children, Christian fellowship will include (1) sharing in our common inheritance of life in Jesus through the Holy Spirit;[61] (2) sharing our common love for neighbor by giving our material and spiritual wealth;[62] and (3) sharing with each other in reciprocal giving empowered by the filling of the Spirit.[63]

Practically speaking, loving fellowship means that people live life together devoted to being a community of people to depend on when times are tough and to rejoice with when times are good. To aid in fellowship, a loving church sees that people intentionally live near one another so they can more frequently spend time together and build loving Christian friendships. Many churches encourage this practice through fellowship groups, following the model developed by John Wesley and the Methodists.

LOVE IN SERVICE

A loving church practices service. In one of the more curious arguments in all of history, Mark 9:33–35 records a debate between the disciples

---

[56]John 13:23.
[57]John 11:5.
[58]Acts 2:42.
[59]Rom. 12:10; 1 John 1:7; Heb. 10:25.
[60]1 Tim. 6:4; 2 Tim. 2:23.
[61]1 Cor. 1:9; 2 Cor. 13:14; 1 John 1:3.
[62]Acts 2:42–47; Rom. 12:13; 15:26; Phil. 1:5; Philem. 1:17.
[63]Eph. 5:18–21. Also see John Stott, *The Living Church* (Downers Grove, IL: InterVarsity, 2007), 86–96.

as to which of them was the greatest. Upon overhearing their arrogant conversation, Jesus responded in a most unexpected manner. Rather than rebuking them, Jesus actually told them how to become the greatest and thereby achieve their objective. His answer was stunning: being a humble servant is the only way to spiritual greatness.

Service is how we can make God's love visible to other people. Christian love is not merely an emotion—it compels us to action. Perhaps 1 John 3:18 says it best: "Little children, let us not love in word or talk but in deed and *in truth*."

We live in an age where service has become a commodity to be bought and sold as a foundation of the national economy. As a result, there has been a decline in personal service to others without employment obligation or financial compensation. Rather than rejoicing in the opportunity to serve freely, we automatically expect payment. For the Christian, however, it is God's love and Jesus' example that compel us to humbly serve in love. Because of how Jesus has served and continues to serve us, our Christian service is not motivated by guilt or duty but rather by gladness and love. As Psalm 100:2 exuberantly proclaims, "Serve the LORD with gladness!" and Galatians 5:13 encourages, "through love serve one another."

Jesus is our perfect model of a humble loving servant. In fact, Jesus' entire ministry is often summarized simply as humble service, which included everything from feeding people to washing their feet and dying on the cross for their sins.[64] Many other Scriptures encourage humble service.[65]

Humble service in the church is so important that Scripture declares that the exercise within the church of all the natural talents and spiritual gifts is simply various ways in which service is conducted. First Peter 4:10 says, "As each has received a gift, use it to serve one another, as good stewards of God's varied grace." Additionally, God not only commanded every Christian to serve, but he also imparted to some the spiritual gift of helps or service so that their love might be visible.[66]

LOVE IN APPROPRIATE SPEECH

A loving church practices appropriate speech. Experts say that an average person speaks two to five thousand words each day in their home.

---

[64]Matt. 20:20–28; Phil. 2:5–11.
[65]Matt. 20:26–28; Acts 9:36; Rom. 16:1; Gal. 5:13; Phil. 2:5–7.
[66]1 Cor. 12:28; Rom. 12:7.

For those who work full-time outside the home, that number may increase to as many as ten to twenty thousand words a day. Our communication also includes innumerable emails, text messages, and such. In short, we speak a lot in both spoken and printed words.

Proverbs has a great deal to say about what we say and is perhaps the most packed book of the Bible on the subject of our speech. According to James 3, our tongue is often the last part of our body to get sanctified. Jesus' brother compares the power of our tongue to the bit in a horse's mouth, the rudder on a ship, a wild beast, and a small spark that could set a fire of destruction as great as hell itself. In Ephesians 4:29 we are told to speak "only such as is good for building up, as fits the occasion, that it may give grace to those who hear." Jesus also said, "People will give account for every careless word they speak, for by your words you will be justified, and by your words you will be condemned."[67]

The Bible is filled with examples of condemnable speech, including cursing God, blaspheming God, falsely accusing someone, perversity, rashness, harshness, wickedness, boasting, lying, flattering, bitterness, nitpicking, adulterous flirtation, busy-bodying, gossip, nagging, whining, complaining, needless quarreling, and plain old foolish stupidity in its innumerable forms. On the other hand, the Bible also speaks of speech being an opportunity for worship, prayer, grace, teaching, counsel, preaching, kindness, truth, comfort, love, healing, sweetness, encouragement, mercy, hope, gentleness, conviction, and faith. As Proverbs 18:21 says, "Death and life are in the power of the tongue."

In many ways, the tongue is an indicator of the heart, because, as Jesus said, "out of the abundance of the heart the mouth speaks."[68] The disciple of Jesus learns to speak under the discipline of the Holy Spirit, who enables him or her to speak truthfully in love in a manner that is appropriate for both the hearer and for Jesus, who is listening to our words. The key is to get our time listening to God through his Word so that when we do speak, we echo Jesus with loving words.

LOVE IN SABBATH-KEEPING

A loving church practices sabbath rest. To practice *sabbath* is to rest from one's labor. The first Sabbath day was a Saturday: "And on the

[67]Matt. 12:36–37.
[68]Matt. 12:34.

seventh day God finished his work that he had done, and he rested on the seventh day from all his work that he had done."[69] The first recorded command for humans to keep the Sabbath is in Exodus 16:23, and the Sabbath is listed as the fourth commandment in Exodus 20:8–11.

Sabbath rest has benefits for all people. Workers and animals are permitted to rest as an act of justice and compassion to ensure the dignity of God's creation. Both rich and poor are invited to stand in equality for one day as they rest from their labors, knowing that our sovereign God is on our side and is able to hold the universe and our lives together even when we rest and sleep.

Some have maintained that the Sabbath should be celebrated on Saturday like the Hebrews did, which was the final day of their week. However, the early church abruptly changed the day of worship to Sunday to commemorate the resurrection of Jesus from death[70] and the coming of the Spirit on Pentecost[71] on that first day of the new week.[72] Sunday remained a workday in the early church until Emperor Constantine instituted it as an official day of rest in AD 321. In America there was a debate as to whether the Jewish Sabbath of Saturday or the Christian Sabbath of Sunday should be recognized, and the compromise was to keep both, which is why we have two-day weekends.

Legalistic attempts have been made to rob the Sabbath of its worship and joy by carefully mandating what can and cannot be done. However, Jesus intentionally lived out a model of the Sabbath contrary to that given by other legalistic teachers. Jesus healed on the Sabbath,[73] taught on the Sabbath,[74] and promoted evangelism on the Sabbath.[75] Jesus demonstrated that the Sabbath is not to be enforced legalistically, but that it exists for worshipful fun and rest. Furthermore, our true Sabbath is not in a day but ultimately in a saving relationship with Jesus, in whose finished work we can rest from trying to earn our salvation.[76] Therefore, the Sabbath is not a law for believers to obey but instead a grace to enjoy.

By setting aside a day, we are showing that we are a people who are

---

[69]Gen. 2:2.
[70]Matt. 28:1; Mark 16:1–2; Luke 24:1; John 20:1.
[71]Acts 2.
[72]Acts 20:7; 1 Cor. 16:2.
[73]Matt. 12:1–14; John 9:1–17.
[74]Mark 6:1–2.
[75]John 7:21–24.
[76]Matt. 11:28–30; Rom. 4:5; Col. 2:16–17.

set aside (holy) and who rest in Jesus. Worshiping is our primary objective, and our weeks are purposefully ordered around worship. On the Sabbath, we make it a priority to grow in our loving relationship with God and people.

LOVE IN WORSHIP

A loving church practices worship. Worship is living our life individually and corporately as continuous living sacrifices to the glory of a person or thing. This connection between glory and worship is clear in places such as Romans 11:36–12:1, which says, "To him be *glory* forever. Amen. I appeal to you therefore, brothers, by the mercies of God, to present your bodies as a living sacrifice, holy and acceptable to God, which is your spiritual *worship*." In this packed section of Scripture, Paul connects a number of vital truths regarding worship. First, we hold a person or thing in a place of glory. Second, we then worship that person or thing. Third, our worship of that person or thing that we hold in glory is done by means of making sacrifices.

Glory means weightiness, importance, preeminence, or priority. What we hold up in glory is our greatest treasure, deepest longing, and fountain of hope. The glory of God is the radiance of his presence.[77] Christians glorify God both by proclaiming his greatness and radiating his character. People can and do hold various people and things in a position of glory and then worship them by making sacrifices. Because we have limited resources (time, energy, money) we must allocate those things to what we consider most important or glorious to us and in so doing make sacrifices for our functional god. Whatever we hold in the position of highest glory is by definition our god(s).

The first two commandments state that there is only one God, and that God alone is to be worshiped.[78] According to Martin Luther, we break the rest of the commandments only *after* we have broken the first two. What he means is if we have only the one true God as our God, and we worship only that God, then we will not end up committing idolatry and worshiping our job at the expense of taking a Sabbath, worshiping our anger and becoming violent, worshiping sex and committing adultery, worshiping things and stealing them, or worshiping success and

---

[77]Ex. 40:34–35; Ezek. 10:4, 18; Hag. 2:7–9.
[78]Ex. 20:1–6.

coveting what other people have. If we worship God alone, we will not be tempted to go to a demon god that masquerades as an angel or to a spirit being for knowledge, love, healing, or success in business.[79]

The opposite of worship is idolatry or the worship of something or someone other than the one true God of the Bible or the worship of God that is contrary to his Word. This theme of worship versus idolatry is in some ways the theme of the entire Old Testament. Romans 1 articulates the pattern of false worship as failing to glorify God, which leads to an overinflated and arrogant view of self that ends in worshiping created things rather than the Creator God.

Jesus lived a life of perfect glory to his Father and thus we can look at everything in his life, from the ordinary to the extraordinary, as born out of a life of ceaseless worship that glorified God the Father. Jesus' life destroys any notion that worship is a sacred thing we do at a special time in a special place. All of life is to be lived as ceaseless worship; cutting our grass and cleaning our dishes are as sacred and God-glorifying as raising our hands in church. Jesus himself modeled this; he spent roughly 90 percent of his earthly life doing chores as a boy and carpentry as a man. Paul sums up the life of unceasing worship best in 1 Corinthians 10:31: "So, whether you eat or drink, or whatever you do, do all to the *glory* of God."[80] Simply, in worship we actively love God above all else as our greatest treasure and source of joy.

LOVE IN EVANGELISM

A loving church practices evangelism. Evangelism is speaking and showing the transforming power of the grace of the gospel of Jesus Christ to people who do not yet know him. Evangelism is the natural overflow of a life lived in joy as a worshiper of God. Sadly, evangelism is often portrayed as something that Christians must do as a duty, rather than something that they get to do as a delight.

Jesus set the example for us in his role as the Evangelist. Jesus explained his earthly mission in evangelistic terms, saying, "For the Son of Man came to seek and to save the lost."[81] When he called his first disciples, he said to them, "Follow me, and I will make you fishers

---

[79]1 Cor. 10:20–21; 2 Cor. 6:15–17.
[80]See also 1 Cor. 6:20.
[81]Luke 19:10.

of men."[82] As we go to work, school, and the grocery store, we are to assume that Jesus is always with us, preparing people to hear the gospel. His work of evangelism has not ceased but has expanded to include us as we share Jesus in love with others.

Love in Mercy

A loving church practices mercy.[83] Mercy is the capacity to feel and express unusual compassion and sympathy for those in difficult or crisis situations and to provide them with the necessary help and support to see them through tough times. A merciful church is empathetic and compassionate to those who are hurting, struggling, suffering, and in need. A merciful church finds its inspiration in the mercy it has received from God and the loving example of Jesus. Jesus repeatedly had compassion[84] and was so filled with mercy that he sometimes wept.[85] Jesus' mercy included an attentiveness to and concern for children.[86] Jesus also taught on mercy.[87] Jesus' teaching on the Good Samaritan is the classic story on the subject of mercy.[88] Practically speaking, a merciful church will reflect Dorcas who "was full of good works and acts of charity."[89] Practically speaking, a merciful church seeks out, welcomes, and aids those who are needy, hurting, sick, disabled, suffering, dying, mourning, or elderly with visible compassion to demonstrate the love of God.

Love in Hospitality

A loving church practices hospitality.[90] Hospitality is the ability to welcome strangers and entertain guests, often in your home, with great joy and kindness so that they become friends. Hospitality is patterned after the life of Jesus, who spent time befriending social outcasts[91] and eating with his disciples, and who has welcomed us into the family of God, which includes an eternal home[92] and an eternal party.[93]

[82]Matt. 4:19.
[83]Rom. 12:8.
[84]Matt. 9:36; 15:32; 23:37; Luke 7:13.
[85]John 11:35.
[86]Matt. 19:14.
[87]Matt. 5:7; 9:13; 23:23.
[88]Luke 10:30–37.
[89]Acts 9:36.
[90]Rom. 12:13; Heb. 13:2; 1 Pet. 4:8.
[91]Matt. 11:19.
[92]John 14:2.
[93]Isa. 25:6–9; Rev. 19:6–9.

In the church, hospitality is supposed to include one's family,[94] friends,[95] Christians,[96] and strangers who may not be Christians.[97] The pattern of hospitality is supposed to be established by the elders-pastors and their families.[98]

Loving hospitality includes open homes, condos, apartments, and dorms where people are welcomed in to visit, eat, talk, hang out, play video or board games, and watch sporting events. Subsequently, church members consider such things as available parking and entertaining space when deciding where to live because they see their home for both personal and communal purposes. Conversely, hospitality is not supposed to be extended to false teachers and such who are a danger to the life and health of a church.[99]

Love in Prayer

A loving church practices prayer. Prayer is reverently speaking to God about the joys, toils, and concerns of life, either silently or verbally. Prayer includes praise, adoration, confession, thanksgiving, petition, and intercession. In prayer we go directly into the presence of God, giving attention to him. Prayer raises my mind from the all-consuming concerns with the immediate issue and allows me to see reality from God's perspective and priorities. What we pray for is very seldom what we really need. We need God's presence far more than his provision.

Similarly, the psalms come in many moods: reverence, sadness, anger, hope, remorse, devastation, abandon, protection, lament, and joy, to name a few. This example encourages our complete authenticity in prayer, so that we bring our most real self to him. To try to hide something from an omniscient God is the highest level of dumb.

A praying church takes its cues from Jesus, who was often in prayer,[100] and the Bible records some of Jesus' prayers.[101] In the life of the church, prayer is to be naturally woven throughout the entire life of God's people. Colossians 4:2 commands the church to "continue steadfastly in prayer" and 1 Thessalonians 5:17 exhorts us to "pray without ceasing."

---

[94]1 Tim. 5:8.
[95]Prov. 27:10.
[96]Gal. 6:10.
[97]Lev. 19:34.
[98]1 Tim. 3:2; Titus 1:8.
[99]2 John 10–11.
[100]Luke 5:16.
[101]Matt. 6:5–15; John 17.

Just as the Trinitarian God is in continual communication, God's people are not to consider prayer as merely an aspect of their life but as the essence of their very being. In summary, a loving church is filled with innumerable spoken and unspoken prayers, continually prayed out of love for God and people.

LOVE IN GIVING

A loving church practices generous giving.[102] Our wealth includes everything we have, such as our finances, houses, products of our land, businesses, automobiles, and personal items.

Fully 25 percent of Jesus' words in the Gospels are related to our resources and stewardship of them. This accounts for twenty-eight passages in the four Gospels. Surveying the entire Bible, there are over eight hundred verses dealing with a wide variety of financial topics, including planning and budgeting, saving and investing, and debt and tithing. According to Jesus, how we spend our money is ultimately an indicator as to whether we love God above all else or worship money and possessions in place of God.[103] Practically speaking, money is a critical component to the growth and health of the church. As Ecclesiastes 10:19 says, "Money answers everything."

Money is simply a tool, and the Bible gives us a framework for how to use it. The biblical uses of money include loving and honoring God,[104] providing for the needs of your family,[105] advancing the gospel, showing tangible love to people, and simply having some fun and enjoying God's grace.

A giving church views all of its individual and collective wealth as ultimately belonging to God.[106] The members of a giving church see themselves as stewards. Stewards are people who by God's grace belong to God. Because they belong to God, they recognize that ultimately everything they are and have belongs to God and has been given to them as a gift. Therefore, they seek both to enjoy the gifts God has given them and to invest those gifts in others and the future by distributing them wisely. There are three categories that we must steward: our time, our talents, and our treasure.

---

[102]2 Corinthians 8–9.
[103]Matt. 6:21.
[104]Prov. 3:9.
[105]1 Tim. 5:8.
[106]Deut. 8:17–18; Pss. 50:10; 139:13; Hag. 2:8; James 1:16–18.

A giving church does not enforce tithing as practiced in the Old Testament, but it does support generous, grace-based giving as demonstrated in the New Testament.[107] The word *tithe* literally means a tenth of all that one earns as wealth. The total tithe in the Old Testament was not 10 percent; it only began with 10 percent of one's gross income given to fund the Levite priests' ministry.[108] There was an additional 10 percent paid for festivals[109] and 3.3 percent was given to help the poor.[110] Furthermore, there were crop gleanings for the poor and aliens,[111] as well as occasional additional tithes above and beyond regular giving.[112] In total, the "mandatory" Old Testament tithe resulted in over 25 percent of a family's gross income.

In the New Testament generous, grace-based giving supersedes tithing.[113] There we read that everything we have belongs to God and is to be stewarded biblically. Giving is a joy and honor. It should come from our firstfruits or gross income and be done regularly, cheerfully, and sacrificially. Grace-based giving means that it is a heart issue, one tied to our proportion of faith, and it is to be an amount settled between us and God. In a loving, giving church, people not only give generously to their church, but they go beyond that to share God's grace in the form of giving money and possessions to individuals.

LOVE IN HUMILITY

A loving church practices humility. Because it understands that its salvation, and everything else it enjoys, is solely a gift of God's grace, a loving church follows the humble example of Jesus. Philosophers from Aristotle to Friedrich Nietzsche praise highly competent self-sufficiency, ignoring or castigating humility as a perverted morality that exalts servility and denies genuine humanity. Jesus' pattern of humility is neither self-destructive nor self-centered but requires accepting ourselves as we really are before God. We are "not to think of [ourselves] more highly than [we] ought to think, but to think with sober judgment, each according to the measure of faith that God has assigned."[114]

---

[107]2 Corinthians 8–9.
[108]Num. 18:21–29; 27:30.
[109]Deut. 12:10–11, 17–18; 14:22–27.
[110]Deut. 14:28–29.
[111]Lev. 19:9–10.
[112]Neh. 10:32–33.
[113]2 Corinthians 8–9.
[114]Rom. 12:3.

We have strengths and gifts as well as weaknesses, guilt, and needs. We happily give to others out of our strengths and freely receive from others where we have needs.

The Bible records that Jesus came as the most humble person who will ever live.[115] Subsequently, a humble church is one that is filled with people who look out for the needs of others in addition to their own and boast in the person and work of Jesus over and above who they are or what they have seemingly accomplished. Because the loving church is well loved by God, it is able to celebrate rather than covet the success of others, is more concerned with Jesus' glory than its own, and prefers confidence to arrogance as a virtue to be pursued. A humble church knows that even if its doctrine is pure, its witness will be tainted by pride because pride is the satanic root of all other sin and repugnant to the gospel.

Lastly, a loving church takes to heart the words of 1 Peter 5:5, which command churches, "Clothe yourselves, all of you, with humility toward one another, for 'God opposes the proud but gives grace to the humble.'"[116] A humble church is filled with members who, because of their understanding of the gospel, speak truthfully and humbly to one another about sin. Those who are lovingly confronted in sin humbly respond with repentance as needed.

MUCH TO OFFER

Overall, the loving church has much to offer, as the historian Rodney Stark has written:

> To cities filled with the homeless and impoverished, Christianity offered charity as well as hope. To cities filled with newcomers and strangers, Christianity offered an immediate basis for attachments. To cities filled with orphans and widows, Christianity provided a new and expanded sense of family. To cities torn by ethnic strife, Christianity offered a new basis for social solidarity. . . . People had been enduring catastrophes for centuries without the aid of Christian theology or Christian social structures. Hence I am by no means suggesting that the misery of the ancient world caused the advent of Christianity. What I am going to argue is that once Christianity did

[115]Phil. 2:1–11.
[116]See also James 4:6.

appear, its superior capacity for meeting these chronic problems soon became evident and played a major role in its ultimate triumph. . . . For what [Christianity] brought was not simply an urban movement, but a *new culture*.[117]

A loving church is a visible manifestation of deep Trinitarian love where people can connect to and live out the inner life of the Father, Son, and Spirit on their mission of fulfilling the great commission. And the only way to witness this firsthand is to be active in a church seeking evidences of love and being, oneself, loving in word and deed.

---

[117]Rodney Stark, *The Rise of Christianity: A Sociologist Reconsiders History* (Princeton, NJ: Princeton University Press, 1996), 161–62.

Answers to Common Questions about Love in the Church

Church . . . Loving? You Must Be Kidding!

It is true that many churches are not loving. It is often because they have given up the gospel of grace for the practice of religion.[118] This is what Jesus warns against in passages such as Luke 11:37–12:3. Paul echoes this warning often, most powerfully in Galatians. "Religious" churches would do well to think carefully about the points in this chapter.

Sometimes the hurt comes from the gospel itself, which convicts of sin and points out the secrets of the heart (1 Cor. 14:24–25; Heb. 4:12–13). If this conviction comes in a context of grace instead of religious judgmentalism, it is painful, but not really hurtful. It is love in action.

On the other hand, many people have let bad experiences with one church ruin their whole picture of God and his people. Worse yet, there are some who have heard the horror stories about churches and believed them wholesale with no attempt to find the grace that characterizes many churches that humbly follow the Bible.

No church is as loving as it should be. Every church sinfully fails to carry out the commandments of Jesus. Listening humbly to people who have been hurt is a mark of a good church. Sometimes the church can repent and do ministry better. Other times the hurt is an inevitable result of fallen human interaction.

It may take some effort to locate a church that is true to the Bible and also loving and gracious, but it is worth the effort. Ask people at the rescue mission or Christian counselors where they go to church. The barista at your favorite coffee shop or servers at restaurants often know which churches are real. Visit and see for yourself. Does the pastor preach from the Bible? Do the people carry Bibles, hang around after the service, and seem to enjoy being together? Do they talk about differ-

---

[118]See chap. 4 in Mark Driscoll and Gerry Breshears, *Death by Love* (Wheaton, IL: Crossway Books, 2008).

ences rather than fighting over them or hiding them? Do they listen and care when you talk to them? If so, you are likely in a loving church.

WHAT SHOULD I DO IF I ATTEND A CHURCH THAT IS NOT VERY LOVING?

First, prayerfully examine your assessment that the church is unloving. Is the problem really the church or is there a relational issue that needs to be resolved? In other words, perhaps it is not the whole church but a couple of people in the church who are hurtfully unloving. Are you carrying hurt that you have not brought to the light of grace? If the hurt is in you, it may be really hard for you to feel love from other people. Dealing with difficult people will be even harder. Is it just you that feels the unlovingness, or do you discern that others also experience it?

If the church really is unloving, it needs to be dealt with. The best way to begin is to talk with the leaders. See what they are doing. Sometimes they are working to change the culture of a church. You can join them in that good project. If they are unaware of what is happening, tell them respectfully what you experience. Use concrete examples whenever you can. Insofar as possible, speak from your personal experience and perception. The proverbial "they say" or "some feel" is usually not helpful in achieving resolution. It takes courage to do this, but you can be the Spirit's agent for growth in grace.

If they defend their unloving ways, then it may be time to bring a more formal response or even a grievance (1 Tim. 5:19). Are there two or three other Jesus followers who agree with your assessment and have tried to promote change? Be careful not to gossip or undercut the leaders as you find these people. The biblical pattern is to speak with the people involved before you go over their heads. Come to the leaders with much prayer and humble respect but also with clear statements of what you are seeing.

If this also fails, it probably is time to find a church that expresses the holy love of Jesus, one where you can bring your unsaved friends. Leaving is often painful, but in the long run it's probably better.

WHAT DOES THE BIBLE MEAN WHEN IT TELLS US NOT TO LOVE THE WORLD?

When John 3:16 says God loved the world enough to send his Son and 1 John 2:15 tells us "do not love the world or the things in the world" and that "if anyone loves the world, the love of the Father is not in him," you know there's something going on. Clearly, they are not talking about the same thing.

When John tells us not to love the world, he is not speaking of the world of people, as in John 3:16, or the created world, as in John 17:24 or Ephesians 1:4, but the evil system that is the domain of the devil. This world hates Jesus and his followers and opposes the progress of the gospel and the worship of God (John 12:31; 14:30; Eph. 2:2; 1 John 4:3–5; 5:19). It is full of temptations and threats to Christians who seek to live the life of Jesus.

John is not talking about the selfless love that compels us to preach the gospel to people so they can be reconciled to God (Mark 16:15–16; 2 Cor. 5:13–14), but the self-indulgent love where our evil desires respond to the seductive temptations of evil. Similarily, it was Demas's love of the world that brought him to desert Paul (2 Tim. 4:10).

The warning not to love the world means not to be infatuated with the values and lifestyles of the dominion of darkness and not to long after or indulge in its sinful pleasures and passions. We are vulnerable to the enticing allure of sinful values and activities of the world. We must recognize that the world is not a neutral place, but one that worships and serves other gods.

Some Christians interpret the command not to love the world to mean we must draw away from evil and separate ourselves from non-Christians, their evil culture, and their evil government in all aspects of life—physically, geographically, socially, and spiritually. But if we do this, we refuse to emulate the lifestyle of Jesus, who regularly ate and drank with tax collectors and sinners (Matt. 9:10–11; 11:19; Luke 5:30; 15:1–2; 19:7).

The bottom-line question is, "Do we as Christians influence sinners toward Jesus or do they influence us toward their sinful values and practices?"

IS THERE ANYTHING I CAN DO TO DEEPEN MY UNDERSTANDING OF THE TRINITY?

You certainly are not the first to be perplexed by this truth, if that is any comfort. The biggest problem is that no one has ever seen God, as Jesus told us (John 1:18). Despite God's self-revelation, our knowledge of him is like seeing someone in a dim mirror (1 Cor. 13:12). Also the Trinity is absolutely unique, so we have nothing to give us perspective.

This is a place where Deuteronomy 29:29 fits well: "The secret things belong to the LORD our God, but the things that are revealed belong to us and to our children forever, that we may do all the words of this law." What we do is meditate on the biblical teachings of the one God who is a trinity of persons, as expounded in this chapter. God's revelation in passages such as John 17 will engage your mind and spirit deeply. Resist the temptation that has plagued Christians throughout the centuries to fill in the blanks with philosophy and speculation. You can find that history in any good systematic theology.

One helpful book for thoughtful beginners is Millard Erickson's *Making Sense of the Trinity* (Baker, 2000). He answers three basic questions: "Is the Trinity biblical?"; "Is it rationally coherent?"; and "Is it at all relevant to anything?" Another book is Bruce Ware's *Father, Son, and Holy Spirit: Relationships, Roles, and Relevance* (Crossway, 2005). If you compare these two books, you will find some significant differences. However, they are in areas we can hold to loosely, or in an open hand. A more technical work is Robert Letham, *The Holy Trinity: In Scripture, History, Theology, and Worship* (P&R, 2005). Lastly, be sure you read these books with your Bible open!

CHAPTER NINE

WHAT IS A MISSIONAL CHURCH?

**"You are the light of the world.
A city set on a hill cannot be hidden."**

MATTHEW 5:14

✝

Cool young pastors with some sort of facial hair, a Mac on which they write blogs, and at least one tattoo frequently claim to be doing missional church ministry. When asked what that means, most start stammering, nervously looking at their feet like the kid in school who got asked a really big word in the first round of the spelling bee.

Thankfully, the mission of the church is not that complicated. The mission of the church comes directly from the command of Jesus who, after his resurrection and just prior to his ascension, said, "Go therefore and make disciples of all nations, baptizing them in the name of the Father and of the Son and of the Holy Spirit, teaching them to observe all that I have commanded you. And behold, I am with you always, to the end of the age."[1] Jesus speaks of going, evangelizing, making disciples, and planting churches that plant churches to continue the process. Therefore, the mission of the church is nothing less than bringing the entire world to Christian faith and maturity.

A missional church must strategize how to carry out the mission in today's increasingly non-Christian culture. Early leaders in the missional movement saw that many contemporary evangelical churches

---

[1]Matt. 28:19–20; see also Mark 16:15–16; Luke 24:46–49; John 20:20–31; Acts 1:5–8.

had slipped into an attritional ministry philosophy focused almost solely on bringing people into church buildings and events. Such churches lacked a missional philosophy focused on sending Christians out of the church into the world to evangelize and disciple people. Subsequently, the Western church had, sadly, become overly attached to and defined by buildings, programs, staff, services, and institutions that only strategize ways to do "attractional" ministry. To correct this problem, the term *missional* was adopted to emphasize that the church exists to go into the cultures and nations of the earth and live sacrificially for the good of others. Subsequently, popular terms such as *Jesus followers* address our identity as disciples committed to being like Jesus by adopting a missionary stance in relation to our culture.

One of the heroes in the missional church world is a man named Lesslie Newbigin who is now in heaven with Jesus. He returned home to England after nearly thirty years of missionary work in India to find that the previously Christian culture he had left had become pagan, pluralistic, secular, and non-Christian. Using missiological insights gained from so many years on the mission field, he ascertained that the "Christian" West had become a culture in need of missions—it was now as lost as the unreached cultures of the world.

As a young church planter, I read everything I could find by Newbigin, along with the work of an organization called The Gospel and Our Culture Network (GOCN), which came into existence to work out in detail many of the issues raised by Newbigin. The work of the GOCN culminated in the publishing of a landmark missiology book titled *The Church between Gospel and Culture*.[2] Another book was then published by the GOCN called *Missional Church: A Vision for the Sending of the Church in North America* in early 1998.[3] The GOCN conversation was very helpful but was dominated by older theoreticians from primarily mainline denominations struggling with liberalism in dying churches, so it was not directly applicable to younger evangelical church planters.

Young pastors, including me, picked up on the work of the GOCN, which led to the start of what is now known as the emerging church. *The*

---

[2]George R. Hunsberger and Craig Van Gelder, eds., *The Church between Gospel and Culture* (Grand Rapids, MI: Eerdmans, 1996).

[3]Darrell L. Guder, ed., *Missional Church: A Vision for the Sending of the Church in North America* (Grand Rapids, MI: Eerdmans, 1998).

emerging church is a broad term referring to a wide variety of evangelicals seeking to be the missional church. In contrast, *Emergent* is an organization promoting a more theologically liberal and non-evangelical version of the missional church that often does not even meet the definition of a church that we set forth in this book.

The discussion about the missional church in evangelicalism has grown. What began as a conversation among a handful of young church planters is now more than half a million Google hits for "missional" and "missional church." A host of conferences, Web sites, books, and related products and events have come into existence around the concept of the missional church. Subsequently, even the word *missional* has been co-opted so often that it has lost its clarity. One of the greatest missional church researchers is a dear friend named Ed Stetzer, who addressed this issue, saying:

> A missional church is not any one thing. It is not simply a new style or model of doing church. And there is not one formulaic amalgamate (that means "word") that sums up its meaning. The landscape of the missional debate is filled with questions, assumptions, and opinions— along with hard pressed critiques on wider issues such as leadership styles, congregation sizes, vocational/bi-vocational ministry, building church-based or house church-based as well as core theology.[4]

Ed Stetzer and David Putman express the core of the shift to missional thinking like this:
- from programs to processes,
- from demographics to discernment,
- from models to missions,
- from attritional to incarnational,
- from uniformity to diversity,
- from professional to passionate,
- from seating to sending,
- from decisions to disciples,
- from additional to exponential, and
- from monuments to movements.[5]

---

[4]Ed Stetzer, "Thursday is for Theology of Missions—Meanings of Missional, part 3," EdStetzer. com blog, posted on August 29, 2007, http://blogs.lifeway.com/blog/edstetzer/2007/08/thursday_is_for_theology_ of_mi.html.
[5]Ed Stetzer and David Putman, *Breaking the Missional Code: Your Church Can Become a Missionary in*

To understand the missional church one must first understand the cultural shift from a thousand years of Christendom and the way that culture is created in the post-Christian world.

In Christendom, the values of culture reflected those of Christianity; the culture was pervasively Christian and thus stigmatized non-Christian beliefs and behaviors. This did not mean, however, that individuals were necessarily regenerated Christians who knew Jesus. A brilliant thinker and kind friend, Tim Keller, pastor of Redeemer Presbyterian Church in New York, has provided some helpful insights regarding the nature of our post-Christian world that merit quoting at length:

> The advantage [to Christendom] was that there was a common language for public moral discourse with which society could discuss what was "the good." The disadvantage was that Christian morality without gospel-changed hearts often led to cruelty and hypocrisy.... Also, under "Christendom" the church often was silent against abuses of power of the ruling classes over the weak. For these reasons and others, the church in Europe and North America has been losing its privileged place as the arbiter of public morality since at least the mid 19th century.
>
> One of the reasons much of the American evangelical church has not experienced the same precipitous decline as the Protestant churches of Europe and Canada is because in the U.S. there is still a "heartland" with the remnants of the old "Christendom" society.... In conservative regions, it is still possible to see people profess faith and the church grow without becoming "missional." Most traditional evangelical churches still can only win people to Christ who are temperamentally traditional and conservative. But... this is a "shrinking market." And eventually evangelical churches ensconced in the declining, remaining enclaves of "Christendom" will have to learn how to become "missional." If it does not do that it will decline or die.
>
> We don't simply need evangelistic churches, but rather "missional" churches.[6]

To that end, it is important to define the characteristics of a missional church. We propose the following eleven marks as being those that

Your Community (Nashville: Broadman and Holman, 2006), 48.
[6]Tim Keller, "The Missional Church," June 2001, http://www.redeemer2.com/resources/papers/missional.pdf.

identify a missional church, one that is on God's mission to make disciples of all nations.[7]

1) A MISSIONAL CHURCH IS BIBLICAL

A missional church not only believes that Scripture is God's Word of truth, but lives out all that the Bible teaches to the best of its ability. A missional church has a deep trust in and affection for the Bible and seeks to anchor all of its teaching and life in the storyline of sacred Scripture and preserve truth.

Because it is biblical, a missional church contends for those parts of Scripture that are most essential to the gospel of Jesus Christ and does so with grace and humility so as to be biblical not only in doctrine but also in demeanor. In our day this means that we not only contend for the doctrines that older creeds (e.g., the Apostles' Creed and Nicene Creed) defined, but also for biblical answers to newer assaults on biblical truth. Thus, it is important today to contend for doctrines such as:

- Scripture, as God's speaking inerrant, timeless truth in human language and history;
- The sovereignty and foreknowledge of God;
- True humanity, which is made in the image of God, though it has become pervasively depraved because of sin;
- The virgin birth and bodily resurrection of Jesus;
- Jesus' death as our penal substitution, triumph over the powers of darkness, and model for every believer's life;
- Jesus' exclusivity as the only possible means of salvation;
- God-designed, complementary male and female gender distinctions and the sinfulness of all sexual activity outside of heterosexual marriage;
- The conscious, eternal torments of hell for unbelievers;
- The preeminence of God's kingdom over human culture;
- The recognition that Satan and demons are real and at work in the world.

Lastly, because a missional church is biblical, a missional church is always, only, solely, fully, passionately, uncompromisingly, wholeheartedly, unwaveringly, and continually all about Jesus as God, Savior, Lord, Hero, Hope, and Friend! The missional church does not want to

---

[7]Many of these marks are adapted from Guder, *Missional Church*, 11–12.

use vague terms and titles such as *God* into which non-Christians and false teachers can pour their own unbiblical meaning, so in missional churches the name of Jesus is often used instead.

2) A MISSIONAL CHURCH PRACTICES AND PREACHES REPENTANCE

Because it has a high view of Scripture, a missional church has a corresponding high view of the preaching and teaching of God's Word. In teaching God's Word, leaders of a missional church regularly call believing sinners, unbelieving sinners, and especially religious people to repentance.

For believing sinners, this includes calling them to acknowledge that they sin by both omission and commission in their thoughts, words, deeds, and motives. By the power of the Spirit, in the community of the church they can change their deeds out of their newness of heart as God grants them "repentance leading to a knowledge of the truth, and they may come to their senses and escape from the snare of the devil, after being captured by him to do his will."[8]

For unbelieving sinners, this includes calling them to gospel repentance, which fundamentally means changing their mind about who God is and what is really important. Through the gospel they come into living relationship with Jesus. Then their lives change out of their new heart-level love for the Lord. Like Paul, we proclaim that "they should repent and turn to God, performing deeds in keeping with their repentance."[9]

For "religious" people, this includes calling them to repent of their religion. "Religion" attempts to obtain righteousness apart from or in addition to the gift-righteousness given through the cross of Jesus. Religion instead seeks righteousness through piety and religious devotion to various unbiblical legalisms that culminate in formal and informal lists of what holy people do and do not do. Liberal religious people do this when they accept homosexuality, and move beyond evangelistic, interfaith friendships to interfaith prayer and worship with people of other religions. Conservative religious people do this when they live in a smug, self-righteous separatism that denounces all alcohol consump-

---

[8] 2 Tim. 2:25–26.
[9] Acts 26:20.

tion as sinful and ignores mainstream entertainment—television, movies, music, sports—except to criticize it as godless while lacking any heart to learn from it in order to relate to lost people for evangelistic purposes.

The missional church seeks to call both lost sinners to repent of their sin and religious people to repent of their religion for three reasons. First, both pursue righteousness apart from Jesus' grace, which is an offense to the gospel. Second, if only so-called sinners are called to repent, then these "sinners" wrongly think the church is trying to make them into religious people, while the religious people fail to see that they are sinners too who need to repent and live humbly by grace. Third, it was the religious leaders whom Jesus most sharply rebuked and was most violently opposed by; if we are to follow the example of Jesus, we must be just as forthright with the religious while accepting that they will likely be our most vocal critics and opponents.

Finally, to set an ongoing example for all, the leaders of a missional church openly confess their own past sin as well as their ongoing struggles and failures. This kind of demonstrable repentance also occurs at least occasionally in the pulpit by the preacher. He must be honest about what God is teaching him and how God is convicting him to make sure that everyone knows Jesus is the perfect hero in the church, and the pastor is merely a humble servant. The hope is to establish a culture of humility and honest repentance in the church that gives everyone an opportunity to follow the leaders in personally acknowledging their need for Jesus' saving, forgiving, and transforming grace.

3) A MISSIONAL CHURCH GOES INTO CULTURE

A missional church knows that God has sent it on mission to a time, a place, and a people. Paul stated this very fact to the Athenian court of Mars Hill in Acts 17, explaining how God not only created us but also determined when and where we would live according to his providential hand. Knowing that when we are born and where we live are part of God's purpose for our lives, together as the church we pay careful attention to where God has sent us.

To build on a biblical theme, if the gospel is the seed of God's powerful work in our lives and world, then the culture is the soil into which it is planted. Therefore, before doing any ministry, a missional church first examines the culture, or proverbial soil, in which they seek to have the gospel take root. Understanding the soil helps the missional church know which weeds of moral sin and theological error will need to be pulled up so as not to choke out the growth of the gospel and church.

A missional church goes to great lengths to understand the people God has sent them to. It seeks to know the culture and people better than any other organization, even businesses, so that Jesus can be most effectively, persuasively, and winsomely introduced. The opposite of a missional church is a church that simply copies the best practices of other churches in other cultural contexts and seeks to import them into a different time and place. Such churches are often as successful as a farmer determined to grow oranges in Alaska after seeing so many of them on a trip to California.

The elder who leads a missional church must be not only a missionary but also a missiologist. A missionary is someone who can bring the gospel to people in an effective cultural way. A missiologist is someone who studies the various cultures and subcultures in a community to help train all the missionaries to be effective. A missiologist intentionally investigates the local culture surrounding his or her church in an effort to find the opportunities and obstacles for the gospel.

The key is to do as Paul did when he arrived in Athens: go into culture and see what is happening in an effort to uncover the idols and understand the people. Like Paul, I pray that the Spirit would enable me to see how the gospel is truly the only answer to their longings for security, spirituality, love, friendship, and joy. Therefore, I engage culture not for entertainment but rather for theologically motivated missional observation, with the purpose of finding the sins and idols that have replaced the gospel of Jesus as the source of hope and object of worship. All the while I am praying to keep a clear heart and mind so as not to be corrupted by worldliness. That being said, it is helpful for a good missiologist to regularly do the following in order to see culture and its effects.[10]

---

[10]Some of these points are adapted from James Gilmore's presentation "Decoding the Future, the Phoniness, and the Shifting Sands" at the Resurgence Conference 2008: Text and Context. You can download audio and video of his presentation here: http://theresurgence.com/text_and_context_media.

WATCH TELEVISION

Missiologists watch everything on television, minus pornographic material of course. To do this you will need a TiVo or other device that records various television shows. In our house we have three TiVos, one for our five children with age-appropriate shows and two for me, guarded by passwords. I record a smattering of literally everything and try to keep up with the most popular shows for various age and gender groups. I also look for pioneering shows, those created as experiments to see if a new market can be created. Having the ability to fast-forward through shows is a great timesaver, and I always slow down to watch some of the ads because they too are insightful. As I watch, trying to learn about the culture, I pray and take notes in the journal I carry with me everywhere.

SURF TALK RADIO

I do not drive very much, but when I do I use the time to surf various talk-radio stations geared to Christians, non-Christians, women, men, Democrats, Republicans, sports fan, and others. I am able to hear which issues various people groups are most passionate about. This proves to be insightful, especially to the preacher looking for real-life cultural examples to connect with biblical truths.

WALK THE MALL

There may be more missional learning opportunities at the mall than anywhere. One of the best ways to learn at the mall is to go during school hours. The mall is empty then, and the store clerks are incredibly bored and happy to tell you about those who come into the store, what they buy, and what they talk about.

PAY ATTENTION AT THE GROCERY STORE

Since everyone goes to the grocery store, it is a fascinating place to learn about people—especially the folks in the organic section. Also, grocery stores are ideal places to observe what sells and how it is positioned for marketing purposes. One grocery store I studied has a small restaurant in it, along with an open coffee shop with a big fireplace and lots of comfortable couches. Many people stay there all day, not buying any groceries at all.

HANG OUT AT THE MAGAZINE RACK

At large magazine racks, such as those in bookstores, there are hours of free learning to be had. I spend my time first observing the various magazine categories because they represent tribes of people. I then observe the various covers because each is some tribe's view of heaven. Thus, having a great body, new car, home theater, or nice house is nothing less than a false heaven being sold through magazine evangelism. Then, I open the magazines to read about what people are thinking and are concerned about and committing themselves to in a worshipful way. All the while I am praying and asking God to show me their idols and how to offer the gospel as their only answer.

PAY ATTENTION TO KIDS

For better or worse, cultural trends tend to start with young people. This means that the parents of teenagers are at a strategic cultural advantage because they live in closer proximity to new slang, fashion trends, technological innovations, and moral behaviors. Anyone who is not in relationship with teens is not in a strategic position to be a good missionary who sees where culture is going.

TALK TO THE PEOPLE

Talk to the people who talk to the people. There are people in your local culture who broker relationships and information. Bank tellers, grocery store clerks, realtors, guidance counselors at the public schools, news reporters, and others are in constant contact with large numbers of people and continually learn vital information.

GO ONLINE

Online you can see where people are spending their time, what Web sites they are frequenting, and how they are describing themselves in various social networks. The odds are you can learn a ton about people in your own neighborhood by asking them where they go online and if they blog, and then reading what they post and reading what they read or watch online.

BREAK YOUR ROUTINE

Too many people live their life by a predictable routine and at times need to go out to places they otherwise would not to observe what other people are doing. I was once in a major city outside of the United States preaching Sunday morning services at a large church filled with mainly older people. I was curious where the young people in the city were, so when I arrived back at the hotel, I asked the young bellhop where people his age hung out. He said there was an entire block of bars and clubs that were virtually empty until just before midnight. So, planning to be out all night, I took a nap and then went out with a few other pastors to walk the city and see the block. That city block was absolutely packed with thousands of young professionals who lived and worked in the city—what an opportunity for church people to hang out in a way that brings Jesus to this block.

4) A MISSIONAL CHURCH CONTEXTUALIZES THE GOSPEL

A missional church seeks to follow the example of Jesus, who is the greatest missionary ever to engage culture. He left one culture and came into another and participated in it fully by using a language, participating in various holidays, eating certain foods, enjoying various drinks, attending parties, and befriending people, while never crossing a line into sin. Jesus' life is the perfect and model missionary life lived for God in culture that we are to emulate, without falling into the pitfall of liberal syncretism or fundamental sectarianism. It deserves to be noted, however, that in the eyes of those who were fundamental and separatist in their thinking, Jesus simply went too far. They viewed his actions as sinful, and they falsely accused him of being a glutton, a binge drinker, and a supporter of sin.[11]

The undeniable truth is that contextualization is not something done just by Christian missionaries in other nations, but it is something done by every Christian in every culture even if they don't recognize it. On this point, Paul said in 1 Corinthians 9:19–23:

> For though I am free from all, I have made myself a servant to all, that I might win more of them. To the Jews I became as a Jew, in order to win

---

[11]Matt. 11:19.

Jews. To those under the law I became as one under the law (though not being myself under the law) that I might win those under the law. To those outside the law I became as one outside the law (not being outside the law of God but under the law of Christ) that I might win those outside the law. To the weak I became weak, that I might win the weak. I have become all things to all people, that by all means I might save some. I do it all for the sake of the gospel, that I may share with them in its blessings.

In the world of missiology we call this *contextualization*. That is, churches should be aware of the cultural context in which lost people around them live, and they should make every effort to bring the love and truth of Jesus in word and deed and to be "all things to all people" using "all means" to "save some." Rather than being a compromise, such labor is "for the sake of the gospel," which means that any church that only does evangelism without first studying the culture in an effort to contextualize does not fully care about the gospel. Too many churches are built solely to accommodate religious people, even though their culture and cultural methods of ministry are not welcoming or hospitable to those outside their Christian culture. Contextualization is about making the church as culturally accessible as possible without compromising the truth of Christian belief. In this, what is sought is timeless truth and timely methods. In other words, contextualization is not making the gospel relevant, but showing the relevance of the gospel.

Practically, this means that a missional church speaks the language and sings the style of the culture without using pious talk, or what one pastor calls "dearlybelovedisms," because it is biblical. When God inspired the writing of the New Testament, the options were academic or street-level Greek, and God chose to have his Word written in the language of the street. Paul also argues for comprehensible Christianity in 1 Corinthians 14; many of God's people were speaking a language that lost people simply could not understand, and Paul rightly commanded them to speak intelligible words in the church so that lost people could comprehend and be saved.

At this point, it is important to distinguish between relativists and relevantists. Relativists are willing to compromise Christian truth in the name of relating to lost people. This is a problem because they seek to change Jesus, wrongly believing he is not relevant to people and their lives. Conversely, relevantists know that Jesus is relevant to every person, time, place, culture, and circumstance. They are committed to breaking down every cultural barrier that raises its head against the power and truth of the gospel. They use any moral means so people can clearly hear the message of Jesus and see the relevance of Jesus.

Furthermore, we are not promoting seeker-sensitive churches where doctrine is downplayed. Rather, we prefer seeker-sensible churches. This means that a church does not stop using the words of the Bible, which are packed with theological meaning (e.g., *sin*, *propitiation*, *wrath*, *judgment*, *hell*), but does make every effort to explain those words. It also winsomely defends against lost people's objections so that they understand what Christians believe and why, while they are invited to believe as well. By contextualizing, the missional church is not compromising but rather obeying the example of Paul, who rebuked Peter for his sinful attempt to have a church only for Jews that did not welcome Gentiles and their culture.[12]

As faithful missionaries, Christians have been adapting the methods and culture of church throughout the history of the church. While in India some years ago I was asked to preach at a rural village church. They met in a very simple cinder block building. Everyone sat on the floor, and the women and men sat on different sides of the church. Their Bible was not any version I had ever seen; it had been contextualized via translation into vernacular that they could understand. Children were included in the service, as there was no nursery. The singing time included instruments and songs I had never heard. I found it strange that the church service did not start on time or have any set length. I was told that we would wait patiently and graciously for everyone to show up before starting, and we would end when it seemed like it was time. As a result, we started very late and stayed very long; but unlike in American churches, no one seemed to mind and no one left early but used the time to visit and build relationships.

To preach I was asked to sit up front on a slightly raised platform guru-style with my legs crossed and wait for the translator to contextualize my words to the people. Being about as flexible as a hyper-Calvinist, I was unsure how I could possibly preach that way, but I made a sincere effort out of a love for the people and a desire to respect their cultural

---

[12]Gal. 2:11–14.

forms, which were not in any way forbidden in Scripture and therefore permissible. However, had they asked me to sacrifice an animal as their Hindu counterparts down the road were doing to appease their gods, I would have declined because to be a good missionary means that we do all we can, short of sinning, to make the church culturally accessible. My guess is that in reading this story, few people, if any, would object. Yet many people are prone to make severe moral judgments about any cultural accommodation in their own church in things such as aesthetics, dress code, music style, service times, and service orders.

Why? Because they still live under the myth that missions is something that happens across the world rather than across the street, and that missionaries are special people and not normal Christians. This is a sin to be repented of. Every church is surrounded with cultures, subcultures, and tribes of people who are just as lost and culturally different from Western evangelical Christianity as an Indian villager who sits on the floor, eats with his hands, and plows his field behind an ox. Since we are to love our neighbor, we should have a church that is culturally contextualized as an act of love.

Admittedly, as the gospel passes from one culture to another there is the very difficult matter of determining what is to be rejected, what is to be received, and what is to be redeemed. This is true in both the culture that is sending and the culture that is receiving the gospel; the gospel will not be held captive to any culture, including church culture, without continually calling it to repentance.

This is one of the reasons we have the New Testament Epistles. Much of their content deals with the questions and conflicts regarding what was to be rejected, received, and redeemed as the gospel moved from the Jewish to the Gentile culture. Therefore, the New Testament is in itself a missiological example of the difficult theological work of contextualization. Today, questions about contextualization include mode of dress, tattoos, piercings, plastic surgery, music styles, use of technology in church, entertainment that includes television and film, smoking, drinking, language, homosexuality, and sexual deviancy of every conceivable type.

Because the early church was missional, it answered the questions of their day faithfully and contextually. And in our day we must do the same.

5) A MISSIONAL CHURCH LOVES SINGLES AND COUPLES

On many church Web sites are photos of loving couples and families with children. Many churches promote their program as being tailored to the whole family. In many churches nearly every leader at nearly every level of the organization is married. During most church services, the preacher's points are all about how to improve one's marriage and family.

However, for the first time ever, a slight majority of Americans are single. Practically speaking, this means that a missional church is not solely built for families; it also takes into serious consideration how to minister to those who are unmarried.

For too long the church has assumed that most people are married with children, or will get married and have children. But with divorce, widowhood, people waiting longer to marry, some people never marrying, some not wanting children, others delaying children, and still others struggling with infertility and the like, the assumption that people in general, and lost people in particular, are or will be a typical family is incredibly outdated. As a married father of five, I wholeheartedly believe that marriage and children are a blessing, but since most people are not there we need to meet them where they are.

A missional church knows not only that most people are single, but that most single people are not Christians. This means that a missional church gladly considers unmarried people in everything from how it advertises to when services are offered. This does not necessarily mean that a missional church adds a singles' ministry as an aside, as if the married people were normal and the unmarried people were abnormal and in a temporary life stage that will be outgrown like puberty. That kind of thinking makes singles feel like second-class citizens, which is especially insulting when many of them are well educated, vocationally successful, and affluent. At Mars Hill Church roughly half our people are single. Our largest service is at 7 p.m. on Sunday nights and does not offer childcare at all but does attract a lot of college students and singles.

6) A MISSIONAL CHURCH TRAINS CHRISTIANS AS MISSIONARIES

One of the ways a missional church seeks the glory of God is in the conversion of lost people. Too often, what is called a missional church is nothing more than a hip, trendy gathering of the disgruntled children of other churches, where few if any true conversions and life transformations are experienced. This does not mean that a church exists solely as an evangelistic ministry for lost people, as the seeker movement has extolled. But a healthy missional church knows the gospel is true, powerful, and compelling, and it should be seeing people saved regularly.

Tragically, the need for the missional church is incredibly great because evangelism seems to be a dying ministry. Liberals tend to think evangelism is not necessary since they falsely assume generally everyone is heaven-bound, while conservatives are huddled up in their church busy preaching to the proverbial choir instead of leading them on a mission to reach people in their local culture. Researcher Thom Rainer confirms this fact:

> Church leaders are becoming less evangelistic. A survey of pastors I led in 2005 surprised the research team. Over one-half (53 percent) of pastors have made no evangelistic efforts at all in the past six months. They have not shared the Gospel. They have not attempted to engage a lost and unchurched person at any level.[13]

A missional church accepts its responsibility for being the primary vehicle that God has chosen to be on mission with him in making disciples of all nations. As a result, it takes a missionary outlook on all of life and ministry. Because it loves lost people, a missional church considers non-Christians in all that it does.

Members of a missional church are expected to serve on the frontlines of cultural missions. They are witnesses to the world about Jesus and their church every day, and the only question is whether they are good or bad witnesses. Because they are on the front lines of ministry, like Jesus was, Christian members of missional churches are trained in hospitality, theology, and apologetics so that they can practice 1 Peter 3:15–16, which says:

> In your hearts honor Christ the Lord as holy, always being prepared to make a defense to anyone who asks you for a reason for the hope that is in you; yet do it with gentleness and respect, having a good conscience,

---

[13]Thom S. Rainer, "First-person: The dying American church," *SBC Baptist Press*, March 28, 2006, http://www.bpnews.net/bpcolumn.asp?ID=2197.

so that, when you are slandered, those who revile your good behavior
in Christ may be put to shame.

Peter describes the missional lifestyle as loving Jesus as Lord over
all and living in relationship with lost family, friends, neighbors, and
coworkers in such an authentic way that they are compelled to ask
questions about Jesus. Christians should be sufficiently taught by their
missional church so they have biblical answers to those questions and
the character to answer them in a way that is gentle and respectful so
that Jesus' loving grace is not only articulated theologically but demonstrated practically. This loving grace, Peter says, is most often put to
the test when missional Christians are opposed, mocked, and despised
for the biblical answers they give. Instances of opposition are wonderful
opportunities to show that our gospel has really transformed our lives
and has enabled us to love even our enemies as God in Christ loved us
when we were his enemies.

Lastly, because the members of a missional church see themselves
as missionaries, their ministry expands beyond their local church.
As a result, a missional church is truly "glocal"[14] in that its leaders
and members are both missionaries locally and missionaries globally.
Therefore, a missional church finds itself more easily aligned with missions work around the world regardless of cultural context than with
many non-missional churches in its neighborhood.

7) A MISSIONAL CHURCH IS SUPERNATURAL

Luke describes the church as a supernatural community: "And awe
came upon every soul, and many wonders and signs were being done
through the apostles."[15] Some would limit the performing of wonders and signs to the apostles, but the miraculous Samaritan revival
was led by a deacon, Philip.[16] Likewise, we should assume that the
activity of the Spirit is a normal part of the Christian church. In fact,
the whole distinction between natural as normal life ruled by the
laws of nature and supernatural as the abnormal breaking in of God,
which underlines so much erroneous thinking, comes more from

---

[14]For more on the concept of "glocal," see Bob Roberts Jr., *Transformation: How Glocal Churches
Transform Lives and the World* (Grand Rapids, MI: Zondervan, 2006).
[15]Acts 2:43.
[16]Acts 8:6–13.

the mechanistic worldview of Enlightenment deism than from the Bible.

Just like the church in the Bible, it is normal for God to be visibly at work in and around the church. Therefore, the missional church refuses to settle for superficial faith, preferring to pursue a life of Spirit-filled, Spirit-led, and Spirit-empowered living. This does not mean that the missional church chases signs and wonders. The church in Corinth considered itself to be very spiritual because of strange supernatural manifestations in its midst. However, God judged the members of that church because their unguided frenzy made unbelievers think they were out of their minds.[17] If God is present, his working will be wonderfully normal because the kingdom of God has come among his people through the power of the Holy Spirit and the gospel of Jesus Christ.

This means that the missional church does pray for people to be physically healed, and it will see healings. But it will never focus on them, nor will they result in frenzy. This also means that the missional church believes in all of the spiritual gifts mentioned in the New Testament and seeks to exercise them in a way that is both humble and biblical. It will value those things that build, encourage, comfort, and edify. Furthermore, it also means that demonic activity is not uncommon, and while not everything is blamed on Satan, there is a recognition of real, ongoing spiritual warfare between the kingdom of light and the domain of darkness.

8) A MISSIONAL CHURCH IS COUNTERCULTURAL

God's people are to live out their lives as a countercultural community whose citizenship is ultimately in God's kingdom. They live in culture to reveal Jesus their King and the difference his kingdom rule makes. The purpose of such countercultural kingdom living is threefold. First, countercultural kingdom living worships God by obeying the teachings of Scripture. Second, countercultural kingdom living trains younger generations in missional living so that there is a legacy of faith that continues after one's death. Third, open and public countercultural kingdom living provides lost people an alternative and attractive way of life with Jesus and his people, the church.

---

[17] 1 Cor. 14:23.

Jeremiah 29:4–9 describes what this countercultural kingdom living looks like:[18]

> Thus says the LORD of hosts, the God of Israel, to all the exiles whom I have sent into exile from Jerusalem to Babylon: Build houses and live in them; plant gardens and eat their produce. Take wives and have sons and daughters; take wives for your sons, and give your daughters in marriage, that they may bear sons and daughters; multiply there, and do not decrease. But seek the welfare of the city where I have sent you into exile, and pray to the LORD on its behalf, for in its welfare you will find your welfare. For thus says the LORD of hosts, the God of Israel: Do not let your prophets and your diviners who are among you deceive you, and do not listen to the dreams that they dream, for it is a lie that they are prophesying to you in my name; I did not send them, declares the LORD.

We can glean six aspects of countercultural kingdom living from these verses.

1) Countercultural living includes loving the people and the place where God has providentially put us, no matter how hard that might be. In the day of Jeremiah, God brought his people to the godless city of Babylon. Babylon was founded by the godless man Nimrod.[19] Symbolically, it came to be associated with the counterfeit kingdom of Satan and the haven for all sin.[20] God's people in Jeremiah's day wanted nothing more than to leave Babylon. By calling his people to love Babylon and the Babylonians, God was asking them to show the gospel to their enemies.

2) Countercultural living requires becoming a stakeholder in the culture. As in Jeremiah's day, this includes buying houses for oneself and one's family, along with other real estate for one's business and church. This, combined with the command to plant gardens and eat what they produce, demonstrates the idea of permanence. In our transient day when people come and go, the missional church and its members purchase real estate for their family, business, and church as stakeholders in the culture. This gives lost people the clear affirmation

---

[18]I want to thank Tim Keller for really helping to illuminate the importance of this text of Scripture in our personal conversations over the years.
[19]Gen. 10:10.
[20]Rev. 18:2, 10, 21.

that Christians do not intend to use the culture or pass through it while moving elsewhere but rather to settle in for a lifetime of service.

3) Countercultural living includes honoring marriage. This includes preaching and practicing abstinence before marriage and chastity in marriage so that the marriage bed is honored and kept pure as Scripture commands.[21] It also means that parents are intimately involved in raising their children to love God and ensuring they marry people who also love God so that the legacy of missional service to the city continues for generations to come.

4) Countercultural living includes celebrating children as God's blessing. The Bible connects sex, marriage, and children in a way that the culture at large does not. In the missional church, countercultural living means that abortion is not accepted and that adoption (as Joseph did Jesus) is done in love as a demonstration of the gospel whereby God the Father adopts us into his family the church.

5) Countercultural living includes doing good not only for fellow Christians but also for the common good of all people, so long as it does not require sinning or condoning sin. This means that the gospel should be shown in deeds of generosity, kindness, and mercy, especially to the poor and suffering. This kind of selfless living is contrary to the incessant selfishness and tribalism that marks typical fallen living. Practically, this also means that power and money will be wielded in a countercultural way so that the entire community can be blessed and served, rather than one person or group of people prospering at the expense of the well-being of all people.

6) Countercultural living includes not fearing the greater culture. This lack of fear does not negate wisdom or discernment as if sin and its effects were not real. Rather, it believes that the gospel truly is the power of God and that our goal is to be faithful to our calling rather than fearful of our challenges.

Perhaps the most fitting metaphor for the missional church as a countercultural kingdom community is the one we are most fond of at Mars Hill Church—we are a city within a city. We take the analogy from Jesus who said, "You are the light of the world. A city set on a hill cannot be hidden."[22]

---

[21]Heb. 13:4.
[22]Matt. 5:14.

Picking up on this theme of the missional church as a city within a city, the church father Augustine wrote an entire book titled *City of God*. In it he says, "Accordingly, two cities have been formed by two loves: the earthly by the love of self; even to the contempt of God; the heavenly by the love of God; even to the contempt of self. The former, in a word, glories in itself, the latter in the Lord. For the one seeks glory from men; but the greatest glory of the other is God, the witness of conscience."[23]

In the city within the city, Jesus rules above all, men are called to lead in masculine love, women are cherished, heterosexual marriage is honored, sex is celebrated but only within marriage, children are a blessing, and an alternative vision of life is offered in love and hope of attracting the city to consider a countercultural way of life with Jesus and his people. For the city within the city to thrive, the burden for demonstrating a kingdom lifestyle among God's people has to be placed on the men, especially the young men, because so much of culture rises and falls depending on the quality of the men.

9) A MISSIONAL CHURCH MULTIPLIES

Because it cares about people getting saved, about the well-being of the local church, and about the health of the whole church the missional church is innately reproductive. The missional church expresses this through the sharing and giving of resources (e.g., leaders, people, facilities, finances, training) in four ways.

1) A missional church is committed to planting other churches. This commitment is visible with the release of people, money, and other resources.

2) A missional church is open to starting other campuses as an extension of its ministry, if and when that is possible. As a general rule, though, a church should not seek to open another campus unless it is nearing capacity at multiple services in their current facility, growing numerically, and raising up enough leaders to sustain the existing campus while other leaders are sent out to pioneer the new campus.

[23]Augustine, *City of God*, book 14, chap. 28. For further reading on how the early church and other great expressions of the church in history have been cities within cities, the following books are helpful: Rodney Stark, *Cities of God: The Real Story of How Christianity Became an Urban Movement and Conquered Rome* (New York: HarperCollins, 2006); Wayne Meeks, *The First Urban Christians: The Social World of the Apostle Paul* (London: Yale University Press, 2003); Richard Fletcher, *The Barbarian Conversion: From Paganism to Christianity* (Los Angeles: University of California Press, 1999); and Lester De Koster, *Light for the City: Calvin's Preaching, Source of Life and Liberty* (Grand Rapids, MI: Eerdmans, 2004).

Furthermore, the church should be in a season of health, open to change, and have the financial resources to cover the expenses of both the existing and the new campus, which will have many costly start-up expenses.

3) A missional church practices unity on a local level to the degree that faithfulness to God isn't compromised. Regarding partnership, churches should work with non-Christian agencies and organizations such as food banks and require no theological agreement with those that do not claim to be Christian. For organizations and churches that do claim to be Christian, however, we must not expect them to agree with us on every point but must require that they adhere to the essential Christian beliefs such as the Trinity, the deity of Jesus as God, and the need to repent of sin and trust in Jesus for salvation.

4) A missional church helps other evangelical churches improve in their maturity inwardly and evangelism outwardly. Because a missional church sees itself as part of the larger church, it serves not only its well-being but the well-being of the whole church. Accordingly, a missional church will give resources to help other churches outside of its network, denomination, or theological tradition, especially for the cause of church planting. Thus, the missional church sees its theology and heritage as a home, not a prison. As a home, the missional church is free to visit the proverbial physical and theological home of other churches and thereby seek to learn while serving without losing its distinct convictions.

10) A MISSIONAL CHURCH IS MESSY

The missional church is much like the early church. The early church struggled with marginalization in its society, surrounded as it was by spirituality, paganism, and sexual deviancy of every sort and kind. The early church also wrestled through the questions that were raised when the gospel jumped from Jewish to Gentile culture, which included topics such as circumcision, Sabbath day and festivals, meat sacrificed to idols, and sexual propriety. Arguably all the New Testament Epistles are missional letters intended to help local churches either get on or stay on mission with God.

A reading of the New Testament reveals how truly messy the first missional churches were. It seems that every reform and revival movement in the history of the church has sought to return to the pattern of the New Testament church. While this is wise in principle, the result in practice is often an unrealistic and idealistic reading of the New Testament that overlooks the messiness. Admittedly, the New Testament does speak of a few decent churches in generally favorable terms, such as the churches in Philippi and Thessalonica. However, the churches and Christians in the New Testament are anything but the utopian dream that too many Christians somehow see when reading their Bible. The church at Galatia, for example, was filled with legalistic, false, demonic doctrine.

In summary, the reason the Bible has so many exhortations to live out the new life of the Spirit is because so few Christians and Christian churches obey. Religion responds to such debauchery with more rules and shouted threats of punishment. But the Bible calls us back to the reality that we are members of the kingdom of the beloved Son and new creatures in Christ, with a gift-righteousness that includes a regenerated heart with godly desires empowered by the indwelling Holy Spirit. As we remember these things, we move toward Christlikeness out of genuine love for him and out of joy for what he is doing for us, in us, and through us. Any accurate reading of the New Testament must include a humble recognition that we and our churches have a lot of sanctification to experience.

Living as Christians, the missional church seeks the welfare of the broken and sinful culture while never condoning sin in the church. We remind Christians and Christian leaders that the missional church is willing to take risks, make changes, and suffer through mistakes as needed. We commit to become what Jesus ultimately desires for the church to be and do as it is led by leaders filled with the Spirit and guided by the Scriptures.

ANSWERS TO COMMON QUESTIONS ABOUT THE MISSIONAL CHURCH

IF A CHURCH TRIES TO BE RELEVANT WON'T IT BECOME WORLDLY?

Ironically, many Christians who are most concerned about worldliness have imbibed a form of it that provoked Jesus to wrath: the worldliness of the man-made religion of the Pharisees (Matthew 23; Luke 11:33–12:3).

First, worldliness is in what we love, the ideals we use to interpret and evaluate the society around us. Worldliness can be seen in our priorities that influence which activities we will do. We are worldly when we worship other gods and adopt their practices (Ex. 20:3; 23:13; Deuteronomy 13; Matt. 6:24; 1 Cor. 10:20–21; 2 Cor. 6:14–17). Worldly values include rugged individualism expressed in self-sufficiency, seeing wealth or physical beauty as the key to status, and personal freedom apart from restraints of morality. Study such passages as Ephesians 4:17–6:9, Colossians 3, or 1 Peter 4:1–9 to get the biblical picture of worldliness.

Second, we have to determine how to be relevant. If we play the significance game by the rules of the contemporary culture, trying to gain attention by its values, we are being tainted by worldliness. We simply cannot adapt the gospel to the values of popular concerts, TV, and movies. The problem is that unchurched people are so caught up into their here-and-now priorities that they don't even see Jesus. We can and must communicate the gospel to these people, so we use contemporary topics of conversation as points of contact for the gospel as Paul did on Mars Hill (Acts 17:16–34). We join their conversations, speaking biblical values and truth to awaken them to Jesus.

Being relevant means lowering the cultural barriers of Christian jargon, dress, topics of conversation, and musical genre that tell unchurched folk they don't fit here. It means addressing their real issues without falling into the trap of adapting to please them. It means taking the gospel into the world of the people who live around the church. We are like Jesus, who went where the people were, hung with them, ate and drank with them, and talked seriously with them.

Being relevant never means easing the offense of the gospel. It means making the connections so people who are occupied with every-day cares and concerns of their "real" world can hear the powerful truth of the *real* world.

DIDN'T JESUS TELL US TO GO TO ALL NATIONS? WHY IS IT THAT MISSIONAL CHURCHES SEEM TO FORGET ABOUT MISSIONS?

The simplest answer is that missional churches see local needs so clearly that they can get locked into their community. But the problem is not just on the side of the missional church. Missions churches can get locked in too. An overly simple comparison may help clarify. Missions churches see the mission field as being an ocean away. The "all nations" of Matthew 28:19 refers to all people groups in all the countries of the world. Missionaries are Christian superheroes who go to China or Africa, learn a foreign language, adapt to living in a very different culture, and win very foreign people to Christ. They come back every five years to show slides of their work. We marvel at what God is doing through them, knowing we could never be like them.

Conversely, missional churches see the mission field as being next door. The "all nations" of Matthew 28:19 refers to all ethnicities and cultural groups in their neighborhood. All Christians are missionaries who must learn the language and culture of their neighbors so they can win them to Christ. They constantly share the demands and joys of their mission as they live and worship with the other missionaries in their church. There really is no "us" and "them."

Missions is defined as sending people to geographically distant places across cultural barriers for the central purpose of making disciples of Jesus Christ by proclaiming the good news about Jesus for the purpose of evangelism, church planting, leadership development, and church development. Missional churches usually see the mission as broader, thereby including personal and community renewal, justice, cultural transformation, and closer, following along natural relationship lines.

It is unfortunate that foreign missions is not a part of the vision of many missional churches. Losing the world focus gives away a global dimension that is essential to Jesus as Lord of all nations. When church members connect with a missionary serving abroad, they can learn a lot about the cultural differences in churches. A world that is increasingly interconnected economically and culturally also should be connected by the church. It is also unfortunate the local community is lacking from the vision of many missions churches. The outreach is often long-distance and short-term. Subsequently, their youth spend ten days building a house in Mexico rather than doing repairs on the run-down apartment building across the street. Even something as simple as a call to volunteers to do community service projects never appears in the church bulletin.

We believe the church's vision must be what pastor Bob Roberts calls "glocal," taking the message and life of Jesus to the community and the world and uniting people "from every tribe and language and people and nation" (Gen. 12:2–3; Phil. 2:9–11; Rev. 5:9).

CHAPTER TEN

WHAT IS A MULTI-CAMPUS CHURCH?

"Go therefore and make disciples of all nations."

MATTHEW 28:19

✝

I started Mars Hill Church with my wife, Grace, as a clueless, newer Christian and naïve twenty-five-year-old. I believed that the gospel was true and Jesus was alive, and because God loves glory, I expected that for him to show up in a city as jacked-up as Seattle was not a big request. You can read about the entire fiasco in another book I wrote,[1] but the gist is that we started as roughly the same size as a Mormon family and met in the living room of our rental home in the city. Before long we moved into a building and kept moving during the early years because we were flat broke and were never able to secure a church home of any kind.

After a few years, by God's grace, we eventually grew to a few hundred people in an evening service at a rented church downtown. At that time, we were given a church building free of charge in another part of the city. I wore a suit and carried a King James Bible in an effort to be a good missionary to conservative, Jesus-loving grandmas who stayed on in the church when we took it over. Around that same time one of our

---

[1]Mark Driscoll, *Confessions of a Reformission Rev.: Hard Lessons from an Emerging Missional Church* (Grand Rapids, MI: Zondervan, 2006).

elders purchased a small theater in yet another part of the city near the University of Washington.

We decided to put a small core—a few dozen people—in each of the two new locations. I preached live at each location, driving between them in my old pickup, which had more than two hundred thousand miles on it and a huge dent in the side from a portable baptismal loading accident. We experienced the most rapid growth at the donated church building; our core of maybe three or four dozen exploded to some eight hundred people in less than a year, despite the fact that our main building seated only about 150 people, had only one parking spot, and was in a remote area of the city. To accommodate the growth at that location, we went to multiple services and threw up a very poor video feed of the sermon from a home-movie camera onto a screen in the basement.

All of this occurred during the late 1990s before the video phenomenon. Without really thinking about it, we became a multi-site and video-venue church. Before long, each of our three locations was growing, reaching different kinds of people with different music and styles that organically emerged at each place based upon who was getting saved there and stepping up to serve.

Reflecting on those experiences now, it is clear that we were in many ways following the pattern of the New Testament. Many of the New Testament letters were written to networks of churches scattered throughout a particular city (e.g., Corinth, Galatia, Thessalonica, and Philippi). Some of the instructional letters, such as Hebrews, James, and the epistles of Peter, are called general epistles because they were intended to be read and obeyed at multiple churches. Furthermore, the New Testament seems to indicate that churches spread across regions as a linked network of congregations. For example, 1 Peter 1:1 refers to churches in the areas of "Pontus, Galatia, Cappadocia, Asia, and Bithynia." While the circumstances in the New Testament era are not the same as what we are doing today, the variety of venues there indicates that the early church was quite flexible, meeting and worshiping in distinctive situations to meet the needs and opportunities of their time.

Likewise, throughout the history of Christianity there have always been networks, denominations, and movements in which multiple churches were linked together in various ways and to various degrees for the benefit of the forward progress of the gospel. Historically, preachers have even traveled between churches to provide preaching and pastoral leadership. One such example is the Methodist circuit riders, who would travel on horseback to preach at multiple churches. Each of the meeting places had local identity and leadership, with the pastor serving successively at each site. Francis Asbury (1745–1816), the founding bishop of American Methodism, traveled more than a quarter of a million miles on foot and horseback, preaching about sixteen thousand sermons as he worked in his circuits. These men were generally a rugged bunch; their average life expectancy was only thirty-three years due to the constant exposure to the elements.

With increasing advances in technology, we are now seeing the principles of one church meeting in multiple locations exponentially applied. The result has come to be called the "multi-site church revolution," which includes the controversial advent of "video venues." In many ways this is the circuit-riding preacher model renewed by technology. This chapter is devoted to exploring these two phenomena in both theological and practical detail.

MULTI-SITE CHURCHES

The experts at Leadership Network who are thoroughly researching multi-site churches[2] define a multi-site church as "one church meeting in multiple locations—different rooms on the same campus, different locations in the same region, or in some instances, different cities, states, or nations. A multi-site church shares a common vision, budget, leadership, and board."[3] Multi-site churches can take a variety of forms or models:

> For some churches, having multiple sites involves only a worship service at each location; for others, each location has a full range of support ministries. Some churches use video-cast sermons (recorded or live); others have in-person teaching on-site. Some churches maintain a similar worship atmosphere and style at all their campuses, and others allow or invite variation.[4]

---

[2]See http://www.leadnet.org for their extensive research.
[3]Geoff Surratt, Greg Ligon, and Warren Bird, *The Multi-Site Church Revolution* (Grand Rapids, MI: Zondervan, 2006), 18.
[4]Ibid.

Thus, there is a great variety of methodology applied to multi-site churches. My friends at Leadership Network have been the most aggressive researchers of the phenomenon and networking facilitators of those churches pioneering it. According to their research, five key multi-site models have emerged:

1) *Video-venue model*: creating one or more on-campus environments that use videocast sermons (live or recorded), often varying the worship style.

2) *Partnership model*: partnering with a local business or nonprofit organization to use its facility beyond a mere "renter" arrangement.

3) *Teaching-team model*: leveraging a strong teaching team across multiple locations at the original campus or an off-site campus.

4) *Regional-campus model*: replicating the experience of the original campus at additional campuses in order to make church more accessible to other geographic communities.

5) *Low-risk model*: experimenting with new locations that are low-risk because of the simplicity of the programming and small financial investment but have the potential for high returns in terms of evangelism and growth.[5]

The size and pervasiveness of the multi-site revolution may surprise some readers. The experts claim that among Protestant churches in the United States:

- Well over 1,500 churches are already multi-site;
- One in four megachurches [2,000 or more people] is holding services at multiple locations;
- One in three churches says it is thinking about developing a new service in a new location;
- Seven of the country's ten fastest-growing churches offer worship in multiple locations, as do nine of the ten largest churches.[6]

Furthermore, "the multi-site movement is represented in every area of the country, across many denominations, and in churches of all sizes, especially those with attendances of 250 and up. The dramatic growth of interest in the multi-site approach is nothing short of a revolution in how to reach people for Christ."[7]

The experts do not expect this revolution to recede. In fact, they

---

[5]Leadership Network, *Innovation 2007: Connecting Innovators to Multiply* (Dallas: Leadership Network, 2007), 13. Also available at www.leadnet.org/innovation2007.
[6]Surratt, et al., *The Multi-Site Church Revolution*, 9.
[7]Ibid.

predict that "30,000 American churches will be multi-site within the next few years, which means one or more multi-site churches will probably be in your area. . . . [and] estimate that one-third of the churches in America could succeed as multi-site congregations.[8]

Perhaps the most controversial aspect of many multi-site churches is the use of video for the preaching. This is done in any number of ways. First, some churches simply play back their Sunday sermon a week later at other campuses. Second, some churches capture a Saturday night service for replaying at campuses on Sunday. One church at which I have preached goes so far as to put an employee on an airplane every Saturday night to fly the hard drive with the sermon to another state for the Sunday morning services. Third, some churches broadcast the sermon live to their campuses via the Internet or television satellite, which is what we do at Mars Hill.

Four points must be made regarding the use of video.

1) Every church that exceeds roughly four to five hundred people per service is forced either to add another service, if they can, or to use video, because beyond roughly sixty feet, the human eye has a difficult time seeing facial expressions and such. Therefore, a larger room in which the people are sixty feet or more from the preacher requires at least image magnification on side screens with close-ups of the preacher's face if he is to be seen by everyone.

2) People wrongly subscribe a moral value to a church size. People who prefer small churches (however they define "small") criticize big "fancy" churches with "impersonal" preachers who are on screens and denounce the lack of loving community. Conversely, some who prefer large churches (however they define "large") criticize small "mom and pop shop" churches for having "pathetic" preaching, music, and programing and disparage their lack of conversion growth and evangelism. Such bantering is no more helpful than parents arguing whether their tall child or their short child is better and more loved by God. At best, it reflects pride, immaturity, and judgmentalism that is detrimental to Christian unity among churches.

3) In the days of the New Testament, the apostles used the technology available to them to speak to churches at which they were not present. They sent letters by courier to the churches they were responsible

---

[8]Ibid., 11–12.

for. Some of those letters had universal authority and were immediately canonized and became the New Testament Epistles.

One example of pastoral leadership being exercised remotely is found in 1 Corinthians 5:3. The church had affirmed an alternative sexual lifestyle, so Paul wrote them a letter to be read aloud to the church: "For though absent in body, I am present in spirit; and as if present, I have already pronounced judgment on the one who did such a thing." Perhaps if the apostles had video they would have used it; at the very least their example permits what Scripture does not condemn.

4) Effective churches have always bucked their critics and have quickly adopted new technology, ranging from the early movie theaters to radio to TV to satellite broadcasting. Today we are in an age where people are used to getting video messages on screens ranging from mobile devices to TVs to theaters. It is foolish stewardship not to at least consider using some of those screens for the preaching of the gospel.

MULTI-SITE LESSONS FROM MARS HILL CHURCH

For a few years in the 1990s, we were doing six services in three different parts of the city. Some were on Sunday morning and some were on Sunday evening. I frantically drove between the locations to preach all of the services live, and because my sermons are more than an hour in length, it made for a long and exhausting day. To make matters worse, the campuses were growing simultaneously, filling up the services, which required even more services, growth which I could not accommodate because, unlike Jesus, I am not omnipresent.

In an effort to alleviate the problem, we moved to the teaching-team model and established a preaching team. Besides me, the team included two very godly men, cofounding Mars Hill elders who had done some preaching since the beginning of the church. I handed off one location to one man, combined two locations into one to oversee myself, and sent out the other man to start a new service in another part of the city with the church members who lived there. That location became a successful church plant; the other location struggled financially because it was made up of mainly homeless indie rockers and college students; and the campus I oversaw exploded from a few dozen to maybe a thousand people in a very small building in a very short time. I say this not to boast but to point out the complexities of what we were dealing with despite a sincere effort to have a truly shared pulpit.

At that time, no one was doing video, so we did not consider that option. Instead, we purchased an old warehouse, allegedly built by a Mormon guy to house a hardware store, and built it out as a church with thirteen hundred seats. Much of our renovation was done by volunteer labor, and we were so broke that people had to bring their own chairs to our first services there, which meant that our room was filled with lawn chairs, dining chairs, and every other sort of ghetto seating imaginable. We entered that building as a church of about twelve hundred after shutting down the other location for financial reasons. Every year thereafter we grew by twelve to fourteen hundred people until we were at five services and had over five thousand people. Ours had become one of the fastest-growing churches in one of America's least-churched cities.

As an aside, we did try to manage our growth with church planting. We have planted churches through our Acts 29 Network and were even honored as the second most prolific church-planting church in America. Furthermore, we have always given 10 percent of our church income to church planting, which now amounts to more than one million dollars a year, to fund churches wherever the lead pastor senses God's calling, even if that may be across the street from one of our campuses. Our sole goal has never been growing our church, but as Scripture says, God loves a cheerful giver, and for every person we sent out, he brought ten more in, and we feel like the little boy who gave his lunch to Jesus.

We then searched for a larger building that would enable us to stay in the city. However, civil limitatations have essentially zoned out large churches. Hence, we were left with three options. One, we could leave the city and abandon our vision of reaching one of the nation's least-churched sities. Two, we could simply stop growing, cap the number of converts, and literally continue to shut the doors and turn upwards of a hundred people away from a service, as we were doing on some Sundays. Three, we could find another option. The possibility of planting more churches had not presented itself, because while we had actively pursued possible church planters, the ones we sent out and supported felt called to areas around the city but not to the city itself, as we felt called.

LESSONS FROM VIDEO

It was around this time that I was introduced to Pastor Larry Osborne through my friends at Leadership Network. Pastor of Northcoast Church in San Diego, he is a laid-back, easy-going ex-hippie who loves Jesus and has a brilliant mind for leadership and administration. He has been kind enough over the years to speak wisdom into my life, for which I am deeply grateful. He is regarded as the father of the multi-site and video-sermon models.

He began encouraging me to trust him and experiment with multi-campus video services. To be honest, I had serious doubts that it would work, but our elders decided it was worth pursuing to see what Jesus might do. We decided not to use the video-venue model on our campus because we did not have a room big enough to house any service of note. So we chose to try the partnership model.

A ministry called Crista, in a suburban neighborhood roughly twenty or thirty minutes north of our urban campus, agreed to let us use their auditorium, which seats maybe 350 people, and the adjacent daycare for children's ministry, free of charge. We gathered the people who live in that area and had about one hundred nonstaff people at our informational meeting. We put some money into the room for new carpet, paint, seats, sound, projectors, and screens. We did not put any full-time paid staff on the project and started with one morning service, which was a DVD playback of the first morning service brought to the campus by a guy on a motorcycle riding like he was in some video game. As of this writing, this campus celebrated their two-year anniversary and now has two morning services and one evening service with more than seven hundred people in attendance.

After that we connected with a church planter who had been given an old church building in the westernmost part of our city. It seats one thousand people, but it needed a lot of work because it had been neglected for many years. He had planted a church there, but was worn out from his wife's ongoing battle with cancer. He was a great man whom we loved, and the thought of partnering with him seemed like a win for him, his church, and ours. He humbly chose to partner with Mars Hill and gave us the building and joined our staff, along with his other elder. Those people who wanted to become a Mars Hill campus stayed, and some folks from our church who lived in that area joined the core.

We raised 1.8 million dollars in one offering from the other two campuses and upgraded the entire building. While construction was underway, I stopped preaching the at-capacity 11 a.m. service at our main campus and turned it into a video service so I could go and build the core for the new campus, which was meeting temporarily at a high school. Since we could not do video there due to logistics, I intended to get the campus up and going, which worked. By the time we opened the new building in the spring of 2007, it was quickly filling up. So, to allow more services I stopped preaching live and returned to the main campus. The new campus went to two video services and did not lose people but actually grew and is running roughly one thousand people a week in its first year. Furthermore, the elders we adopted from that campus have been an enormous addition to our team, and we have all benefited from their wisdom. More than the building, the elders we received were the greatest blessing.

Our next campus was in the eastern part of our city where we purchased a building from a denomination. Having been open just a few months, meeting in a room that seats maybe 250 people, there are now four hundred people in two services. We are confident that the campus will fill up three services and reach a more isolated but densely populated part of the city under the leadership of one of our pastors who was saved and baptized in the early days of our church.

At the same time we began the eastern campus, we purchased a former nightclub in downtown Seattle, just a few miles from our main campus. It had been shut down by the city for repeated criminal violations, including drugs, prostitution, shootings, and underage drinking. It was a sleazy club; when we converted it to a church we replaced the bathroom condom dispenser with a baby changing table and turned the go-go dancer cage into a coat rack. A crack pipe fell from the ceiling onto the pastor's desk when the tech guys were installing the Internet wiring. The nightclub's big night had been Sunday, which they promoted as "Sin Sunday." We intend to continue using that marketing slogan for the campus. It opened just before Easter 2008 with roughly 750 people in attendance and some great local media coverage from neighbors who are glad we have redeemed the space.

Admittedly, by the time this book is published we will be doing things differently and likely will have added even more campuses. In sum, since our experiment with video two years ago, we have grown to a church with a peak attendance of eight thousand people spread across sixteen services on six campuses with the capacity to double our attendance in the coming few years. Half of our attendance already participates via video, and in the coming years video will be the primary way in which people hear me preach the gospel. I now preach live four times on Sunday at our main campus. Some weeks I prerecord the sermon if I am traveling, in which case all services are video, and if I am sick or need a break I can just preach the morning services, which is a great relief.

Based on the five ways of doing multi-campus church, we are doing the partnership model at one of our seven campuses, the teaching-team model roughly 20 percent of the time across all campuses, and the regional-campus model. We also have some smaller informal gatherings both in the U.S. and around the world experimenting with the low-risk model to see if there is potential to make Mars Hill a national and international church.

We are by no means experts at all of this, but we have learned some things that I believe are helpful.[9] Therefore, the following suggestions are offered as observations—not obligations—for those considering doing multi-campus church.

MULTI-CAMPUS OBSERVATIONS

1) Each campus must be treated as a church plant with a clear mission to reach its community. It must be more than just an overflow room for a main campus; it must be a missional extension of a church into a culture or area with programming and style that is most effective for contextualizing the gospel. A campus does not simply replicate what is done elsewhere, like a franchise. In addition, a campus is not set up for church consumers; people have to do all the grunt work that normal church plants do, such as remodeling, setting up and tearing down, and generous giving.

We repudiate the idea that a group of people can gather to watch a sermon on a screen and call it church. If you spoil people and give them

---

[9]Seeing how friends such as pastors Ed Young Jr., Craig Groeschel, and Larry Osborne do their campuses has been very helpful.

everything up front, they end up like bratty kids. The best thing is to make every campus struggle to some degree, as do the church planters we support, so that their people own the mission and sacrifice for it. In this way, we have seen that campuses actually cause our people to give and serve more than ever before, and they respond generously.

2) Each campus must have its own paid staff appropriate for a church its size such as a campus administrator and children's leader, along with some unpaid elders and deacons to administer such things as premarital counseling, small groups, and membership. For this to happen each campus must have its own budget that the campus pastor and other elders spend as they see fit, within certain established guidelines for all campuses such as salary compensation criteria. Mars Hill is legally one church that employs all the staff and issues identical benefits packages and such.

3) If a campus is to be rooted in a community, it ultimately needs a facility that can handle both Sunday and midweek programming and other events as needed. Such a facility can be purchased or rented. Without such auxiliary programming and events, those who attend the campus will always feel like second-class citizens, although they are not. The specific ministries will vary from campus to campus depending on whom they are reaching. For example, an urban campus may have little if any student ministry, whereas the exact opposite is true for a suburban context. And, every campus needs what we call community groups that meet weekly in homes.

4) Each campus needs its own office space, either at or near where it gathers on Sunday.

5) Each campus needs the freedom to adopt the musical style that is best suited for its cultural context. Each campus needs its own worship leaders and bands that are vitally connected and committed to the campus; the musicians must be worshipers at the campus, not just performers showing up for a gig. This also promotes the ownership that contributes to community of the Spirit at each campus.

6) Each campus of one hundred people or more must have a full-time paid campus pastor to lead the mission. That campus pastor opens and closes services and is available after the service along with the campus elders to pray for and counsel people. The campus pastor also covers the pulpit ten to twelve weeks a year when the main preaching pastor

is out of the pulpit. The campus pastor is the first-among-equals lead pastor at that campus and has the full authority to lead the mission as a uniquely gifted leader of leaders. In this way, every campus has a visible leader who can speak to its needs and issues. He has a long-term commitment to the people there and the ability to assume the pulpit every week if needed, should the primary preaching pastor no longer be able to preach due to something such as severe illness or death. He oversees the elder team at his campus and does all of the biblical pastoral functions, with the assistance of the campus deacons.

7) Each campus must use some Sundays each year for family business conducted by the campus pastor, such as baby dedications, baptisms, new leader installations, and new member introductions. Therefore, the preaching schedule has to include ten to twelve annual opportunities for the campus pastor and other elders to preach live at their campus, thereby dealing with issues at the campus level by the campus pastors. Without this, we fear that a campus will not really be a church but rather just an event. Truly, each campus is essentially a church unto itself that is networked together in love and mission with the other campuses that also function as churches.

8) All the campuses must be served by a unifying central support staff that focuses on the Web site, printed materials, training, human resources, and best practices. This also means there are Web sites for each campus on which the staff can post their blogs, announcements, and event calendars, all of which link back to the main church Web site.

9) Each campus should be plugged into the main broadcast campus so that when there are training events and conferences, people can attend their normal campus and receive the training rather than drive to the main campus for such events. When John Piper came to speak at our Resurgence event in February 2008, he was simulcast live to every one of our campuses. More people saw him on video than in person since he was broadcast to a wide geographic area, and more people were able to hear him.

10) Church membership must be tied to a campus. People need to be committed to one campus at which they will be members, attend services, give generously, join a community group, and serve, and to which they will bring others. Of course, it is also permissible for some-

one to attend training and the like at another campus as needed, since some campuses have ministries that others do not. Many of our people enjoy their commitment to one campus but also visit the others just to see what is going on and to be encouraged. If people are not tied to a campus on a mission to reach their community, they invariably become consumers only, which is a sin.

11) A large, geographically spread church that remains male-elder led and governed requires working elder teams broken up by campus with clear delegated authority for decision-making. Only a few times a year does the entire elder council convene from all campuses. Nearly all decisions are made at the campus level where the campus pastor leads his elders, deacons, and members on their mission to reach and disciple their community. The campus elder teams meet at least once a month, and some meet weekly for prayer and Bible study as a brotherhood.

12) Insofar as technology goes, we have chosen to use television broadcast technology rather than other options such as Internet broadcasting because we find it cheaper and more established and reliable. We have a large television satellite dish on the main campus, and the stage there is essentially set up like a television studio with proper lighting, a rotating set design, and camera angles fit for switching views. The sermon is broadcast live from that campus via satellite to other campuses. They receive it on their satellite dishes with a buffering system similar to a TiVo, which allows them to start the sermon whenever they like. Some churches, such as Northland Church in Florida, do not use a buffering system and as a result require all of their campuses to have the same service time and format schedule, which is far too complicated and limiting for us to pull off but worked well for that church, as I saw when I preached there.

13) Not every campus needs to do the same thing. During our most recent Christmas season some of the campus pastors wanted to do Christmas Eve services for their people and others did not. I wanted to be home with my family. We all did what worked best for each campus. The campuses that chose to hold Christmas Eve services did so to packed rooms because people from all our various campuses attended there, which was a great joy for everyone. Since Mars Hill is one church in multiple locations, it is a relief that different campuses take care of different needs, and our people gladly visit another campus.

Most multi-site churches that I am aware of have a Saturday night service at which the sermon is captured for playback at various campuses on Sundays, thereby negating the need for a live satellite feed. After discussing this with our elders, I refused to add Saturday night services solely for the purpose of capturing the video for Sunday. I was already preaching multiple Sunday morning and Sunday evening services. Ultimately, I consulted my wife, Grace, and our five children. I asked them what they thought about daddy canceling Saturday Sabbath (a.k.a. "pajama day") and family movie night forever, and they all cried, which caused me to cry also. At that time I refused not to have a day off when my kids are home from school, which meant we had to find another option to accommodate our growing church. I told the church we needed to raise the money to do a live satellite feed because my family was more important than the church, and our church graciously responded by cheering and giving generously, knowing that I already work a full six days each week and am working upward of sixteen hours on Sundays.

14) Not every service at every campus needs to start at the same time. The benefit of video is that campus pastors can set their own service times. This allows the campuses to have sufficient time to turn things around between services, or start services at unusual times.

Admittedly, not every church can or should use video or be multi-campus. For those who view these models as a new and second form of church planting, though, we have found it to be a wonderful way to expand the gospel alongside traditional church planting. Still, there are many common objections and questions that merit rebuttal.

OBJECTIONS TO VIDEO AND MULTI-CAMPUS MODELS

While I was on a preaching tour of Scotland, a godly Christian pastor asked me how I respond to the charge that churches like mine are simply cults of personality. I responded that just because the preaching pastor has a strong personality and is able to lead does not make his church a cult. A cult is formed when one person has virtually all of the power, is accountable and submissive to no one, and makes himself the focal point of adoration rather than humbly pointing to Jesus. I, too, share this concern, and it is one reason we emphasize plural leadership. Also, I have not turned our church Web site into www.MarkDriscoll.com, nor is my face on or in any of our buildings or promotions. I am subject to an annual performance review, and I always introduce myself on Sunday as "one of the pastors." Furthermore, I have repeatedly told our people that if the day comes when the elders discipline or fire me, they should trust their elders and submit to them even if I disagree, because the authority resides with the entire team and not just one man, especially me.

On the other hand, large and small churches alike are almost always shaped by the personality of their pastor, much like Peter was the charismatic leader of the early Jerusalem church. In our church, people attend because they learn about Jesus from my preaching, and though they have never met me, they do not really care because they have pastors who love them and Christian friends who walk with them, and are part of our mission to see people and culture transformed by Jesus. Likewise, in a small church there are people who love their pastor not because he's a world-class preacher, but because he has loved, served, taught, and encouraged them. In either instance the issue is not whether people are coming because they like the pastor but why they like the pastor. The only reason the guy with the big church is criticized is because his name is more widely known and he preaches from a stage so people can get better aim.

A dear friend who pastors a small church said it bothered him that I was not physically present in the room with those who listened to the sermon. When I pressed him for a biblical reason, he admitted that he had none. In the end, he said his real concern was that the people were only consuming information and not in community experiencing transformation. I agree wholeheartedly, which is why we emphasize community life on each campus. We intentionally connect the pulpit to our community groups so that after I preach, our people gather in homes to discuss the text or topic and share meals, friendship, prayer, accountability, love, support, and worship, not unlike house churches. In this way, we have essentially established our campuses as churches networked together for resource sharing, support, accountability, and training.

One woman who loves Jesus and meant well was concerned that we were trying hard to make our church into a big deal. Her pointed questions were really about the heart and motives of our leadership. I explained to her that our goal has always been to point as many people to Jesus as effectively as we can and that we rejoice when more people are attracted to Jesus than we can handle. It is constantly baffling that some Christians complain when lots of people get saved. My guess is that the 120 people who made up the early church included some who were really bent out of shape when 3,000 people got saved at Pentecost and took their parking places and normal seats at services.

Yet another godly pastor who is gifted at biblical counseling asked how a pastor can have a big multi-campus church and preach to a camera and remain humble. I told him a pastor can the same way as a biblical counselor, who has people praise him for his love and support, remains humble—continually confessing his sin and pride and pursuing humility by the grace of God. The fact is that when our church was small, I, like many jealous, petty, and ill-informed young bucks who know everything but have done nothing, liked to take my shots at well-known pastors of large churches. Now that I am one, I must confess that I was much like the out-of-shape guy with a bowl of chips sitting at home on the couch watching television and criticizing trained professional athletes, which is far easier than actually playing the sport.

Over the years I have had the privilege of meeting thousands of pastors from around the U.S. and the world. They range from pastors of very small churches to pastors of the largest churches in America. The truth is I have seen no correlation between church size and pastoral humility. I have met more than a few church planters who are young, arrogant, brash, and overconfident (this is curiously the same kind of guy who is most likely to plant a decent church) whose entire church membership could fit in a phone booth. I have also met some pastors of tens of thousands who are so beyond their ability and entirely reliant upon God's grace while surrounded by critics and enemies that they are exceedingly humble and humbling to be around. We must never forget that Jesus is the biggest deal ever, and also the most humble, thereby demonstrating that ministry size and minister humility are not necessarily in opposition.

REASONS WHY MULTI-SITE AND VIDEO CHURCHES WILL INCREASE

There are many reasons why multi-site and video churches will increase. Based on my observation and experience, they include the following.

1) More people need to meet Jesus. This simple fact means that, as Paul says, we must use "all means" to win as many people to Jesus as possible.[10] If multiple campuses and video are ways that God the Holy Spirit chooses to reach more people for Jesus, then we would be wise to not criticize or oppose it, even if our church decides not to do it.

2) More people are commuting longer distances to church. By starting campuses closer to their homes, it allows them to be more missional and evangelistic and start reaching the community that they normally just drive through.

3) It is just happening. One thing we have seen by putting the sermons online in audio and video format for free is that people use them however they see fit. As a result, we are getting reports from all over the world of people gathering in homes, churches, missionary outposts, dorms, apartments, condos, fire stations, and even tents on the front lines of war to have church, using the videos of my sermons as their teaching. Some even call themselves Mars Hill and are asking how their group can be considered a campus. We are trying to formulate an answer, but we cannot keep up with what God is doing. Rather than control it, we are simply trying to figure out what is best for Jesus and people. The key is that we do all we can to replicate Spirit-led communities, not just people listening to podcasts by themselves.

4) A church with a well-known name is at a unique advantage to succeed. Most churches are not well known and as a result have a difficult time growing, or even surviving. However, churches with well-known names are going to continue to grow and in so doing will continue to spread out wherever they can, using whatever technological means they can to reach people for Jesus. This is especially true of churches in which the people are excited about Jesus and their church and aggressively grow their church by bringing people in. While there have always been hucksters who pander the gospel for personal profit,[11] there are also celebrity-type preachers of notable character who draw enormous crowds, such as Billy Graham, Greg Laurie, and Luis Palau.

Assuredly, some people will lament the franchising of things, so there will always be a need for boutique restaurants, coffee shops, churches, and the like. But it is illogical for the average person who

---

[10] 1 Cor. 9:22–23.
[11] 2 Cor. 2:17; Titus 1:11; 2 Pet. 2:1–3; 2 John 7–11.

knows nothing of Jesus and church to visit churches not knowing what to expect until they find one that makes sense to them. If some churches with good names in their community can multiply and use their good name to compel more people to worship Jesus, then even if you do not consider that ideal, it is better than unknown, empty churches, which are so common.

5) As was noted earlier, Jesus Christ is the senior pastor and Chief Shepherd of the church. Jesus' three offices of prophet, priest, and king are megathemes from Genesis to Revelation. As prophet, Jesus preached and taught Scripture with authority. As priest, Jesus cares for people and deals with their sin compassionately. As king, Jesus demonstrated his rule over creation through miracles while on the earth and today rules and reigns over his people through church leaders, principles, and systems by the Holy Spirit and his Word.

As leaders who are not Jesus Christ, we are an imperfect combination of these three roles and tend to be strongest in just one or two. Rarely does someone have a high capacity in every area.

In my experience most pastors are priests. Priests have a deep understanding of human suffering and are compassionate and merciful in tending to the needs of hurting people so that they are loved to spiritual maturity. Priests are masters at resolving conflicts so that there is reconciliation through the gospel. The weakness of priests is that they are so people-focused that they tend to be disorganized. Without kingly help, they run from crisis to crisis without building other leaders and systems to care for people in large numbers. Without prophetic support, they can be merciful and patient to the point of enabling people in their sin and not calling them to an urgent repentance.

This explains why many churches are small and struggling but led by a nice pastor who loves God and people. Such pastors may be better served by being part of a multi-campus church where the central support systems oversee the kingly aspects, such as systems, policies, procedures, technology, and finances. They may also benefit from a prophet who can preach via video. Prophets tend to be strong at vision, study, preaching, teaching, doctrinal truth, refuting error, and calling people to repent of sin.

I believe that in the coming years more and more struggling churches that are led by priests will become campuses of larger churches. Such partnerships will allow the pastors in those churches to be free from what they are not good at, such as the air war of preaching, and focus their time on caring for people in the ground war. Chart 10.1 shows how I often distinguish between what I call the air war and the ground war.

CHART 10.1

Air War	Ground War
Leads the mission	Follows the air war
Has a primary visible leader	Has multiple, less-visible leaders
Requires prophets and kings	Requires priests and kings
Deals with the masses	Deals with individuals and small groups
Is event centered	Is relationship centered
Is the church's front door	Is the church's living room
Draws people to the church	Connects people to the church
Proclaims with authority	Explains with accountability
Provides general principles	Provides personal applications

The air war includes preaching and teaching at gathered church services and other large events such as church-based conferences, retreats, and training events. Central administration (bookkeeping, payroll and benefits, and legal counsel) also falls under air war. The air war at our church includes our Web site, vodcasts and podcasts, and publishing.

The ground war includes home-based Bible studies, smaller training classes, individual counseling appointments, and recovery groups for addictions and sexual abuse.

In my experience, most church leaders are good at either the air war or the ground war. For a church to succeed, though, it must have both an air war and a ground war. A church with only an air war will have large Sunday meetings but will not see the kind of life transformation in people that can only come through the intense efforts of a well-organized ground war. Conversely, a church with only a ground war may have mature people but will not grow or see new converts meeting Jesus regularly.

By having those who are most skilled at such tasks provide the air war, leaders at various campuses are free to build a very successful ground war. With so many churches struggling at the air war, more people than ever would be better cared for if the air war strategy could be brought to them so as to enable them to focus on the ground war. In the near future many ground war churches, which are usually led by a priest, will partner with and become campuses of larger churches that specialize in the air war.

6) Specialization allows for better stewardship. In a larger church spread out among various campuses there is increased specialization so that more things are done with focused excellence. As a result, God's resources are better stewarded for kingdom purposes. Subsequently, in the coming years more and more pastors who want to specialize in their area of greatest giftedness will be attracted to the larger multi-campus model of church. Thus they can contribute where they are strong and be part of a team that is strong where they are weak.

7) A growing multi-campus church thrives on learning and risk taking. By pioneering new forms of church, new locations, and new methods, multi-campus churches are able to continue doing what they are successful at while exploring ways to have greater kingdom impact, without risking the entirety of their ministry. By sending out some resources (e.g., people, money, gear) to take risks and pioneer new works, they are able to continually innovate and find new ways to reach new people.

8) Multi-campus churches will continue to attract high-quality, entrepreneurial leaders. The opening of various campuses of various sizes in various communities with various cultures means that there is an ongoing opportunity for leaders to rise up and pioneer new ministries. This kind of opportunity is rare in many established churches where new leaders and new ideas are not always welcome. Where new leaders and ideas are encouraged, trained, and released, though, the result is an ever-growing pool of talented people who are attracted by the opportunities that a multi-campus church provides.

9) People can be better cared for. Having pastored our church from a core of about a dozen people to its present state, I can declare with complete confidence that our people are better cared for now that our church is larger than when it was smaller. I know this is controversial, but it is generally true. The advantages of a small church where people know and care for each other well occur in our small community groups. A larger church also has the resources to ensure that training is

undertaken and systems are built to excellently care for people with a wide variety of personal needs.

In our church this includes paying for hundreds of people to be trained in biblical counseling and having support groups for people with eating disorders, women who have had an abortion, couples fighting infertility, sexual abuse victims, sex addicts, drug and alcohol addicts, people struggling with same-sex attraction, and premarital and marital counseling. When our church was smaller I did the best I could, but in no way could I care for people as well as we do today as specialized teams. By breaking down a church into multiple campuses, people have the benefits of a smaller church in terms of community and access to senior leadership at the campus, along with the benefits of a larger church with good preaching, music, technology, training, and care systems for hurting people. In the end, we have found that multi-campus churches have the best of both worlds.

In conclusion, the multi-campus and video churches are here to stay. As the experts have said, "Fifty years ago, the one-venue option was the norm. Fifty years from now, we believe multi-venue and multi-site will be the norm."[12]

As a result, in many ways some churches will form their own denomination or network and spread across their city, country, and even the world as Jesus opens opportunities. Some of these churches will likely be comprised of hundreds of thousands of people and will implement new technologies that allow them to remain connected despite geographic distance. They will pioneer a new form of church planting that will allow them to plant a church among any people group in the world with greater effectiveness than missionaries have previously enjoyed because they will be connected to a lifeline of support and resources, thanks to technology.

ANSWERS TO COMMON QUESTIONS ABOUT MULTI-CAMPUS CHURCHES

WHY PRESS TO BE A HUGE CHURCH? ISN'T IT BETTER TO PLANT CHURCHES?

It doesn't have to be one or the other. Some people like being a part of a big organization. So we have the megachurch with many different ministries under one organization. Others like the warmth and simplicity of a small church. Still others are entrepreneurialists who always need to be a part of something new; they plant. People are free to choose. We affirm them all for different reasons.

A megachurch does not negate the place and unique ministry of mid-size and small churches. Our neighborhood has the mega-corporate Starbucks and also the small Java Jahn's. Both are outstanding in their own way. The problem comes when people begin to criticize what doesn't fit their preferred ministry style. In the same way that it is wrong to criticize a megachurch because it's not small, it is wrong for megachurches to criticize small churches because they are not large. All churches must strive for excellence in what God has called them to.

DON'T PEOPLE GO TO MEGACHURCHES SO THAT THEY CAN BE ENTERTAINED WHILE REMAINING ANONYMOUS IN THE CROWD?

It's certainly true for some people. Their last desire is to get connected or to get involved in self-giving ministry. They treat the church as a free performance simply to be observed. They can successfully flit in and out unnoticed. The problem is those people, not the church. They must constantly disobey the preached command to get involved. For Jesus followers there is much encouragement and many opportunities for ministry where they can fan into flame the gift of God (2 Tim. 1:6) and maximize their potential.

ISN'T IT BEST FOR MY PASTOR TO KNOW ME PERSONALLY SO THAT HE CAN PROCLAIM GOD'S WORD DIRECTLY INTO MY LIFE SITUATION?

You'll do well being a part of a smaller church. But watch out. If your preacher and the church are good and godly, then it almost certainly will grow. One result is that you'll have less contact with your preaching pastor as he grows responsible for more people. Will you hang in as your care switches from the senior pastor to another? Will you switch churches? Or maybe you'll be a part of a church plant.

One danger is a kind of self-centeredness that demands the senior pastor be your personal pastor. Check yourself to rule out the possibility that you see the church as existing to meet your needs rather than as a body on a Spirit-empowered mission to promote the King of kings.

HOW IS A LARGE VIDEO CHURCH ANY DIFFERENT FROM HOLLYWOOD MERCHANDIZING A PERSONALITY?

There could be a lot of truth to what you say. But consider the reasons behind the video. Hollywood is out to make a profit for the owners. It uses, abuses, and disposes of people for the sake of the corporation. It does whatever is popular for the sake of drawing a crowd. If the church falls into this trap, then it deserves the condemnations of Jesus we read in Revelation 2 and 3.

A godly church will give away money in ministry. It builds and protects people, including the preaching pastor. It seeks to be popular only to Jesus. The preaching and doctrine isn't shaped by opinion polls to see what people are buying today.

The point is to maximize the gifting of some unique individuals. Pastors of multi-campus megachurches are a little like Moses and David in Israel. They are all "larger-than-life" individuals who oversee large groups that gather in smaller units for much of their life under God.

WHERE DOES MULTI-CAMPUS STOP AND DENOMINATION BEGIN?

Perhaps the key difference is between the single multi-campus pastor and the denominational bishop and the type of organization that forms around them. The commonality of the multi-campus church will come in the prophetic work of a preaching pastor, whereas the commonality of a denomination will come in the organization headed by an administrative officer, often called a bishop.

If multi-campus is done well, each campus will have the feel of being its own church with campus leadership, identity, and belonging, as we have already developed. But the campuses share one preacher and a single corporate organization with all the policies and structures required by state and federal governments. As a large group, it can lower the cost of health insurance along with other costs. Such costs can easily overwhelm a small church.

CHAPTER ELEVEN

HOW CAN A CHURCH UTILIZE TECHNOLOGY?

**I have become all things to all people,
that by all means I might save some. I do it all for
the sake of the gospel, that I may share
with them in its blessings.**

1 CORINTHIANS 9:22-23

Not far from my home is a small church that has struggled for years. Every time I drive by that church I pray for it because I love the church, in general, and I know that this church, in particular, has a long history of loving Jesus and believing in the Bible. But it got stuck in a cultural cul de sac, so it couldn't adapt as culture changed. Younger people couldn't connect so they didn't come. The people died off so that virtually no one was left. The pastor was discouraged and struggled to know what to do. So I decided to try to meet the pastor to see what I could do to encourage and serve him. Thus far I have had no success, despite repeated efforts. Their lack of technology is part of the problem.

I have stopped by the church office several times during the past two years and never found anyone on the church grounds. I have called repeatedly, but no one has ever answered the phone. There is no answering machine. I have also tried to email but cannot because the church has no Web site and no email address.

I will continue trying to meet the pastor there because I feel burdened to do so. Still, I lament the fact that with a little bit of technology they could open up a new world of resources for me and others in the neighborhood who are more likely to visit their Web site before ever visiting their church.

Admittedly, churches do some incredibly goofy things when they pursue relevance for the sake of being uber hip and ultra cool. One pastor I know got so many piercings that he looked like a rack of lures at the Bass Pro Shop and started skateboarding, despite the fact he was a grandfather. He was not relevant but ridiculous. The hard truth is, as Christians, we cannot be all that cool anyway. When *cool* is defined as making an amateur naughty movie with Paris Hilton while in rehab to be leaked on the Internet for free viral advertising, reading our Bibles, praying, and loving our enemies is admittedly going to seriously limit our chances of being voted Most Uber Hip at the MTV Video Music Awards ceremony.

Therefore, the church should not pursue innovative methods for the sake of coolness but for fruitfulness. Every church is culturally contextualized; the only difference is to what year. A brief and admittedly less than precise historical survey of cultural adaptations in church culture and methods will illustrate this point well. Remember that each of these changes was met with resistance by some Christians who confused culture and Christ and could not see how to keep Christ while changing culture.

The early church likely met either very early on Sunday morning or very late on Sunday evening, because for the first few hundred years of our faith, Sunday was a workday. Furthermore, during that time Christians tended to meet in homes, which meant their gatherings generally were not very large, perhaps no more than one hundred people.

During the first few hundred years of the church, Christianity was also opposed:

> Widespread persecution of the early Christians was frequent, beginning at least as early as the reign of Nero in the mid-first century. The final effort to eradicate Christians from the Roman world took place under Diocletian in 303. It failed, and with the Edict of Milan in 313 Christianity became an officially recognized religion in the Roman Empire. Moreover, by the end of the century the Roman rul-

ers had decreed that Christianity was the sole official religion of the empire.[1]

Many changes took place after the legalization of Christianity. The church could meet more publicly and freely without threat of violence. The church could also meet on Sundays because Sunday became a day of worship recognized by the government. Furthermore, with state support, the church began building larger and more expensive buildings, opening more formalized schools for theological training, and enjoying many cultural benefits as the favored religion. Over time, many other cultural adaptations were made to contextualize the church.

As a general rule, Christians who attended church were expected to stand throughout the entire service. This began to change when some churches introduced benches in the thirteenth century and pews in the fourteenth century, with seating becoming more popular in the fifteenth century.

Musically, the church's corporate worship also changed dramatically in the fourteenth century. It was then that the first organ was permanently installed in a building. While some churches were quick to include it in their service to augment congregational singing, other churches rejected it as an instrument of the devil because it was also used in pubs to accompany drunks singing bar tunes. When some Christian hymn writers began using not only the organ but also the bar tunes with rewritten lyrics, the feces and the fan interfaced.

In the fifteenth century it was the invention of the printing press that in many ways fueled the entire Protestant Reformation. With its invention, various translations of the Bible were culturally contextualized to cultures and their language, and this, along with other Christian books and materials, literally changed the world. People could read and study for themselves rather than depend on tradition and spiritual leaders who were often corrupt or erroneous. This radically liberating opportunity was made possible by embracing the new technology.

In the nineteenth century electricity became available at roughly the same time that large concert halls came into existence. The combination allowed for large meetings, which paved the way for everything

---

[1]R. D. Linder, "Church and State," in *Evangelical Dictionary of Theology*, ed. Walter A. Elwell (Grand Rapids, MI: Baker Books, 1984), 234.

from evangelistic crusades to megachurches, as well as for city-wide meetings for prayer and worship.

In the late nineteenth century the first loudspeakers and microphones were invented. By the early twentieth century the modern version of loudspeakers and microphones came into existence, and by the mid-twentieth century the first box-enclosed loudspeakers were invented. By adopting this technology the church became more fruitful because more people could gather to hear the gospel of Jesus and worship together as God's people. By way of comparison, the great Reformed evangelist George Whitefield reportedly preached some eighteen thousand sermons to an estimated ten million people. Many of his sermons were in open air without amplification, and as many as thirty thousand people at any one time heard him preach. The strain on his voice from preaching without amplification was so severe that some biographies report he would cough up blood after preaching. Conversely, Billy Graham was able to preach live to 210 million people in some 185 countries because he enjoyed the benefits of such things as airplanes and amplified sound.

In the late nineteenth century the first radio signal was sent. By the early twentieth century the first telegraph of the letter *S* was sent across the English Channel. By the early twentieth century the human voice was sent out over the radio. That invention revolutionized the preaching of the gospel; no longer must a preacher be physically present with his audience to communicate Jesus. Since the invention of radio the preaching ministry of some men has increased in effectiveness, and the number of hearers has exploded exponentially.

It is curious to note that the movie camera was invented by the Christian Thomas Edison, who sought to give the patent to his church, but they rejected it. In the late nineteenth century the first public movie was released in the United States, and in the early twentieth century the first public movie theater opened. The church was among the first to use the new technology for the gospel, which explains why seven of the first ten movies made had the word *passion* in the title—they were about the life, death, and resurrection of Jesus.

In the early twentieth century, television as we know it came into being. The church again used the technological opportunity for the gospel, with admittedly varying results. Thankfully, great men such as Billy Graham have used the medium of television to preach Jesus. Regrettably, guys in white suits sitting on gold thrones alongside wives with big hair and enough makeup it seems they lost a paintball war have also made their way onto television to talk about "Jezuz." This goes to show that no matter what the medium, the message needs to be clear.

In 1990 the Internet came into being and was made available to the public in 1995. This revolution was so altogether transforming that it is difficult to overstate how the free exchange of information has been radically altered. One result of this revolution is that preachers use the Internet as a major source of their sermon preparation. In fact:

> Nine in ten pastors use the internet in sermon preparation, with more than half using web gleanings extensively. Only 8% never use the web. The most common resources sought online are illustrations and stories (78%), historical background (51%), statistics (50%), and humor (45%). Even the grunt work of plumbing commentaries has gone electronic for 4 out of 10 pastors. And about one-third are looking for artistic images, media clips, and references to pop culture. Only 1 in 5, however, listen to sermons by other preachers.[2]

These technological advances throughout history have impacted how we communicate with one another. We are now in the "third age of communication":

> The first age was oral communication, when history and theology were captured in stories and shared around campfires and tables. The second age was written communication, when the stories were committed to papyrus and sheepskin and paper and finally mass-produced, thanks to Gutenberg. Now comes the third age. You might call it the age of Spielberg.... "Many centuries after the shift from oral to written culture, we are now well along in the transition to visual culture—where the predominant mode of communication is images rather than words."[3]

Some churches have been quick to adopt these various technological advances and their consequence—a visual culture—while others

---

[2]Eric Reed, "Visualcy: Preaching by Faith and by Sight," (The *Leadership* Survey) *Leadership*, Summer 2007, 27.
[3]Ibid., 25.

have not. No matter where one's church is on the continuum, the undeniable fact is that every church is contextualized to culture. The primary issue is whether they are doing everything they can to be as fruitful as possible, as Paul commands.

It is interesting to note that even the use of particular visual media and technology has changed over the years. While the use of images in preaching and corporate worship is up, the use of PowerPoint is down. Pastor Leith Anderson says:

> PowerPoint has been largely a Baby Boomer phenomenon. Younger adults wonder about the validity and credibility of anything perceived to be canned. Authenticity is a critical aspect, especially with younger adults, in the preaching experience. It doesn't seem authentic that a speech is all written out and words appear on the screen at exactly the same time. So PowerPoint is less used with younger adults and becoming more a characteristic of an older generation.[4]

In addition to using technology in the corporate worship service, the church also benefits from taking full advantage of the opportunity for its preaching and other resources to become "sticky" to a larger audience for a longer period of time, thereby multiplying its influence. This includes use of the Internet, which has become the new front door for churches and the place people visit before showing up at any physical location. Indeed, "what people do more than anything online is consume 'content': look at videos and photographs, read the news, and get the lowdown on friends and celebrities at MySpace or Facebook."[5]

Admittedly, not a lot of pastors are interested in the specific details about new technology. However, consider why it matters to churches. First, nearly everyone is on the Internet. Second, while on the Internet people are primarily looking for content and connection—two specialties of the church. In short, technology gives the church an opportunity to provide gospel content and relational connection to more people than ever before.

At Mars Hill Church in Seattle, we have been blessed in this arena. By virtue of our location near Microsoft and the related tech industry we have an army of highly gifted creative people, both in paid and

---

[4]"Visualcy: Is PowerPoint Fading?" Interview with Leith Anderson, *Leadership*, Summer 2007, 37.
[5]Brent Schlender, "Dawn of the Web Potato," *Fortune*, September 18, 2007, http://money.cnn.tv/magazines/fortune/fortune_archive/2007/09/17/100251021/index.htm.

volunteer ministry positions. They have allowed our church to capture sermons, classes, conferences, interviews, and the like in audio and video format and post them online free of charge. We are thus able to provide content to the world through our own Web site and places such as YouTube, iTunes, MySpace, and Facebook. Our technology gurus have also created a new Web site community called The City that allows us to connect as a church online while also welcoming people to our network from around the world.

I offer this chapter as something of a field guide for those churches that want to wisely determine how to utilize various technologies for the benefit of the gospel. In offering specific counsel I am well aware that much of it will quickly become dated as innovation continues, but I offer it nonetheless in hopes of being helpful. My point is not that our church is cool and yours can be too, but that there are some great new ways to reach more people for Jesus that are worth considering for every church.

To begin with, before worrying about how to distribute gospel content, you must have good content and lots of it. Just as it makes no sense for a horrible band to play on an expensive sound system because it only amplifies their awfulness, so increasing the channels for content distribution is in vain if the content (e.g., preaching, teaching, worship music) is not biblical and well done.

That being said, we can now examine some guiding principles for deciding what your church should do in terms of utilizing technology. Because the preached Word is the most important aspect of the church service, and because it is also the most visible and distinguishing aspect of a church, I will generally limit my points to the pulpit, although they do have applications for worship music, class teaching, and other content.

When considering what (if any) technology to include in one's preaching, keep the following points in mind.

1) As the great communication theory pioneer Marshall McLuhan said, for some people the medium is the message. That is, how the message is communicated is a message in and of itself. For some people, a preacher who uses video clips from television in a sermon means he is acting worldly and proud, whereas for other people it means he is living in their world and being relevant. No matter what you do, you will

draw some people and repel others, so don't be grieved when you lose people. Rather, decide whom you intend to draw and whom you are willing to repel.

2) As you incorporate more technology, more of your time will be required. In order to use technology well, you will need to understand its benefits and potential downfalls and do more than just show up and preach. You must also think through how to maximize the opportunities technology brings and how you want to both present and distribute the content.

3) The more technology your church uses, the more money you will spend. Not surprisingly, good gear costs money and is quickly outdated and needs replacement.

4) The more technology your church uses, the more staff you will need. Volunteers can do some things, but even if you can find good volunteer audio editors, camera operators, video editors, and others, they still need someone on staff to manage them.

5) The more technology you use in your preaching, the more it will affect how you preach. Because my sermons are broadcast live to campuses and posted on the Internet, it affects what I wear, how much I can move around on stage, what I can say about time and location, which audience I am speaking to (beyond just the room I am in), the lifespan of the content (which is now indefinite), and the opportunities available for critics to gather more rocks to throw since they actually know what I am saying and doing on Sundays.

There are also various ways in which technology can be used to enhance the communication of the gospel, all of which should be considered. I am focusing on the Sunday service as the centerpiece of a series of events that together are vital for every pastor to think through if they hope to contextualize well. The process I will outline is the product of a late-night conversation with James Gilmore following our last Sunday evening service. He is a great Christian brother and a brilliant thinker and writer on our experience economy.[6] He said that events such as Sunday church services should be thought through in stages or phases in order for the experience to be compelling.

[6]For more information about the experience economy, you can find articles and audio or video downloads by James Gilmore at www.theresurgence.com. We also recommend his books *The Experience Economy: Work Is Theater and Every Business a Stage* (Boston, MA: Harvard Business School Press, 1999); and *Authenticity: What Consumers Really Want* (Boston, MA: Harvard Business School Press, 2007).

PHASE 1: ATTRACTING

The question here is, how will you let people know that your church exists and then compel them to attend a service or event? Church-growth experts have encouraged such things as mass mailings and phone calls from telemarketers. These methods are more expensive than viral and buzz methods of getting the word out about your church. Yet, in my experience, mass mailings are no longer as successful as they once were, particularly among younger and more urban people. Rather, they tend to attract primarily churched folks shopping for a better place to get religious goods and services. Also they are considered by many to be rude. Furthermore, among strong environmental types such as we find in my city, any church that kills a lot of trees is more likely to get picketed than visited. In some communities door knocking still works, although it is increasingly dangerous and difficult to find anyone at home anymore, and it is considered rude by many and nearly impossible in urban areas with condominiums and apartments where access is denied to anyone who is not a resident or invited guest.

In order to attract people to your church, two things need to occur. First, you need to generate some name recognition in your community. In my experience, the best way to do this is through the media (e.g., Christian and mainstream television, radio, and print). With a degree and background in journalism, I know that the media is often criticized for being anti-faith and therefore is often open to running religious stories. You can facilitate the media coverage you get by introducing yourself to the local reporters (especially religion reporters); tell them what you are doing, ask them if you could send them any newsworthy stories, and tell them you are available for quotes when they need one from a Christian on various social and cultural issues. If the media responds favorably, you can benefit from the enormous investment they have made to communicate with people through technology.

Most media outlets are visually oriented and want a good shot for the paper or nightly news, so when we have something that we think is newsworthy, including a good photo opportunity, we send out press releases to notify the media. They have repeatedly responded to our invitations to cover our mass outdoor baptisms that we hold each summer in various public parks because they make for great photos. As a result, we have been on the cover of both major newspapers in our town.

At our last mass baptism, where more than two hundred people were dunked, God did something amazing. Our crew arrived at the beach to set up the stage, sound, and lights to accommodate thousands of people to hear the gospel and see the baptisms. However, a baby seal that had been left on the beach by its mom had taken over the area where they were supposed to set up. So some government agency showed up to block off a large perimeter around the seal, which meant we had to move down the beach. The next thing you know all the media outlets showed up to cover the event and to let everyone in our city know that we were having a huge baptism next to the baby seal. This upset the environmental rights activists who showed up, which, along with the gawkers and media, made for quite a spectacle. We were informed that if we plugged in our band for worship, we would make too much noise and scare the seal's mother away permanently, meaning we would be responsible for the death of a seal, which in our town is as bad as it gets.

In faith, we kept setting up for our event, asking Jesus to send the seal away to his mom before we needed to start meeting. By God's grace, the seal went back into the water and swam away happily on his own just minutes before we started. The media circus stayed around to cover our baptism, thereby giving us massive amounts of free advertising on television, radio, print, and the Internet. You never know what God may do when you send out a press release.

Furthermore, a good relationship with the media is helpful in other ways. Ultimately, it is an opportunity to see reporters and photographers meet Jesus, as we've seen at our church. A good media relationship is also helpful if and when criticism, tragedy, or conflict involves your church. Finally, sometimes a pastor is even invited to join the media, as I did writing for the Faith and Values section of the *Seattle Times* for roughly two years. I got to write about Jesus and promote our church, which was a great honor. The overarching principle is that the media is a tool that can be friend or foe, depending on how a church relates to them.

Second, once your name is out, people need to be invited to your church. The best ways to do this are through personal relationships and your Web site. People in your church should be speaking to family, friends, coworkers, and neighbors constantly about their life with Jesus in a natural and nonreligious way. They should feel free to invite them to church to meet other Christians and learn more about Jesus. To help this occur, your church must have a good Web site where people who hear about you through the media or word of mouth or are directed there through a search engine can find out who you are and what you believe and get a taste of your teaching and music. They will feel encouraged to visit in person after walking through the digital front door. It is very helpful to promote special events, such as Christmas and Easter, and new sermon series on your Web site. You can also include electronic invitations on the site for viewers to send to others. Your Web site needs to be built with the visual in mind so that it looks good. It must be updated regularly to be of any use; if not updated, it will backfire and be counter-effective. It must list service times along with directions and links to online maps so it is helpful practically. Lastly, it should include answers to common questions that visitors ask, such as whether childcare is available.

Online social networks are an increasingly effective place to meet and gather people. These are also a great resource for inviting people to your church. Facebook is a site that many church planters have successfully used to gather and mobilize entire core groups. College ministries also thrive on Facebook since virtually every college student has a profile there.

Providing a question-and-answer section on your Web site can actually give site visitors an opportunity to help shape a sermon or sermon series. While preaching through 1 Corinthians some time ago, I was struck by the fact that the letter was a series of answers to various questions that the people in the church asked. I assumed there were more questions than Paul answered in the letter, but somehow the questions he did answer were deemed to be of great interest and importance. I thought it might be interesting to do something similar and preach a series answering the big questions and issues in our own day. So I preached a series that solely answered people's questions.

We tried an experiment by opening up a section of our church Web site for people to post any question, make comments about posted questions, and vote up to ten times a day for their favorite question or questions. In the end, 893 questions were asked, 5,524 comments were made, and 343,203 votes were cast. I preached on the top nine questions in a series called "Religion Saves and Nine Other Misconceptions." Our attendance swelled, the bloggers went nuts, and the traffic to the Web site doubled immediately. We were forced to beef up our video and audio download capacity because the demand for the sermons each week was higher than we had expected.

PHASE 2: ENTERING

Is your church approachable from the outside? Will there be sandwich-board signs directing attendees from blocks away, and when they arrive, will there be good signage telling them where to park and where to enter the building? Will any identifiable people from the church be on hand to answer questions, direct people, and escort single mothers with their hands full?

In addition to the touch of a human greeter, what will people experience when entering your church? Will there be any music playing, and if so what? Will you hand them a bulletin or do as we have done and send one to them via email if they sign up online or fill out a visitor card? Will there be good signage to direct them through the building to restrooms, childcare, and the auditorium so they don't feel lost and awkward? Will you have screens in your lobby with rolling announcements in addition to the screens in the main room? Will you have a room designated for nursing moms with an audio and video feed of the service? Will you have computer kiosks for event registration? Will your building have Wi-Fi so people can bring their laptops to take notes and register for events online during the service? Will your stage have a different set design for each book or series you are studying so that there is variety and thematic consistency? Will your building have decent paint colors and lighting so it looks and smells like something other than a retirement home? Will you live-stream the sermon over the Internet so that people can enter without coming into the building? Will you create a "second life" church online where people can attend virtually?

PHASE 3: ENDURING

Once in a church service, how can technology be used to keep attendees focused? Will you use PowerPoint? Will the preacher have a large screen on stage with him, like a late-night talk show host does, so he can interact with various media content shown simultaneously on larger screens? Will the images on the screen(s) include photos, cultural statistics, television clips, personal video footage, testimonies, "man on the street" interviews, or historical biographies? Will your sound system be sufficient so as to enhance but not distract from the teaching and singing, and will it be run by a trained and competent sound engineer?

When you do such things as baptisms and baby dedications in the service, will you include video close-ups so attendees can see the faces, or will you have a photographer on hand to capture such events for the church Web site so that people can see the good things that are happening in your church? Will you use props based on the Scriptures, such as a sword and trowel when preaching Nehemiah, or a two-by-four and toothpick when preaching about Jesus' plank-speck comedic rant?

To make the service less predictable and more informative, will you allow people to text message questions while you preach and have someone filter out the best ones and then send them to the preacher to answer live on the spot during or at the end of the sermon? We first tried this at our latest Sunday evening service that has no childcare and mostly very young people. Their questions were amazing. The sermon was about sex the first week we tried this, and a woman who was pregnant as a result of rape asked if she could have an abortion. I answered her anonymous question, we stopped to pray as a church, and we have followed up with her for pastoral care, since we want to be pro-life for the baby and pro-love for the mommy.

PHASE 4: EXITING

As people are leaving the church building, what things can be done to send them out into the world as missionaries with Jesus to continue their worship throughout the week? Will you hand them anything on the way out? If you use props in a sermon, give them away, because it is a fun memory and gives people great stories to tell. For a sermon I did on dating righteously and maintaining appropriate physical boundaries, the prop I used was an enormous bubble suit that could actually be worn around the entire body; it was a comedic way of mocking hyperconservative, Christian-dating legalisms. We brought it out on stage during the sermon and gave it away to the person who had the best idea for how to use it for the gospel. In the end, people want curious stories to tell their friends, and if your church is able to tell good stories about

Jesus and peoples' lives, along with the occasional good laugh, then those stories will be repeated.

PHASE 5: EXTENDING

Once people have left the church service, how can you extend your teaching to them? Will you have a blog on your church Web site where you offer them more resources for study on the text or topic, answer people's questions in person or via email, or transcribe your sermon or write a summary of it? Will you have small group materials such as Bible study questions that follow the pulpit for folks to use in their weekly groups? Will you have a place on your main Web site for people to discuss the sermon or ask questions? Will you have a password-protected members' site for people to pray for one another, chat about life, share goods and services, find the church directory, and ask you questions about the sermon? Will you make use of other social networks such as Facebook in which you or some other church leaders invest in people digitally in ongoing relationships?

You should make sure your sermons are recorded and distributed, possibly along with your band's live or prerecorded worship music, if it's good enough. The best thing to do is give away your preaching and teaching free of charge. Any pastor who fails to distribute his content runs the risk of being seen as dated as well as greedy, if he charges for it. Generally speaking, the distribution should not be done through a tape or CD ministry. Such distribution methods are expensive, time consuming, and outdated. Your sermons should at least be on your church Web site in audio format. This allows people who missed church to catch up and send links to friends they think would benefit from the sermon, and it archives your teaching on a text or topic for new people who will come in future years. These files can be put on iTunes and similar online portals in addition to your main church Web site. If you capture the sermon on video, you can also post that on your Web site and iTunes and then pull out shorter clips to post on YouTube, Facebook, and other sites.

The opportunities for creativity are endless. For those who want to see their church do a better job of using technology to contextualize the gospel, I would offer the following principles. (1) Experiment before you commit to long-term use of any technology. Make sure it does what you want it to do. (2) Rent gear (e.g., audio, video, and lighting) and see what you like before purchasing it, because if you buy the wrong gear you will waste a lot of money. (3) Be humble enough to visit lots of churches and businesses to see what will work for you. (4) If you hire consultants, be careful to make sure they serve your needs rather than imposing their way of doing things on you. (5) Do not fall into a rut or feel stuck with anything, but use the technology as a tool, making changes as needed. (6) Before beginning, count the cost to your time, staff, and finances and make sure you can pay the price to operate at whatever level makes most sense for your culture.

It makes sense to conclude this practical chapter with a few stories I have received via email from people who are connected to our church by means of technology only. Some Christian soldiers from the front lines of war download the video sermon each week and then gather in a tent to watch it and have church together since there is no pastor with them and no church to attend. A number of missionaries around the world, pioneering ministries to unreached people groups, download our teaching to help them continue learning as they teach others. Others around the world suffering in hospital beds with terminal illnesses appreciate being able to watch or listen to the sermons for some encouragement while they are fighting death. Lastly, one new Christian wrote, "Realizing that I am a sinner, the nature of my sins, and knowing that Jesus paid the price has given me the greatest joy and inner peace that I've never felt in my entire life. And I thank all of you for working so hard to get the message out there for all through this digital media. Believe me, it worked for me, and I'm sure your efforts are paying off for others as well."

Technology is a tool for the church to connect with people and provide them with gospel content about Jesus. Now more than ever, churches that want to reach out effectively to lost people, particularly young people, don't necessarily need to love technology but must learn to use it to connect with people they love. Any church that is willing to use technology well is demonstrating love by approaching lost people in a way they are accustomed to. This technological hospitality is the practical outpouring of Jesus' love for our neighbor.

ANSWERS TO COMMON QUESTIONS ABOUT TECHNOLOGY

WHAT PRINCIPLES SHOULD GUIDE A CHURCH WHEN MAKING DECISIONS ABOUT THINGS, SUCH AS TECHNOLOGY, OF WHICH THE BIBLE DOES NOT SPEAK?

The first principle is what the Bible commands us to be and do, we must do, and what it tells us not to be and do, we don't do. When the Bible speaks, it is God himself speaking to us. The Bible tells us that the church is a body of Spirit-empowered believers who proclaim Jesus to the world. We don't have an option to modify that in order to meet cultural needs.

Second, if the Bible describes how the early church did things, we should look for principles in those examples and use them to guide our decisions (Acts 15:15–21; 1 Cor. 10:6–11). The Bible tells us how the early church selected servant leaders (Acts 6) or dealt with doctrinal controversy (Acts 15). These stories are in the Bible to show us how to deal with similar issues today. We are wise to follow these patterns as closely as possible.

Third, God was purposely silent in many areas to give us freedom to follow wisdom and the leading of the Spirit to be the church and accomplish our mission. He said nothing about what time the church service should begin, how long it should last, or even the specific components of a service. That he says nothing does not indicate his "No," but rather his encouragement to develop practices to meet the varying needs of different cultures and times. What one church does will differ from what another church chooses to do because churches are different. We ask if technology will help us accomplish our mission of taking biblical Christianity to the people he commands us to reach. Will it help leaders build up the body so we "attain to the unity of the faith and of the knowledge of the Son of God, to mature manhood, to the measure of the stature of the fullness of Christ" (Eph. 4:13)?

When evaluating new practices, it is a mistake to say either yes or no simply because the practice is innovative. Innovation itself is neither good nor bad, though many think so! We must evaluate practices wisely by asking ourselves if they help us be the church and accomplish our mission.

DOESN'T THE USE OF TECHNOLOGY INCREASE IMPERSONALIZED MINISTRY RATHER THAN LOVING COMMUNITY?

It certainly can. Indiscriminate use of technology can reduce a person to an impersonal bit of data to be manipulated or allow people to remain anonymous. I know I'm unknown when I get something addressed to *Ms.* Gerry Breshears. When technology reigns, people are shaped to fit the needs of technology. Our feelings and priorities are irrelevant or merely marketing statistics tracked to sell products.

Technology can be undeniably helpful. As I write this, I am listening to Celtic Christian music on Internet radio. One song speaks deeply to my spirit. Using technology I was able to get this music for a very low cost. Similarly, I can learn from great teachers whose lessons were taught far away when they are vodcast to my mobile device.

When my wife, Sherry, and I went as missionaries to the Philippines in 1969, we had minimal contact with our family and friends back home in America. A letter took at least a week to reach home via airmail and was expensive to send. A five-minute telephone call would have taken over 10 percent of our monthly support, and it was often impossible to get through at any cost. Now when I teach overseas, I can talk face-to-face with my family back home every day as long as I want using free Internet phone services and webcams. It is my experience that technological tools such as email, Facebook, and Skype can enable and enhance loving community with friends and family who live all over the world.

Some are very reluctant to use technology, feeling it impersonalizes the communication. They prefer talking in person. But consider that in one sense the Bible itself is technology. It is written words, not God's personal presence. The face-to-face encounter between God and Moses was far more personal than reading Exodus. But I can read my Bible anytime and hear God speaking. There are advantages to technology in communication.

We learn how to communicate in a generational and cultural context. Changing the accepted means of communication can be extremely difficult. As an example, would proposing marriage by a very creative text message be acceptable? In one context it would be unthinkable, while in others it would be "way cool!" Younger couples may use email or texting as effective tools to resolve conflict. The means of communication need to adapt to fit the cultures of the communicators. Intercultural and intergenerational communication requires that both sides work to adapt so that there is no damage to the relationship.

It is essential to keep perspective in this emotionally charged issue. Technology is a useful servant but a terrible master.

ISN'T IT BETTER THAT MY PASTOR KNOW ME PERSONALLY SO HE CAN PROCLAIM GOD'S WORD DIRECTLY INTO MY LIFE SITUATION?

Without a doubt. But pastors have a range of ministry from intensely personal to relatively impersonal large crowds. As soon as the congregation is larger than one, the message will be less specific to my specific issues. There are varying levels of knowledge between teacher and hearer.

It is important to remember that not everyone who proclaims God's Word in my life will know me personally. Truth and its ability to speak into our lives are not necessarily dependent on the speaker's knowledge of the hearer's individual situation. Let's look at the Bible. Jesus had his inner three who shared in his life most intimately (Mark 9:1–8; 13:3; 14:33); the Twelve who were very close and received deeper teaching and did unique ministries (Mark 3:14–19; 6:7–13; 9:35–50; 10:32–45; 11:11–14); the disciples who were committed to him and followed him (Luke 8:1–3); and his hearers, whom he taught in large crowds (Matt. 5:1; Mark 3:7–10; 6:34, 45). When Jesus spoke into the lives of his disciples, it was more personal than when he spoke into the lives of the larger crowds.

Peter did not have a personal relationship with the thousands of people in the church in Jerusalem or with the "elect exiles of the dispersion in Pontus, Galatia, Cappadocia, Asia, and Bithynia" (1 Pet. 1:1). Paul ministered effectively to people in Rome whom he had never even met. But Peter did have deep relationships with his friend John and with his disciples, Silvanus and Mark.

Even in smaller churches, the pastor will not know all the people at the same level. In large churches, the lack of knowledge is magnified. This issue is not unique to the twenty-first century or to megachurches. During the exodus Moses could not know all the people personally, but he was still required to lead them, be responsible for their growth, and speak to them all. So he had the people choose wise, experienced, and understanding men whom he appointed to serve as heads of groups of thousands, hundreds, fifties, and tens (Ex. 18:17–26; Deut. 1:13–18).

This same pattern of gradational ministry is followed in virtually all churches today. A good pastor will be very sure to organize the church so everyone will have a leader who knows and pastors them in very personal ways, even as he gives himself to prayer and preaching the Word to the large group (Acts 6:3, 5). Leaders who oversee home groups, for example, could be equipped by lay pastors, who in turn are shepherded by a pastor of discipleship who keeps close communication with the preaching pastor.

CHAPTER TWELVE

HOW COULD THE CHURCH HELP TRANSFORM THE WORLD?

"My grace is sufficient for you, for my power is made perfect in weakness."

2 CORINTHIANS 12:9

✝

On my first trip to a third-world city I was horrified. I spent a few days in the rural villages observing the work of some pioneering church planters who were starting churches in remote areas where people still lived in huts and plowed their fields behind oxen because there was no electricity. The people there were incredibly kind, the pace of life was slow, the bodies of people were healthy, and the children in the villages laughed and played with great enthusiasm.

Later, a rickshaw driver took me into the city many miles away. As we approached the city, I could see an enormous cloud of pollution hanging over it, dark and ominous. The closer we got, more garbage littered the landscape and more homeless children wandered around begging for food, and the more heartbreaking the picture became.

The final few miles of our journey took us along a vast river that ran through the middle of the city. Nearing the southernmost end of the city, the rickshaw driver took me over a large bridge that crossed over the river.

I will never forget that experience.

The smell was so horrendous that I literally gagged just from breathing the air over the river. The water looked like black coffee and was filled with garbage and feces. On the river's edge were hundreds, maybe thousands, of people. They were bathing in the river, washing their clothes, and cleaning their dirty dishes. Most devastating, children were swimming in the river and invariably drinking some of the water.

Looking at the hellish scene, it was obvious to me that there was simply no way to keep the water clean by trying to fish out all the feces, pollution, and garbage at the end of the city where we had crossed. Instead, the only hope was a complete transformation upstream wherever the filth originally entered the river.

Now some years later, I see cultures that flow through our nations and cities much like that polluted river. Christians from both the left and the right agree on one thing—the river of our culture is polluted, and as a result people are sick and dying. The left tends to lament the lack of community and care for the poor and marginalized, failure to care for creation, and rise of greedy materialism, racism, classism, sexism, and violence. The right tends to lament the lack of sexual mores, respect for sanctity of life, and rise of drug abuse, gang violence, divorce, and general lawlessness. Tragically, both are true, which has led Christians from both the left and the right to cast four visions for how to right what has been made wrong in the world by cleaning up the proverbial river.

FOUR VISIONS FOR THE WORLD

The first vision is *the evangelistic vision*. It seeks to clean up the proverbial river of culture by simply converting as many people as possible to Christianity. Therefore, the focus is on outreach events, personal evangelism, and parachurch ministries. All of these are devoted to seeing lost people repent of sin and become Christians. The underlying assumption in this vision is if more people have new hearts, somehow the world and its culture will change.

However, while the effort to convert people to Jesus is obviously good and right, this vision has failed. Despite the fact that there has always been a high percentage of people who claim to be Christians throughout our nation's history, our river of culture is as polluted as ever. In fact, statistically it seems that Christians are guilty of throwing more junk in the river than they fish out. This vision's push for Christian converts to be trained in a Christian worldview does help individuals' decision making and personal transformation but does not necessarily lead to cultural transformation. Thus, this sincere but simplistic hope will not transform the world and clean up the proverbial river.

The second vision is *the political vision*. This vision seeks to change the world through the powerful means of political influence. This vision believes that if we could simply vote in godly leaders who would enact godly laws, the world would be transformed from the top down by virtue of having a moral conscience and godly law. While Christians should be actively involved in shaping the political landscape, as Joseph did in Egypt and Daniel did in Babylon, this vision alone fails for three reasons. One, true Christians are a minority group, so their candidates struggle to be elected, particularly in major cities, which are far more liberal and secular. Second, politics follows the culture but does not create it, because politics is downstream from the culture. Third, even if the laws are good and just, without regenerated hearts and supporting communities such as churches and families, the laws will not be obeyed, just as God's good laws are regularly known yet disobeyed.

The third vision is *the fundamentalist vision*. This vision asserts that the world is altogether dark, without hope, condemned by God, and destined for imminent destruction by God, who can no longer stomach the wickedness that fills the earth. When combined with a fearful eschatology, this vision is particularly compelling. The practical outworking of this vision is that Christians should separate from the world and its culture as much as possible so as to avoid being stained in any way and to preserve one's personal and familial holiness at all costs. Therefore, large cities, movies, music, television, and the Internet are to be avoided as much as possible because they are "worldly." Adherents of the fundamentalist vision are prone to engage in culture wars, angrily reacting against the filth they see in the cultural river that they abhor. However, they are seen as nothing more than a mean, moral minority that tells others what to do but does not do anything for the common good of all people in the culture.

The fourth vision is *the liberal vision*. This vision seeks to lovingly serve people, particularly the poor and marginalized, in hopes of showing God's love to the culture and eliciting compassion and generosity. The problem with this vision is that it tends to concentrate so intently on deed-based ministry that it neglects Word-based ministry that calls people to repent of personal sin (which contributes to all of the systemic sin). At worst, it becomes so focused on good works that its vision can be little more than generally spiritual people doing good deeds, regardless of their god or religion. Lastly, because the power to transform people and their culture resides in the gospel, the liberal vision, though well intended, lacks the power to truly transform people and cultures.

Each of these four visions is not entirely wrong but, rather, incomplete. Christians and Christian churches should desire to see people converted, laws changed, Christians living in holiness, and Christians serving those in need with loving compassion. The question persists, how can this be accomplished? To answer this question we will now consider a fifth vision for cultural transformation presented by James Davison Hunter, a Christian and professor of sociology at the University of Virginia.[1] In doing so, this chapter is admittedly more technical and academic at some points than the other chapters of this book. But my hope is to share with you a biblically rooted ideology that will help you see the world as it is and world change as it could be.

HOW TO TRANSFORM THE WORLD

Hunter insightfully explains why each of the four Christian visions of culture and cultural change has failed:

> The error . . . derives from at least three sources deep in modern Western thought. The first is "Hegelian idealism," the view that ideas move history; the second is "Lockean individualism," the view that the autonomous and rational individual is the key actor in social change; the third is "Christian pietism," the view that the most important goal in life is having one's heart right before God. There is significant truth in all three traditions of thought, but they have prejudiced our larger view of culture and cultural change in ways that are fundamentally flawed.[2]

[1]James Davison Hunter, "To Change the World," *The Trinity Forum*, vol. 3, no. 2 (June 2002), http://www.ttf.org/index/findings/detail/to-change-the-world/ or http://www.ttf.org/pdf/Bv3n2-Hunter-Text.pdf.
[2]Ibid., 5.

After establishing the deeply held Western myth that one heart fully devoted to God can alone change the world, he makes a very debated point: "If one is serious about changing the world, the first step is to discard this view of culture and how cultures change, for every strategy based upon it will fail—not most strategies, but *all* strategies. This is not to say that the renewal of the hearts and minds of individuals is unimportant. It is just not *decisively* important if the goal is to change the world."[3]

By way of example, if all that is required to transform the world is to have a few hearts, or even a lot of hearts, devoted to a moral cause, then how do we explain something as powerful and culturally transforming as the statistically small homosexual community? Until some thirty years ago, homosexuality was considered a psychological disorder and a social shame. Yet, in a relatively short number of years, a statistically small number of homosexuals and their supporters have in many ways completely transformed the cultural moral opinion about everything from sexuality to marriage. An indicator of the change is that the American Psychiatric Association (APA) first erased homosexuality from the disorder category in its highly authoritative *Diagnostic and Statistical Manual of Mental Disorders* in 1973, completing the process in 1987. Now the APA Ethics Code says that psychologists must never discriminate on the basis of sexual orientation. The current atmosphere paints those who refuse to affirm the full legitimacy of the gay, lesbian, bisexual, and transsexual (GLBT) identity and lifestyle as the ones with a psychological disorder. The question persists, how did so few people create so much cultural transformation so quickly? Is there anything Christians and churches can learn from the homosexual community in order to do for God what they have done against God?

Hunter answers this question by presenting an alternative view of culture and cultural change that is brilliant. He begins by quoting his mentor, the sociologist Peter Berger, who said, "Ideas don't succeed in history because of their inherent truthfulness, but rather because of their connection to very powerful institutions and interests."[4]

As controversial as the statement is, it is insightful. Just as not every person has the same amount of financial clout, so too not every person

---

[3]Ibid., 5.
[4]Ibid., 6.

has the same amount of cultural clout. Simply, when it comes to changing culture, while all people are loved by God and are ontologically equal because they equally bear God's image, some people are more strategic in effecting cultural transformation. Or, to say it another way, some people are upstream and decide what goes in the river, and other people are downstream and have to live with whatever comes down the river to them.

Building on this premise, Hunter offers the following five propositions about culture.

1) Culture is a resource and, as such, a form of power. Like money, there are varying degrees of cultural capital. For this reason, someone with a PhD has more cultural capital than a janitor, and the lead singer of a popular band has more cultural capital than the second-chair trumpet player in a junior high school marching band. Cultural capital translates into power and influence because it is accompanied with credibility and thus authority that causes others to consider that person an expert who names things, and in so doing defines reality itself.

2) Culture is produced. Culture (e.g., music, fashion, morality, architecture, language, technology, law, spirituality) is created and disseminated not by individuals but by cultural elites in the privileged position of being upstream. From their privileged position they decide what is and what is not sent downstream to the masses of people in the culture. The point is that the Western myth of culture being produced almost solely by individuals needs to be reconsidered. We need to rethink how culture is made and thus transformed:

> Most of us are inclined to what could be called the "great man" (or great person) view of history. It is St. Paul, St. Augustine, Thomas Aquinas, Martin Luther and John Calvin, Jonathan Edwards, William Wilberforce, Charles Darwin, Friedrich Nietzsche, Sigmund Freud, and the like, who stood as switchmen on the train tracks of history; it is their genius and the genius of other heroic individuals that have guided the evolution of civilization this way or that; for better or for worse.
>
> Against this view, I would argue that *the key actor in history is not individual genius but rather the network*, and the new institutions that are

created out of those networks. This is where the stuff of culture and cultural change is produced.[5]

3) Cultural production is stratified in a rigid structure of "center" and "periphery." The individuals, networks, and institutions that produce culture with its values and lifestyles are networks of intellectual elites who went to prestigious schools where they not only received excellent education but also became friends with the right people. They live in prominent centers for their culture and work in influential organizations. They gather periodically in the right places, homes, parties, restaurants, or clubs, where they generate ideas as they interact. This is just as true for regional and local culture as it is for national culture. There is an influential group of people who meet over breakfast in the corner café in a small town who set the cultural agenda for the town. Others may respond or reject what they propose, but they don't initiate the culture.

This is true for Christian culture too. For example, the initiation of the emerging church movement came from a small group that met for conversations with the sponsorship of the Leadership Network. And, it was Passion college events that caused Christian musicians such as Dave Crowder and preachers such as John Piper to become incredibly popular with a generation of young people.

This rigid status structure of culture and cultural production flies in the face of the American "one man, one vote" ideal, yet it is true. Those most critically involved in the production of a culture or civilization operate in the center, where prestige is the highest, not on the periphery, where status is low.

4) Culture changes from the top down and rarely from the bottom up. Admittedly, some true political, social, and economic revolutions occur from the bottom up with the masses. However, such cultural transformation is rarely sustained and generally short-lived. Conversely, most cultural creation and transformation begin upstream and flow downstream. This is because the cultural gatekeepers who decide what does and does not go into the river of culture are upstream. They run the law schools, fashion industry, banking industry, political parties, media outlets, and the like. They decide which bands are signed

---
[5]Ibid., 7.

to record contracts and placed on the radio, which films are funded and distributed by the movie studios, which clothes are sold at the store, and which books are published. This is because those who hold the cultural capital are also networked with those who hold the funding capital, media capital, and political capital, and together they are the cultural gatekeepers who decide what goes into the river of culture, how it is introduced, and when.

Hunter goes on to explain that as few as 150 but no more than 3,000 people working in key networks have framed the assumptions that undergird the thinking of the world's civilizations. This is out of roughly twenty-three billion people who have lived between 600 BC and AD 1900, which clearly illustrates that most people live downstream, and only a handful of culture makers and culture keepers upstream truly rule the world.

5) The impetus, energy, and direction for changing the world are most intense where cultural, economic, and often political resources overlap. This is where networks of elites, who generate these various resources, come together in common purpose. Where business, educational, political, and church leaders join their different pools of cultural capital and collaborate, they have the greatest impact. As an example, Hunter says:

> Take the evangelist, Billy Graham—an unknown itinerate preacher whose urban crusades had repeatedly fizzled until William Randolph Hearst ordered his media network to "puff Graham" during the Los Angeles crusade of 1949.
> Within two months of this order, Graham was preaching to crowds of 350,000. No one who has studied the issue disagrees that without the economic and cultural leverage provided by Hearst, we would likely not ever have heard of Graham.
> Again and again we see that the impetus, energy, and direction for changing the world were found where cultural, economic, and often political resources overlapped; where networks of elites, who generated these various resources, come together in common purpose.[6]

This fifth proposition, that world changing happens best when different networks of elites and the institutions they lead overlap, is set up

---

[6]Ibid., 10.

"against Christian pietism, which biases us to see the individual's 'heart and mind' as the primary source and repository of culture; we now see that hearts and minds are only tangentially related to the movements of culture, that culture is much more complicated and has a life independent of individual will; indeed, that it is not individual hearts and minds that move cultures but cultures that ultimately shape and direct the lives of individuals."[7]

Indeed, each of us needs to personally repent of our sin and have ongoing sanctification in our hearts and minds. That is incredibly important on the personal level. Yet, to experience the transformation of the entire world over which King Jesus rules from his throne, this kind of personal, inward transformation must be viewed by Christians and Christian churches as a necessary and inescapable first step that leads to the second step of pursuing cultural, outward transformation. Therefore, because cultures house people who bear God's image, and because the river of culture can make people sick or well depending on what is in it, cultural transformation is to be pursued out of love for God and people here and now in this world.

Furthermore, Jeremiah tells us to shape culture, saying, "But seek the welfare of the city where I have sent you into exile, and pray to the LORD on its behalf, for in its welfare you will find your welfare."[8] Shaping culture requires gaining favor upstream from those leaders who make the culture, which is why Paul tells us to pray for them: "I urge that supplications, prayers, intercessions, and thanksgivings be made for all people, for kings and all who are in high positions, that we may lead a peaceful and quiet life, godly and dignified in every way."[9]

That being said, God does call some churches to be more involved in culture shaping than others, by virtue of such things as their location and resources. Sadly, because they are well known, such churches are often the object of scorn, gossip, and criticism from fellow Christians who do not understand or sympathize with the complexity of the mission God has called them to. Therefore, I am encouraging some graciousness toward churches with more culture-shaping responsibility, because theirs is a difficult task. Loving encouragement combined with loving correction is more helpful to them than mean-spirited criticism.

[7]Ibid., 11.
[8]Jer. 29:7.
[9]1 Tim. 2:1–2.

I also want to be very careful to say I am not in any way denigrating churches that are not near major urban centers with high-impact, culture-making opportunities. I myself was converted and trained in a church that was strategically near my university but was surrounded by farmland for hours in every direction. The church in that small rural town loved Jesus and loved me and changed my life. I praise God continually for that church and the men there who have gleaned a great deal of wisdom from years on their tractors alone with Jesus. Furthermore, Jesus himself never visited a big city and was often mocked for coming from a small town that had not been known for any major culture-shaping influence, which just proves that God can and does work as he sees fit.

God loves everyone, so there must be churches everywhere. Nonetheless, strategically speaking, culture shaping does require planting urban churches to be a kingdom-oriented city within a city.

URBAN CHURCH PLANTING

God made our first parents to worship him, and part of their worship included making culture. In what has been called the cultural mandate, God told Adam and Eve:

> "Be fruitful and multiply and fill the earth and subdue it and have dominion over the fish of the sea and over the birds of the heavens and over every living thing that moves on the earth." And God said, "Behold, I have given you every plant yielding seed that is on the face of all the earth, and every tree with seed in its fruit. You shall have them for food. And to every beast of the earth and to every bird of the heavens and to everything that creeps on the earth, everything that has the breath of life, I have given every green plant for food." And it was so.[10]

As stewards and rulers over lower creation, we were created to make culture and spread across the earth to create culture. Richard Cote says:

> The word "culture" derives its semantic origin from the Latin *cultura*, which initially referred to the cultivation of the soil and then by exten-

---

[10]Gen. 1:28–30.

sion to the cultivation of the mind and spirit. . . . it embraces all aspects of human life in a given society: its values, beliefs, customs, forms of knowledge and art, etc. It is no longer an "elitist" concept of the educated but one that applies to every individual and to all peoples.[11]

Accordingly, culture is not merely something that Christians and Christian churches are to participate in, but also something they are to cultivate, or plow, by living for the kingdom of heaven among the cultures of earth.[12]

In the first two chapters of Genesis we see the elements of this kingdom culture that we are to plow. They include human life lived in harmonious dignity with God and creation, blessing, feasting, masculinity and femininity, goodness, wisdom, work, marriage, song, lovemaking, and lots of children who honor Mom and Dad to the glory of their God. Today we continue to bear the image of God and do what we were made to do, but now we do it marred and stained by sin. Even when we make culture, it has aspects that reflect the glory in which God made us as well as the depravity to which we have fallen. This explains why, for example, a porn-addicted soldier who commits adultery against his wife can also throw himself on a grenade and sacrifice his life to save the lives of his friends.

The culture we were ultimately made to create will be revealed in the new creation. As we wrote in our first book, *Vintage Jesus*,[13] the new creation will not be the idyllic rural lifestyle that has dominated so much American vision of faithful Christianity. Rather, at the center of the new creation will be a grand metropolis from which Jesus will rule over the earth.[14] The entire storyline of the Bible is not from garden to garden, but rather from garden to city.[15] The Bible opens in its first few pages with a beautiful garden paradise. But the Bible closes in its final few pages with the vision of heaven as a dense city filled with people— thus the ultimate goal of creation is an urban paradise.

Sadly, most Christians associate the city with vice, not virtue. In

[11]Richard G. Cote, *Re-Visioning Mission: The Catholic Church and Culture in Postmodern America* (Mahwah, NJ: Paulist Press, 1996), 89–90.
[12]Gen. 1:26–30; 9:1–2, 6–11; Psalm 8.
[13]Mark Driscoll and Gerry Breshears, *Vintage Jesus: Timeless Answers to Timely Questions* (Wheaton, IL: Crossway Books, 2007), 156–157.
[14]Rev. 21:1–2.
[15]I want to thank Tim Keller for many conversations over meals throughout the past years, during which he really helped me to understand God's urban vision for his people.

truth, cities have long been seen as a haven for violent crime, sexual sin, and drug abuse. But sin is often most clearly seen in the city simply because it is more concentrated in the city than in suburban and rural areas. As a result, the correlated need for God is most clearly seen in the city. The rawness of the city makes it exactly the kind of place that God would use to convince people of their need for him. Furthermore, by revealing the unveiling of a city upon his return, Jesus intends for Christians to love cities in the meantime.

In much of the world today, cities are increasingly less Christian, whereas the suburban and rural areas are more Christian. On one hand, this is good because God loves everyone, and so the church should bring the loving truth of the gospel to everyone everywhere. On the other hand, cities are of greater strategic importance because they are upstream where culture is made and changed, yet most Christians today are downstream and subsequently are incapable of effecting cultural transformation. Furthermore, because cities are marked by density and diversity, the city is the most strategic place from which to evangelize and convert a large number of diverse people.

In the book of Acts, which chronicles the spread of the early church, we witness the exact opposite phenomenon. Christianity began as an almost entirely urban movement led by Paul, who moved from city to city to plant churches. In fact, he almost entirely ignored the suburban and rural areas.

Why?

Paul rightly knew that if he reached a city by planting a healthy, gospel-based church there, he would effect change in the culture. Furthermore, Paul knew that a missional church in a city would reach the suburban and rural areas because everything in the city flows downstream to the other areas, carrying in it whatever the city chooses to put in the proverbial water of culture.

Plainly stated, cities are the most strategic place for Christians and the gospel. Because government, law, education, healthcare, information, media, arts, sports, entertainment, trade, travel, population, and industry are concentrated most in a city, cities are the fountains from which culture flows. Therefore, Christians who flee from cities only to complain about the kind of culture that is flowing into the culture from the cities are both foolish and hypocritical. The answer is for Christians to love the city, move to the city, pray for the city, and serve the city until Jesus returns with his city, from which all culture will emanate throughout the new earth.

This is exactly what happened in the early church led by God the Holy Spirit. The historical results are encouraging. Historians like Rodney Stark[16] and Wayne Meeks[17] say that by AD 300, upwards of half of the people living in major Roman cities were Christian, while more than 90 percent of those living in the countryside were still pagan. Curiously, our word *pagan* likely came from the Greek word *paganus*, which meant "someone who lives on the farm." Most of the Christians lived in cities and most pagans lived on farms, which means that most Christians had an opportunity to transform the culture or reach someone who could.

If there is any hope to reach people and transform culture today, churches need to be planted in major cities. Yet, for a church to be effective in the city, it must be wary of flawed models of urban ministry as much as it is wary of flawed models of cultural creation and transformation. On this point, Tim Keller's teaching "The Meaning of the City," based on Jeremiah 29:4–14, is incredibly helpful. He examines various models of urban ministry, each of which grasps some aspect of biblical truth. He argues that a combination of each model is necessary so that the most faithful model of urban ministry can occur. The below is a summary of Keller's models, although I have used more illustrative metaphors.

The first model is *church as bomb shelter*. This church rightly sees that there is great danger for harm in the city. So, the church separates from the city, sadly primarily speaks only ill of the city, and functions as a safe place in which Christians hide from the city. The church forgets that it is called to lovingly serve the city so that it might become a great city like Jerusalem was during seasons of the Old Testament when the city loved and obeyed God and his Word. The strength of the church as bomb shelter model is that it rightly understands the danger of the city. The weakness is that it is not eager to help rescue other people from the

---

[16]For example, see his books *The Victory of Reason* (New York: Random House, 2006); *Cities of God* (New York: HarperCollins, 2006); and *The Rise of Christianity* (Princeton, NJ: Princeton University Press, 1996).
[17]For example, see his book *The First Urban Christians: The Social World of the Apostle Paul* (London: Yale University Press, 2003).

dangers of the city through evangelism and discipleship but is primarily concerned with its own safety.

The second model is *church as mirror*. The strength of this model is its awareness of things in the city that reflect the goodness of God through his common grace and general revelation and the fact that we are made in his image and likeness. The weakness is that it underestimates or even overlooks human sin and its devastating effects. The result is that what the church believes and how the church behaves is nothing more than a reflection of the city. Therefore, such things as homosexuality, sexual perversion, and approval of all kinds of sin, as well as the belief that Jesus was little more than an exemplary man, are tolerated in the name of lovingly relating to the city in a nonjudgmental manner. The sin of the church as mirror is that it has so overly contextualized the gospel that it has failed to also contend for the truth of the gospel, so much so that there is little if any gospel left. Further, rather than mirroring the Scriptures and Jesus by calling the city to repentance, it simply approves of the city in ways that God does not by overlooking the evil of the city as typified in biblical cities such as Babylon.

The third model is *church as parasite*. The strength of the church as parasite model is its awareness of the beneficial resources in the city. However, the weakness is that the church uses the resources of the city for its own benefit but does not care to serve the good of the entire city in any meaningful way. The result is that the church is seen as a drain on the city rather than as a blessing. Church members are dismissed as people who do not live in the city, love the city, or serve the city but merely drive in to the city to attend church events, thereby using the city in an incredibly selfish manner that is repugnant to lost people who love the city. The sin of the church as parasite is its failure to see the city as a battleground between the kingdom of light and the kingdom of darkness and its refusal to live as a city within the city committed to the transformation of the people and culture that make up the city by the power of the gospel. Subsequently, the church as parasite settles for selfishly using the resources of the city but not for the purpose of seeing people saved and their city transformed.

The fourth model is *church as city within the city*. In the church as city within the city there is a love for God, lost people, and fellow Christians simultaneously as Jesus commanded without neglecting any of the three. In the city within the city, life is lived in a countercultural and kingdom manner, taking into account the need to discern when and how to reject the sin and folly of the city. Indeed, the church co-opts the hopes and dreams of the city (for example, racial harmony and generosity to the most needy) by offering the gospel as the true hope for such things. The church partners with the city and its resources with the distinct purpose of doing good for the whole city to make it the best city possible.

A pastor I have never met sent me a very encouraging email. He was in our area visiting some friends while he was here from another country. One Sunday he caught a bus to our church to attend a service. After the service he caught the bus back home and began chatting with the bus driver. He sent me an email reporting their conversation; the bus driver said that although he was not a Christian, he liked our church because "that church really loves our city and wants this to be a great city for all of us." Admittedly, we have a lot to learn, and I have made a lot of mistakes, which means that not everyone in our city would say the same thing. Yet, the fact that some who disagree with us know our heart for them and for our city is hopeful and encouraging.

Sadly, most cities do not have enough churches that are cities within the city. As a result, masses of people do not hear about Jesus, and makers of culture do not hear about Jesus. Therefore, missional churches everywhere need to make a focused effort to concentrate on planting missional churches in cities. In our history as an urban church, this has always been our heart and by God's grace we have seen many other churches planted that are likewise strategically focused on major cities.[18] I want to be clear and stress that God loves all people and we need missional churches everywhere. Still, because of the city's strategic importance, resources such as money and leaders should be sent to the city to plant missional churches as cities within cities on mission for the gospel.

These upstream churches are the best opportunity we have to reach new generations, new residents, new cultures, new subcultures, and new culture creators and transformers. Furthermore, missional urban churches have the opportunity to help reinvigorate struggling and dying churches in the city that love the city but are unsure how to

---

[18]Go to http://www.acts29network.org for more information about our church planting network.

survive and thrive. This is because innovative church plants take risks and pioneer new ministry insights and methods that struggling established churches near them can learn and benefit from. Furthermore, energized new church plants with converts provide an increased pool of potential new leaders to help revive other churches and ministries in the city. Remember, suburban and rural areas along with other cities in the nation and other nations of the earth can be reached from the city because the city is so far upstream.

SEEKING EVIDENCES OF GRACE

Admittedly, the prospect of seeing Christians get and stay on Jesus' mission, non-Christians being converted to Jesus and his mission, the gospel being so contextualized that new churches and campuses are planted, culture creators and transformers upstream being converted, and culture actually being transformed by the gospel all seems daunting and overwhelming. But, before we lose hope and settle in to simply do church, four things are worth mentioning.

1) Jesus' tomb is empty, the Holy Spirit has been poured out, the gospel is the power of God, and therefore anything can happen.

2) Jesus promised that he would build his church and guaranteed that he would never leave or forsake us, which means we are not alone. No matter how bleak it looks, if Jesus is present and committed to his church, anything can happen.

3) In the days of the early church when the *pax Romana* created a government that touched the nations and there was a road system that allowed the free travel of people and information, God chose to birth Christianity as an urban movement. Today, when the cities of the nations are merely a mouse click, phone call, or airplane ride away, it is entirely possible for Christianity to again find itself as an urban people on mission to be the city within the cities, as it originally was.

4) As James Davison Hunter reminds us:

Yet even Jesus created a network of disciples (who, over time, became spiritual and cultural leaders). Though they originated on the periphery of the social world of that age, they moved to the provincial center of Jerusalem, and then, within a generation, to *the* center of the ancient world—Rome. They too created new institutions that not only articulated but embodied an alternative to the reigning ways of life of that time.

We too have the joy and privilege of doing the same in our own generation in humble and faithful obedience to the call God has placed on our lives.

The task is long term and certainly arduous, and the outcome is finally not in our hands. Still, the potential consequences for faithfulness to this task for the common good in this time of uncertainty may be far more than we can ask or even imagine.[19]

I want to close this book with some encouragement, because most of you who are reading it probably need some desperately. One of the greatest failures of my ministry, which was the cause of so much of my anger, grief, despair, pride, and impatience, was revealed to me while writing this book, and so I would like to share it with you.

Like most pastors, I don't really have a pastor in the way that most Christians have a pastor. But occasionally I meet a pastor who becomes something like my pastor. We don't get a lot of time together, but the time we do get is pastoral to me. One of those men is a pastor named C. J. Mahaney. I have found him to be incredibly positive, upbeat, hopeful, gracious, and encouraging, which was perplexing because he is a Calvinist who believes in total depravity, and I was unsure how a pastor who believed in sin could laugh, smile, or do much of anything besides read Lamentations and clean his gun.

Most of my personal and pastoral attention over the years has been spent keenly aware of and frustrated with, if not angered by, sin and its effects. I am continually aware of every minute detail in my life and ministry that is undone, needing work, failing, falling short, not functioning to capacity, lacking, wanting, needing, rebelling, and breaking. Subsequently, I have tended to work too much and play too little. Too often the hope, love, and joy of our little garden called Mars Hill Church has been choked out by my weeds of focusing most of my energies on what I and we are not doing.

Then Pastor C. J. preached a sermon at the Resurgence Conference 2008: "Text and Context."[20] He opened by speaking from the book of

---

[19]James Davison Hunter, "To Change the Word," *The Trinity Forum*, vol. 3, no. 2 (June 2002), 11; http://www.ttf.org/index/findings/detail/to-change-the-world/ or http://www.ttf.org/pdf/Bv3n2-Hunter-Text.pdf.

[20]His sermon is available online for free and is one that every Christian who cares about the

1 Corinthians, which is a book I thought I knew because I had preached it in its entirety. He opened by reminding us of the huge list of faults and flaws in the church, which included sexual sin of every sort and kind, lawsuits, drunkenness at Communion, abuse of spiritual gifts, rejection of spiritual authority, and pride. Painting a dreadfully accurate picture of the urban church as being guilty of the church as mirror, he then read 1 Corinthians 1:4–9:

> I give thanks to my God always for you because of the grace of God that was given you in Christ Jesus, that in every way you were enriched in him in all speech and all knowledge—even as the testimony about Christ was confirmed among you—so that you are not lacking in any spiritual gift, as you wait for the revealing of our Lord Jesus Christ, who will sustain you to the end, guiltless in the day of our Lord Jesus Christ. God is faithful, by whom you were called into the fellowship of his Son, Jesus Christ our Lord.

He then asked how Paul could possibly commend that church for anything, let alone its giftedness, in light of the fact that its great giftedness was being used for great sin and rebellion. He also asked how Paul could have any hope for an urban church as confused, rebellious, wicked, corrupt, and proud as that church.

Not only did Paul have hope for what was perhaps the worst church in the history of churches, but moreover he was certain that they would become a city within that city as a missional church of Jesus. The source of Paul's certainty was the faithfulness of God to unfaithful people: "Our Lord Jesus Christ, who will sustain you to the end, guiltless in the day of our Lord Jesus Christ. God is faithful, by whom you were called into the fellowship of his Son, Jesus Christ our Lord."

Paul was keenly aware of the "grace of God that was given you in Christ Jesus"; this grace enabled him, a pastor full of passion and clarity, to have hope for such a corrupt church. He went on to explain that we cannot lead anyone on mission with Jesus, or rebuke anyone for sin against Jesus, until we first have hope from Jesus for them. This hope is not based on them but on the grace of God in them from Jesus through the gospel.

church would benefit from hearing. You can download audio and video of his sermon here: http://theresurgence.com/text_and_context_media.

The foundation of a missional church that can participate with Jesus in the transformation of people and cultures is Christian leaders who actively, passionately, and continually seek the evidences of God's grace in the lives of their people and their church. Such leaders must then water and nurture the lives of people who are meeting Jesus and growing in Jesus through regenerated hearts. The good stories of where God is at work and of what God is doing must be sought and told by the preacher of God's Word so that God's people learn to seek and celebrate the evidences of God's grace at work in their lives, church, and city.

Furthermore, this culture of hope and encouragement enables a church and its leaders to cut off the dead branches in the church which no longer bear fruit but instead waste valuable resources, prune back the branches that after a season of pain will return with greater health and fruitfulness, graft in the new branches that bring new ideas and experiences to enable even sweeter fruit, and pull the weeds of sin and error that threaten to choke out the life of good things God is growing on the branches abiding in the vine of Jesus. After laying the pastoral groundwork of hope rooted in God's faithfulness and nurtured in the evidences of his grace at work in our midst, Paul does all of these things in the remainder of his letters to the Corinthians.

The evidences of sin and its effects are everywhere in my life and our church. But so are the evidences of Jesus and his grace. I find the more I seek and celebrate the evidences of his grace, the more my heart is rightly prepared to deal with the evidences of sin and its effects—with hope for people, our church, our city, our culture, and our world.

What are the evidences of God's grace in your life today?

What are the evidences of God's grace in your church today?

What are the evidences of God's grace in your culture today?

What are the evidences of God's grace in your city today?

Be encouraged, have hope, vocally tell the stories of God's grace, be the church, and do not stop plowing until you see him face-to-face.

Jesus is alive. Anything can happen.

ANSWERS TO COMMON QUESTIONS ABOUT TRANSFORMING THE WORLD

THE BIBLE COMMANDS US TO SET OUR MINDS ON THINGS THAT ARE ABOVE (COL. 3:1). SHOULDN'T WE BE CONCERNED WITH ETERNAL THINGS LIKE GETTING SOULS INTO HEAVEN? WHY WASTE OUR TIME DEALING WITH TEMPORAL THINGS SUCH AS CULTURAL CHANGE?

In Colossians, Paul is speaking to the source of our values and priorities as we live our lives in this world. He wants our imaginations captured by the invisible reality of the kingdom of light. He commands us to set the direction of our lives toward God. We are to avoid being lured and trapped by the world's pleasures and entangling alliances.

Like Jesus who left heaven to come to a world devastated by sin, we depart the churchly city within the secular city to love the city that has been devastated by sin. We proclaim a whole gospel that speaks to a new life in the community of the Spirit here on earth and a heavenly destination. We proclaim concrete righteousness into the culture by deed and word, exposing its evils in a context of grace. Our eternal salvation is first lived out in our temporal world. So long as we live lives faithful to Jesus in this world, we will impact the culture around us.

We will waste our time if we *only* work for a betterment of culture, abandoning evangelism for social or political action. This embraces the temporal but neglects the eternal. About a century ago many churches adopted the "social gospel," thinking that applying Christian principles to current society was the only thing needed; evangelization was unnecessary. Another major segment of Christianity reacted to this error and committed the opposite error. They distanced themselves from social action and focused merely on evangelism. Both missed the point. As Christians, we are called to live life in the community of the Spirit, which is made possible because of our relationship with Jesus. We are to lead others to know Jesus and to enter this community with us. As we extend our new life as followers of Jesus, we will transform society and culture around us.

WHY SHOULD WE BE CONCERNED ABOUT TRANSFORMING THE WORLD WHEN GOD PLANS TO DESTROY IT ALL ANYWAY?

I suppose this would be like the Samaritan walking past the wounded traveler, reasoning, "Why should I help him? He's going to die someday anyway" (Luke 10:30–37). If you really love your neighbor, then you will have compassion on him and want to improve his broken way of life. If you love your city, you will want to do all you can to overcome its debauchery.

There will be a day when Jesus will come in power and transform this world into either a millennial kingdom (as we believe) or the new earth (as many believe). All who refuse the gracious call to join with Jesus will be destroyed (Pss. 2:9; 21:8–9; Isa. 63:1–6; 66:15–24; Dan. 2:44; 2 Thess. 1:7–10; Rev. 2:26; 12:5; 19:15–21). Until then we are concerned about transforming the world because God is concerned about transforming the world. We, like the Samaritan, choose to stop to help the wounded traveler. These repeated acts of love transform us and the society around us and declare the goodness of God.

ISN'T THE BEST WAY FOR CHRISTIANS TO CHANGE THE WORLD TO WORK WITH PEOPLE OF OTHER FAITHS AND BRING PEACE AND UNITY TO A WORLD TORN BY RELIGIOUS STRIFE?

When we are involved in community or cultural transformation, we will work with all kinds of people. That work will be based on our common image of God. Even though it is marred by sin, that image remains (Gen. 1:26–28; 5:1–3; 9:6; 1 Cor. 11:7; James 3:9). We can work in partnership with people of all faiths, building from principles of freedom and justice that come from our common status as image bearers. We respect all people because they are in God's image. We work together for justice in society including such basic rights as freedom of religion and freedom from abuse and exploitation.

However, when we join in such collaborations, we must always beware of the temptation to downplay or ignore our identity as Christians. There is a temptation to speak only of a common spirituality, as if all religions are the same at their core. Some seem to think that if everyone were just nice and friendly everything would be peaceful or that interreligious dialogue will solve everything.

As we write this, the Dalai Lama is doing a tour of the U.S. It has grieved us to see that some leading pastors who joined with him in the Seeds of Compassion event for a discussion about nurturing youth with spirituality never mentioned the name of Jesus. True Jesus followers do not shy away from the fact that our lives are centered on him.

This does not have to lead to religious strife. Religious wars are usually motivated by tribal, ethnic, or political concerns rather than by allegiance to Jesus. While it is easy to see Jesus commanding us to reason in order to persuade all people to follow Jesus (Acts 17:17; 18:4; 19:26), it is really hard to establish the claim that Jesus told the Crusaders to wage war to reclaim the Holy Land.

One can be positive and gracious and speak positively and graciously while maintaining a clear Christian stance. We can be consciously Christian without a condemning spirit or without constantly reminding people to "repent or you'll burn." We interact with an attitude of personal humility rather than self-righteousness or arrogance. But as we proclaim the gospel and do the work of Jesus, we may be branded troublemakers and be persecuted, as we see with Paul at Philippi or Thessalonica (Acts 16:19–21; 17:5–8). When we speak of Jesus as Lord of the universe, it may be perceived as arrogance. If we are persecuted, it should be because we are unashamedly Christian, not because we are personally antagonistic or offensive in our demeanor.

Isn't it Best for Christians Simply to Separate from Secular Culture Altogether so as to Preserve Holiness?

Only if you ignore the pattern of the life Jesus lived. It is really good that he didn't stay in heaven, separated from our sin and preserving his holiness, but came to earth to connect with us and influence the unholy world in a holy way. Like him, we are in but not of the world (John 15:19–20; 17:14–16; 1 John 4:1–6).

The holiness of Jesus does not make him withdraw from sin-marred life but enables him to spread godliness into that life. Under the law, touching a leper defiled a clean person (Lev. 5:3; 13:1–59; 15:1–33). But when Jesus touched a leper, the defiled man was cleansed (Matt. 8:2–3).

Following 2 Corinthians 2:14–16, an important question is, what do you smell like? Do you spread the aroma of Jesus when you go to school, to work, or to community activities? Or do you spread the stench of the world when you come to church?

Ironically those who are most adamant about withdrawing from contact with secular culture are most likely to fall into the evil trap of worldly religion. The temptation is to develop rigorous rules, detailed lists of prohibited behaviors, and severe punishments in order to prevent immorality. Those deal with external holiness while neglecting the heart. This is the leaven of the Pharisees, which Jesus and Paul warned us about so strongly (Luke 11:33–12:3; Galatians).

Being separate from sin means we neither do sinful practices nor adopt sinful values. We are wise to avoid situations or people that serve as triggers or temptations to sin. Our values and practices must be like Jesus'. Thus Paul tells us to avoid sexual immorality, all impurity or covetousness, filthiness, foolish talk, and crude joking (Eph. 5:3–4).

The holiness of Jesus penetrates to the heart, transforming it, altering our deepest loves so that we live grace-based lives of joyful obedience, reflecting the very character of the Lord of glory.

Sample Church Membership Covenant

†

MARS HILL CHURCH MEMBER COVENANT

INTRODUCTION

> Present your bodies as a living sacrifice, holy and acceptable to God,
> which is your spiritual worship. Do not be conformed to this world,
> but be transformed by the renewal of your mind, that by testing you
> may discern what is the will of God, what is good and acceptable and
> perfect. (Rom. 12:1–2)

As Christians, we are members of God's household (Eph. 2:19) called
to function, participate, and minister in a particular place within the
body of Christ. A healthy body requires that each member does its part
well. A healthy church requires the same: members who are sacrificially
committed and well equipped to do the works of service that God has
prepared in advance for them to do (Eph. 2:10; 4:12). Mars Hill Church
holds its members in high regard; we expect them to lead as missionaries of the gospel to the culture. God, in his sovereignty, placed us in this
city, among these people, in this century, for a reason (Acts 17:26–27).

> For by the grace given to me I say to everyone among you not to think
> of himself more highly than he ought to think, but to think with
> sober judgment, each according to the measure of faith that God has

assigned. For as in one body we have many members, and the members do not all have the same function, so we, though many, are one body in Christ, and individually members one of another. Having gifts that differ according to the grace given to us, let us use them. (Rom. 12:3–8)

Being a member of Mars Hill Church is really about being part of a family. All members are disciples of Jesus, unified by their identity in Christ. This unity is expressed in the way they collaborate in loving God, loving fellow Christians, and loving non-Christians. Members who enter into a covenant with their local church are called to a higher degree of responsibility and service. At the same time, the elders and deacons are covenanted to assist members first and foremost, to love and lead, provide counsel and aid, and pray for, teach, and guide them.

Above all, keep loving one another earnestly, since love covers a multitude of sins. Show hospitality to one another without grumbling. As each has received a gift, use it to serve one another, as good stewards of God's varied grace. (1 Pet. 4:8–10)

WHAT IS A COVENANT?

A covenant is a promise by which we obligate ourselves to one another in such a way that the obligation of one party is not dependent on the faithfulness of the other (Ps. 76:11; Ezek. 20:44; 36:22; Hos. 2:19–20; 3:1; 2 Tim. 2:13). The Mars Hill Church covenant includes a statement of faith, a statement of biblical doctrine, the obligations of Mars Hill Church to its members, and the obligations of members to Mars Hill Church. Though the covenant does define the relationship between members and the church, it is first and foremost a promise made to God as a commitment to his glory and his bride, the church (Eph. 5:25).

STATEMENT OF FAITH

- I am a Christian saved from the eternal wrath of God by faith in Jesus Christ, my Lord and Savior, through his death and resurrection, by which I am assured of eternal life (John 3:16–18; Rom. 3:23–26).
- I believe Jesus Christ is exactly who he claimed to be (Isa. 5:6; Matt. 26:64; Mark 14:62; Luke 22:70; John 4:25–26; 6:29; 8:58; 11:25–27; 14:6–7; 15:5).

- I have repented of my sins and have been made a new creation in Christ (1 John 1:9; 2 Cor. 5:17).
- In obedience to Scripture, I have been baptized to personally identify with the death, burial, and resurrection of Jesus, and to publicly demonstrate my commitment as a disciple of Jesus (Col. 2:12; 1 Pet. 3:21).

STATEMENT OF BIBLICAL DOCTRINE

- I agree with the core beliefs of Mars Hill Church, which are founded upon historic creeds (e.g., Apostles' Creed and Nicene Creed) and expressed in the Mars Hill doctrinal statement.
- I understand the importance of submission to church leadership and will be diligent to preserve unity and peace; I will adhere to Mars Hill Church's position on primary theological issues, and I will not be divisive over secondary issues (Eph. 4:1–3; Heb. 13:7, 17).
- I agree that the sixty-six books of the Bible are the ultimate doctrinal authority on all matters (Isa. 55:11; 1 Cor. 15:3–4; 2 Tim. 3:15–16; Heb. 4:12).
- I understand that Mars Hill Church doctrine is also communicated and specified through various channels, such as sermons, published materials, and other writings distributed by Mars Hill Church.

OBLIGATION OF MARS HILL CHURCH TO ITS MEMBERS

- We covenant that your elders and deacons will meet the criteria assigned to them in the Scriptures (1 Tim. 3:1–13; 5:17–22; Titus 1:5–9; 1 Pet. 5:1–4).
- We covenant to seek God's will for our church community to the best of our ability as we study the Scriptures and follow the Spirit (Acts 20:28; 1 Pet. 5:1–5).
- We covenant to care for you and seek your growth as a disciple of Christ, in part by equipping you for service (Eph. 4:11–13) and praying for you regularly, particularly when you are sick (James 5:14).
- We covenant to provide teaching and counsel from the whole of Scripture (Acts 20:27–28; Gal. 6:6; 1 Tim. 5:17–18).
- We covenant to be on guard against false teachers (Acts 20:28–31).
- We covenant to exercise church discipline when necessary (Matt. 18:15–20; 1 Cor. 5; Gal. 6:1).

- We covenant to set an example and join you in fulfilling the duties of church members (1 Cor. 11:1; Phil. 3:17; 1 Tim. 4:12).

MY OBLIGATION TO MARS HILL CHURCH AS A MEMBER

- I have read and understood the Mars Hill doctrinal statement and will not be divisive to its teaching. I also understand the importance of submission to church leadership and will be diligent to preserve unity and peace (Eph. 4:1–3; Heb. 13:7, 17).
- I covenant to submit to the authority of Scripture as the final arbiter on all issues (Ps. 119; 2 Tim. 3:16–17).
- I will maintain a close relationship with the Lord Jesus through regular Bible reading, prayer, fellowship, and practice of spiritual disciplines. My relationship will be evident through my participation in weekly worship services, communion, Mars Hill community, service, and a life that glorifies Jesus (Pss. 105:1–2; 119:97; Acts 2:42–47; Heb. 10:23–25; 2 Pet. 1:3).
- I will steward the resources God has given me, including my time, talents, and treasure (Prov. 3:9–10; Rom. 12:1–2; Gal. 5:22–26; Eph. 4:1–16; 5:15–18). This includes regular financial giving, service, and participation in community that is sacrificial, cheerful, and voluntary (Rom. 12:1–8; 2 Cor. 8–9; 12:7–31; 1 Pet. 4:10–11).
- I will not function in leadership or as a member in another church family (Heb. 13:17).
- I covenant to submit to discipline by God through his Holy Spirit, to follow biblical procedures for church discipline in my relationships with brothers and sisters in Christ, to submit to righteous discipline when approached biblically by brothers and sisters in Christ, and to submit to discipline by church leadership if the need should ever arise (Ps. 141:5; Matt. 18:15–17; 1 Cor. 5:1–5; 2 Cor. 2:5–8; Gal. 6:1–5, 8; 1 Tim. 5:20; 2 Tim. 2:25; Titus 1:9; 3:10–11; Heb. 12:5–11; Rev. 2:5–7, 14–25).
- I agree, by God's grace, to walk in holiness as an act of worship to Jesus Christ, who has saved me from my sin so that I could live a new life (2 Cor. 5:17). I will practice complete chastity before marriage and complete fidelity in heterosexual marriage by abstaining from practices such as cohabitation, pornography, and fornication (Job 31:1; Prov. 5; Rom. 13:12–14; 1 Cor. 6:9–7:16; Heb. 13:4). I will refrain from illegal drug use, drunkenness, and other sinful behavior as the Bible, my

pastors, and my conscience dictate (1 Cor. 8:7; Gal. 5:19–21). Should I sin in such a manner, I agree to confess my sins to Christian brothers or sisters and seek help to put my sin to death (Rom. 8:13; Col. 3:5; 1 John 1:6–10).

MY COMMITMENT TO THE MISSION OF MARS HILL CHURCH

Mars Hill Mission Statement: Mars Hill Church lives for Jesus as a city within the city: knowing culture, loving people, and seeing lives transformed to live for Jesus.

I have read the mission statement of Mars Hill Church and commit to live out this mission as a diligent, faithful disciple of Jesus, that my identity would be in him, my worship would be for him, my fellowship would be through him, and my interaction with the culture would be for his glory.

I understand that this covenant obligates me to the members of Mars Hill and is an acknowledgment of my submission to the elders of the church. I accept the responsibility to notify Mars Hill leadership if at any time I can no longer commit to this covenant, or if I have any questions, comments, or concerns regarding Mars Hill Church.

General Index

SCRIPTURE INDEX

 # RE:LIT

Resurgence Literature (Re:Lit) is a ministry of the Resurgence. At www.theResurgence.com you will find free theological resources in blog, audio, video, and print forms, along with information on forthcoming conferences, to help Christians contend for and contextualize Jesus' gospel. At www.ReLit.org you will also find the full lineup of Resurgence books for sale. The elders of Mars Hill Church have generously agreed to support Resurgence and the Acts 29 Church Planting Network in an effort to serve the entire church.

FOR MORE RESOURCES

Re:Lit – www.relit.org
Resurgence – www.theResurgence.com
Re:Sound – www.resound.org
Mars Hill Church – www.marshillchurch.org
Acts 29 – www.acts29network.org